Y0-BCM-931

Authority, Piracy, and Captivity in Colonial Spanish American Writing

Authority, Piracy, and Captivity in Colonial Spanish American Writing

Juan de Castellanos's Elegies of Illustrious Men of the Indies

Emiro Martínez-Osorio

Lewisburg
BUCKNELL UNIVERSITY PRESS

Published by Bucknell University Press
Copublished by The Rowman & Littlefield Publishing Group, Inc.
4501 Forbes Boulevard, Suite 200, Lanham, Maryland 20706
www.rowman.com

Unit A, Whitacre Mews, 26-34 Stannary Street, London SE11 4AB

British Library Cataloguing in Publication Information Available

Library of Congress Cataloging-in-Publication Data

Names: Martinez-Osorio, Emiro, author.
Title: Authority, piracy, and captivity in colonial Spanish American writing: Juan de Castellanos's elegies of illustrious men of the Indies / Emiro Martinez-Osorio.
Description: Lanham, Maryland : Bucknell University Press, 2016. | Includes bibliographical references and index.
Identifiers: LCCN 2015046148 (print) | LCCN 2016006987 (ebook) | ISBN 9781611487183 (cloth : alk. paper) | ISBN 9781611487190 (Electronic)
Subjects: LCSH: Castellanos, Juan de, 1522-1607–Criticism and interpretation. | Castellanos, Juan de, 1522-1607. Elegias de varones ilustres de Indias. | Spanish American literature–To 1800–History and criticism. | Latin America–In literature.
Classification: LCC PQ6321.C48 Z75 2016 (print) | LCC PQ6321.C48 (ebook) | DDC 861/.3–dc23
LC record available at http://lccn.loc.gov/2015046148

Printed in the United States of America

For Heather, Amelia, and Elías

Contents

List of Figures

Preface

This book examines the intricate bond between poetry and history writing that shaped the theory and practice of empire in Early Colonial Spanish American society. The book explores from diverse perspectives how epic and heroic poetry served to construe a new Spanish American elite of original explorers and conquistadors in Juan de Castellanos's *Elegías de varones ilustres de Indias* (Elegies of illustrious men of the Indies; 1589). Similarly, this book offers an interpretation of Castellanos's writings that shows his critical engagement with the reformist project postulated in Alonso de Ercilla's *La Araucana* (*The Araucaniad*) and elucidates the complex poetic discourse Castellanos created to defend the interests of the early generation of explorers and conquistadors in the aftermath of the promulgation of the New Laws and the mounting criticism of the institution of the *encomienda* (a Royal tribute grant was awarded to an individual who performed services to the Crown during the campaigns of conquest. In return, the encomendero was expected to protect and evangelize the natives entrusted to his service). In doing so, this book shows the transformation undergone by narrative heroic poetry owing to Europe's encounter with America, and illustrates the contribution of learned heroic verse to the emergence of a distinctly Spanish American literary tradition.

There are two well-defined perspectives that guide the critical literature available on the work of Juan de Castellanos (1522–1607).[1] The first one reads Castellanos as an enthusiastic but less talented imitator of Alonso de Ercilla (1533–1594), and the second is shaped by readings that approach Castellanos as a historian, whether trustworthy or unreliable. Both approaches share the assumption that the *Elegies of Illustrious Men of the Indies* are the versification of a chronicle written by Castellanos, a premise that has been repeated frequently but does not withstand close scrutiny.

These misreadings have distorted not only our understanding of Castellanos's writings but also the early reception and impact of the works of authors such as Garcilaso de la Vega and Alonso de Ercilla in the Spanish American colonies, as well as our appreciation of the role of epic and heroic poetry in the ideological disputes over the rights and privileges of individuals who carried out the exploration and conquest of the New World. Although it is accurate to state that there is a close intertextual relationship and "epic continuity"[2] between Ercilla's and Castellanos's writings, the significance of Castellanos's ideological position and depth of his poetic practice is far more complex than what critics have been able to recognize until now. As the title indicates, the *Elegies of Illustrious Men of the Indies*[3] upholds the ideology of domination and shares in the celebration of the Spanish enterprise of conquest, but it does so from the perspective of a warrior class that was outmaneuvered in the administrative and legal battle for the political and economic control of the colonies. One of the central theses of this book is that rather than imitating Ercilla in the post-Romantic pejorative sense of this term, Castellanos took his predecessor to task and in some instances rewrote emblematic sections of the *Araucana* (1569, 1578, 1589),[4] while challenging the literary authority of his predecessor and steering heroic poetry in a radically different direction.

Juan de Castellanos's trajectory in the New World follows that of other colonists who tried their luck in what was then known as *Tierra Firme* (mainland) after the decline of the initial colonies established in places such as Hispaniola. Sometime after arriving in Puerto Rico around 1539, Castellanos embarked on a series of journeys southward that took him to the pearl fisheries on the islands of Cubagua and Margarita, off the coast of Venezuela; later to the Guajira Peninsula and the port of Cartagena de Indias; and finally to Santafé de Bogotá and Tunja in the New Kingdom of Granada. While traversing this vast geographical area, Castellanos shed his humble background and went on to climb the social ladder. He was ordained a priest in 1554 and was later appointed beneficiary of the cathedral at Tunja, whose construction he oversaw. Throughout his life Castellanos was able to accrue enough wealth to live comfortably, including owning houses, farms, slaves, and livestock. For someone who had left Andalucía at a time when a severe drought hit the region and poverty was widespread in the neighboring towns in the Sierra Morena, Castellanos's life and success is a story that demonstrates the social mobility that the New World afforded to those individuals who took risks and persisted, and particularly to those who made their voices heard through the perfection of the craft of writing. At the high point of his career, Castellanos played a major role in the literary, religious, and cultural life of the city of Tunja and was summoned to serve as ecclesiastical judge in the inquiry regarding the apparition of the Virgin of Chiquinquirá.

The *Elegías* is a series of heroic poems about several different campaigns of exploration and colonization of the New World.[5] Unlike Ercilla's *Araucana*, which in its American subject matter focuses on the Spanish efforts to restrain the Mapuche resistance in Chile, Castellanos's writings stretch over a period of more than one hundred years and cover a much wider geographical area that encompasses the Caribbean basin and the northern part of South America in what are now part of countries including Cuba, Dominican Republic, Puerto Rico, Venezuela, Colombia, Ecuador, Peru, and Panama. In some sections of the *Elegías*, Castellanos adopts an even wider geographical scope to narrate events that took place off the coast of Chile and Peru during Francis Drake's expedition to circumnavigate the globe in 1580. From a chronological perspective, the *Elegías* spans from Christopher Columbus's 1492 expedition across of the Atlantic to the administration of Judge Antonio González in the 1590s in the New Kingdom of Granada. The broader geographic and the historical scope of the *Elegías* alone is enough to signal that Castellanos did not intend to reproduce or re-create anything that had already been achieved by Ercilla but intended to cast Ercilla's project as too narrow and incomplete.

Another key premise of this book is that many of the misconceptions surrounding Castellanos's writings are linked to the tendency to disengage heroic and epic poetry from the function it served to defend the *encomendero*'s position in the light of the sixteenth-century debates surrounding the legitimacy of the conquest and the treatment of indigenous people (*encomenderos* were trustees of Indian labor responsible for evangelizing the natives under their supervision). On both sides of the Atlantic, critics have referred to the cultural and intellectual environment in which the *Elegías* emerged and described the city of Tunja as a remote and peaceful place that afforded a beneficed priest the solace to pursue his literary ambitions. To be sure, by the second half of the sixteenth century, Tunja was a center of learning where houses were decorated with exquisite murals depicting classical and mythological figures and with gilded altars in convents and churches that rivaled the ones in the neighboring Santafé de Bogotá, the seat of the Real Audiencia de Santafé (High Royal Court of Santafé). But few Colonial Spanish American towns were ever fully calm, and Tunja was no exception, especially because Tunja served as the stronghold of the encomenderos in the New Kingdom of Granada, and the economic prosperity that made possible the construction of its secular and religious architecture was primarily the result of the exploitation of indigenous labor.

The institution of the *encomienda* was fiercely criticized throughout the sixteenth century, and the will to reform it created social tensions that are palpable on the pages of the *Elegías*. Although Castellanos was never awarded an *encomienda*, his poems are linked directly to the encomendero class from Tunja,[6] and to the local city council in particular. Indeed, the

Elegías constitutes the most unapologetic example of pro-encomendero writing ever to come out of the New Kingdom of Granada, and possibly from anywhere else in the Spanish American colonies. Rather than considering the *Elegías* as a series of poems disconnected from its immediate historical and socioeconomic context, in this study I approach them as the prime example of the use of epic and heroic poetry in the intense disputes that Rolena Adorno has termed the "polemics of possession." Like Bartolomé de las Casas's *Brief Account of the Destruction of the Indies* (1552) and Bernal Díaz del Castillo's *True History of the Conquest of New Spain* (1632), Castellanos's *Elegías* are deliberative, persuasive, and polemical texts aimed to influence "reader's perceptions, royal policies, and social practices."[7] Consequently, the comparison between the works by Ercilla and Castellanos is far from gratuitous. In my analysis I assign priority to the explicit and implicit connections between Ercilla's *Araucana* and Castellanos's *Elegías* because from an idealized imperial vantage point, Ercilla's epic is quite critical of the first generation of explorers and conquistadors, which is precisely the group that is exalted in the *Elegías*. As I hope to make clear in this book, two of Castellanos's original contributions to Early Colonial Spanish American writing are the formulation of a regime of representation whose authority does not derive from the king (as Ercilla's poem does in multiple occasions) and the postulation of conquistadors and explorers as the ideal subjects of the Spanish global monarchy, which is quite different from Ercilla's identification with the values of the aristocracy and his vested interest in advancement at the court. Castellanos might have received the title of beneficiary of the cathedral in Tunja from Philip II, but his description, interpretation, and justification of the conquest, as well as his assessment of the success or shortcomings of the system of the *encomienda*, are the poetic expression of the position defended by the encomenderos. By elucidating the polemical thrust of Castellanos's poems and the sharp ideological fissure that separates the *Araucana* from the *Elegías*, this study confirms that Spanish imperial epic poetry was not a monolithic or univocal discourse and that even on the side of the so-called winners there was room for multiple, alternative, and competing narratives that envisioned quite different colonial projects.

Finally, a third and equally important premise of this book is that the polemical nature of the *Elegías* and their historiographical subject matter do not preclude aesthetic sophistication. Within the larger context of a new poetics of imperialistic expansion that linked the writing of poetry to imperialist and colonialist enterprises,[8] the *Elegías* offers one of the earliest examples of the reconfiguration of some of the main tenets of Petrarchism/Garcilacism, as well as the bold transmutation of dominant poetic discourses that had until then been typically associated with the nobility. On the other hand, since the *Elegías* contain an amalgamate of the literary genres available at the time, they offer a vantage point to examine the fraught relation between history and poetry writing, especially as in his poems Castellanos articulates pioneering strategies to construct the writing subject and to establish authority through the use of the discourses of friendship and captivity.

The sheer monumental length of the *Elegías* (more than 110,000 verses) combined with its disperse subject matter and the abundant digressions that delay the narrative continue to baffle critics. Yet, there is a set of paradigms or organizing principles that resonate throughout Castellanos's writing and provide logic and coherence to what would otherwise appear as random and disconnected. Among those paradigms we can include (1) the construction of a subject position and a poetic voice whose authority to narrate is grounded on firsthand experience and prolonged residency in the New World; (2) the postulation of explorers and conquistadors as the ideal subjects of the Spanish global monarchy; (3) the defense of the economic and political interests of the encomendero class, chiefly those from the New Kingdom of Granada; (4) the rejection of poetic adornment in favor of realism; (5) the subversion of Alonso de Ercilla's use of the conventions of Petrarchist/Garcilacist love poetry as a vehicle to portray Amerindians; and last but not least, (6) the systematic demonization of the indigenous population of the New World. Once we recognize these organizing principles, it becomes evident that each individual poem functions as a variation of the same theme, regardless of whether it narrates events that took place during Christopher Columbus's voyages of exploration ("Elegía I" through "Elegía IV"); during the conquest of Puerto Rico and Juan Ponce de León's expedition to Florida ("Elegía VI"); during the rise and fall of the pearl fisheries on the island of Cubagua ("Elegía XIII"); or during Pedro de Ursúa's campaign down the Amazon River and the rebellion led by Lope de Aguirre ("Elegía XIV"). The analysis and elucidation of how these organizing principles play out in emblematic sections of the *Elegías* constitutes the focus of this book.

In the introduction and the five chapters that follow, I strive to situate the work of Juan de Castellanos within the fertile transatlantic dialogues, exchanges, and rivalries that dominated European expansion to the New World. Chapter 1 opens up a window onto Castellanos's poetic practice by examining the exordium to "Elegía I," the first poem of the *Elegías*, and illustrating how the project proposed by Castellanos's diverges radically from the project announced by Alonso de Ercilla in the exordium to the *Araucana*. In particular, this chapter highlights the novelty of Castellanos's grand approach to the narration of events related to the exploration and conquest of the New World and analyzes the ideological and political implications of the references to friendship that are introduced in the opening of the *Elegías*. In addition, this chapter pays close attention to the use of the signifier *dulce* (sweet) in the poetry of Garcilaso de la Vega and Alonso de Ercilla, and establishes Castellanos's derisive use of this term as an expression of an equally ambitious call for poetic reform. In short, the analysis of the first fourteenth stanzas of the *Elegías* will show how Castellanos appealed to elegiac mode to begin to dismantle the link among the Spanish aristocracy, heroism, and the epic as a literary genre.

Chapter 2 elucidates the contentious relationship between Juan de Castellanos's and Alonso de Ercilla's poems by focusing on two emblematic sections of the *Elegías*. First, I analyze the representation of female indigenous characters in the second canto of "Elegía II," a poem dealing with the fate of the thirty men who stayed at the Fuerte de Navidad after Christopher Columbus returned to Spain in 1493. And second, I explore Castellanos's transformation of the epic topic of the fate of the bodies of warriors who die in battle in the story of an indigenous heroine named La Gaitana. In my analysis of these two sections I identify the multiple intertextual references between the *Elegías* and the *Araucana*, and I show their aesthetic and ideological implications. If up until now scholarship on Castellanos has uncritically misinterpreted Castellanos's expressed intention to imitate Ercilla, my reading of these two sections demonstrates exactly the opposite. Castellanos was a careful reader of the *Araucana*, and he drew quite aptly from the classic and Iberian literary traditions (particularly Jorge de Montemayor and Garcilaso de la Vega) to produce an aesthetically and rhetorically elaborate response from the perspective of the encomenderos. Interestingly enough, Castellanos rejects Ercilla while showing a command of and transforming some of the aristocratic discourses previously employed by Spanish courtiers, including the discourses of friendship, honor, and service. All in all, chapter 2 shows that the passage of the *Elegías* that presumably explains how Castellanos came to write his poems in *octava rima* should be cited not as proof that he had indeed set out to copy or mimic Ercilla but as evidence of a crisis in the poetic practice of *imitatio* (a method of composition predicated on the imitation and emulation of prestigious model texts) triggered by the debates surrounding the conquest and colonization of the New World. [9]

Chapter 3 delves further into Castellanos's poetic practice by examining his depiction of Francis Drake's expedition to the West Indies in 1585–1586. I argue that Castellanos's ambiguous portrayal of the English privateer is grounded on his expressed opposition to monarchical economic and administrative policies. My analysis shows how Castellanos embraced the epic not to praise Hapsburg naval power, as does Ercilla in his famous depiction of the Battle of Lepanto, [10] but to map imperial vulnerability through poetic discourse and especially to challenge the policies of Hapsburg monarchs concerning the administration of the recently established viceroyalties in the New World. I am not aware of any critic commenting on Castellanos's intelligent use of the epic genre in this manner. This chapter also foregrounds Bartolomé de las Casas's writings as another privileged subtext of the *Elegías* and shows how Castellanos's poems bear evidence of an internal ideological fissure that contributed to the emergence of a new sense of self-hood and the demarcation of a new sense of patriotism.

Chapter 4 resumes the analysis of Castellanos's poem about Francis Drake but this time turning attention to the way in which he constructs the New Kingdom of Granada (particularly the cities of Santafé de Bogotá and Tunja) as a bastion of military prowess. In canto 3 Castellanos uses the versification of a letter he sent to the president of the Real Audiencia de Santafé to problematize the function of writing in the colonial context and to place political authority in the hands of the local encomendero class. I also demonstrate how the practice of poetic emulation continues to inform Castellanos's writing by analyzing his description of the parade of the local militias preparing to defend the New Kingdom of Granada in the light of Ercilla's parade of indigenous chieftains from canto 21 of the *Araucana*.

Finally, chapter 5 continues to explore the transatlantic scope of Castellanos's poems but from the perspective of a tale of captivity, one of the most important genres in the early modern Iberian Atlantic as demonstrated recently by Lisa Voigt.[11] In volume 1 of the *Elegías*, Castellanos interpolated a brief narrative, which dislodges and shifts the setting where the threat of captivity exists, from the shores of the Mediterranean and North Africa to the newly discovered islands in the Caribbean basin. In my analysis of this tale of captivity I explore the implications and consequences of the author's decision to cast the encounter between Europeans and Amerindians in a similar conceptual and narrative mold as the one used to depict the confrontations between Christians and Muslims or Turks. The insertion of this captivity tale in the early sections of the *Elegías* is instrumental to cast Amerindians as savages and barbarians, to present the conquest and exploration of the New World as a providential mission entrusted to Spain by God, and to anchor the authority of the poetic discourse on extended residency in the New World and the knowledge and experience of a firsthand witness. Above all, Castellanos's original contribution to this genre of tales of captivity vis-à-vis the epic resides in introducing for the first time a captive (Juan de Salas), who like the author of the *Elegías*, had settled in the New World and whose journey home did not take him back to Spain.

NOTES

1. The *Elegías* have played a key role in discussions regarding the legacy of the colonial period and in shaping the memory of some of the events that took place during the phase of exploration and conquest. Ever since Colombia achieved independence from Spain, the writings of Juan de Castellanos have been commented on or examined by some of its leading cultural figures and literary critics, including Joaquín Acosta, José María Vergara y Vergara, Miguel Antonio Caro, Germán Arciniegas, Mario Germán Romero, Rafael Maya, José Manuel Rivas Sacconi, Ulises Rojas, Juan Friede, and William Ospina. This body of criticism has been helpful to clarify some aspects of Castellanos's biographical information, the eclectic nature of

his sources and reading interests, and the abundant Americanisms present in the *Elegías*, as well as to reveal Castellanos's familiarity and use of the Spanish ballad tradition. Above all, the recurring interest of Colombian critics in the work of Castellanos, combined with the 1955 publication of his *Elegías* by the Colombian Ministry of Education, has elevated Castellanos as a foundational figure in Colombian culture and solidified the position of the *Elegías* within the canon of its national literature tradition. This is illustrated by his inclusion in the mural that adorns one of the walls of the Colombian Academy of Language. Outside of Colombia the *Elegías* have been studied by notable Hispanists such as Juan Bautista Muñoz, Marcelino Menéndez y Pelayo, Marcos Jiménez de la Espada, Antonio Paz y Mélia, Angel González Palencia, Caracciolo Parra, Gisela Beutler, Giovanni Meo Zilio, María Rosa de Malkiel, Isaac J. Pardo, Antonio Curcio Altamar, Nina Gerassi-Navarro, and Elide Pitarello. More recently Luis Fernando Restrepo has examined the relationship between the *Elegías* and the encomendero class from the New Kingdom of Granada and the intersection between cartography and heroic poetry in Castellanos's writings. See the coda.

2. David Quint, *Epic and Empire: Politics and Generic Form from Virgil to Milton* (Princeton, NJ: Princeton University Press, 1993), 3–18.

3. Juan de Castellanos, *Elegías de varones ilustres de Indias*, 4 vols. (Bogotá, Colombia: Editorial ABC, 1955) (hereafter cited as *Elegías*, by volume and page number).

4. Alonso de Ercilla, *La Araucana*, ed. Isaías Lerner, 3rd ed. (Madrid: Cátedra, 2002) (hereafter cited as *Araucana*, by canto and stanza).

5. Only volume 1 of the *Elegías* was published while Juan de Castellanos was alive. It was censored by Agustín de Zárate and published in Madrid in 1589 by the widow of Alonso Gómez, official printer of the Crown. Volumes 2 and 3 were approved for publishing by Alonso de Ercilla and Pedro Sarmiento de Gamboa, respectively, but for unknown reasons never reached the printer. According to the will written by Castellanos prior to his death, volume 4 of the *Elegías* also received approval for publication, but this document does not mention the name of the individual who served as censor. Volumes 1–3 were published in Madrid in 1847 as the fourth installment of the *Biblioteca de autores españoles*. Volume 4 of the *Elegías* was edited by Antonio Paz y Mélia for the *Colección de autores castellanos* and appeared in Madrid in 1886 under the title *Historia del Nuevo Reino de Granada*. Castellanos also wrote a poem to Saint Diego de Alcalá, patron saint of the town of San Nicolás del Puerto, Seville, where he spent a significant part of his childhood, but the manuscript of this poem has not been found.

6. Luis Fernando Restrepo, *Un nuevo reino imaginado: Las Elegías de varones ilustres de Indias de Juan de Castellanos* (Bogotá, Colombia: Instituto Colombiano de Cultura Hispánica, 1999), 75–120.

7. Rolena Adorno, *The Polemics of Possession in Spanish American Narrative* (New Haven, CT: Yale University Press, 2007), 4.

8. Ignacio Navarrete, *Orphans of Petrarch: Poetry and Theory in the Spanish Renaissance* (Berkeley: University of California Press, 1994); Roland Greene, *Unrequited Conquests: Love and Empire in the Colonial Americas* (Chicago: University of Chicago Press, 1999); James Nicolopulos, *The Poetics of Empire in the Indies: Prophecy and Imitation in La Araucana and Os Lusíadas* (University Park: Pennsylvania State University Press, 2000); and Leah Middlebrook, *Imperial Lyric: New Poetry and New Subjects in Early Modern Spain* (University Park: Pennsylvania State University Press, 2009).

9. For an analysis of the practice of *imitatio* in the *Araucana*, see Nicolopulos, *Poetics of Empire*.

10. *Araucana*, canto 24, stanzas 1–95.

11. See Lisa Voigt, *Writing Captivity in the Early Modern Atlantic: Circulations of Knowledge and Authority in the Iberian and English Imperial Worlds* (Chapel Hill: University of North Carolina Press, 2009).

Acknowledgments

In the research and writing of this book I have incurred many debts. Without the invaluable inspiration and guidance from the late James R. Nicolopulos, a comparatist interest in the heroic poems about the conquest of the New World would have never been awakened. I was fortunate to attend his graduate seminars on the "Epics of the Indies" and on Colonial Spanish American poetry at the University of Texas at Austin and to benefit from the remarkable generosity with which he shared his outstanding intellectual prowess. At UT Austin, I was also fortunate to come into contact with professors Jorge Cañizares-Esguerra and Cory A. Reed. I owe to them the broader transatlantic scope of my research and particularly my interest in tales of captivity as a crucial genre in the early modern Iberian Atlantic. I think of them often when I teach.

Several friends and colleagues have shared valuable information or offered suggestions that strengthened my arguments. I'm particularly indebted to Elizabeth R. Wright, Kathryn M. Mayers, Luis Fernando Restrepo, María Piedad Quevedo Alvarado, Jason McClosky, Jaime Humberto Borja Gómez, Anna Nogar, Alejandro Cañeque, Lisa Voigt, Karla González, and Juan Antonio Sánchez Hernández.

During the last four years, I have benefited tremendously from the camaraderie and support of my colleagues at York University, especially Mauro Buccheri, Pietro Giordan, Ellen Anderson, María João Dodman, Shanna Lino, Michol Hoffman, Alan Durston, Shobna Nijhawan, and María Constanza Guzmán. I also acknowledge how much I value the feedback I have received from students enrolled in my course on "Iberian Poetry of Exploration and Empire," especially Luis Quesada, Ana Daniela Ponce Morales, Stefana Sandu, and Tali Yanuka Paonessa. I would also like to express my gratitude to the Faculty of Liberal Arts and Professional Studies at York

University for their financial support, which made possible research at the Biblioteca Luis Angel Arango in Bogotá and the Biblioteca Nacional de España, Madrid.

Special thanks go to my editor, Greg Clingham, and to the anonymous reader for Bucknell University Press. It was a privilege to learn from them, and I'm deeply grateful for their commitment and enduring support for this project. Their insightful observations and suggestions tremendously improved the quality of the book.

A section of chapter 2 appeared in Spanish in *Cuadernos de Literatura*, and an earlier version of chapter 3 appeared in *Calíope: Journal of the Society for Renaissance and Baroque Hispanic Poetry*. I'm grateful to the editors of both journals for their permission to include that material in this book.

I owe a remarkable debt of gratitude to my friends Tim F. Lytle and Luis Rafael Zarama Pascualeto, and to my family in Colombia and the United States. I have been fortunate to enjoy their support while I completed this project. At all times during the writing of this book I was nourished by the love and friendship of my wife Heather Nicole White, who has read and touched every page of this book. I dedicate this book to her, and to our children, Amelia Rose and Elías Joaquín, not the least for their sense of humor and their constant disposition to seek new adventures.

A Note on Editions
Consulted and Translations

Juan de Castellanos's *Elegías de varones ilustres de Indias* is grouped into four separate volumes, which appeared jointly in print for the first time in Caracas, Venezuela, in 1930 with an introduction by Caracciolo Parra. There is, however, no definite critical edition of Castellanos's writings. Unless otherwise indicated, all references to the *Elegías* are to the 1955 edition published in Bogotá by the Biblioteca de la Presidencia de Colombia with a prologue by Miguel Antonio Caro. All references to Castellanos's *Discurso del capitán Francisco Draque* come from the 1921 edition published in Madrid by the Instituto de Valencia de Don Juan with an introduction by Angel González Palencia. All references to Alonso de Ercilla's *La Araucana* are to the edition published by Cátedra (Madrid, 2002), with an introduction by Isaías Lerner. For ease of reading I have modernized spelling.

All translations from Spanish are my own except otherwise indicated.

Introduction

Don Alonso de Ercilla cuenta algunas amorosas historias de los indios de Chile y yo tengo por cierto ser ficciones en que mostró su mentira como en lo demás de su obra.
—Diego Dávalos y Figueroa, *Primera parte de la miscelanea austral* [1]

Don Alonso de Ercilla narrates a handful of amorous episodes among Indians from Chile, and I am convinced such episodes are fictions in which he showed his falsehood as he does in the rest of his poem.

The starting point of my approach are the implications of the depiction of indigenous characters in the *Araucana*, particularly the poem's elevation of the bravery of the Mapuches and its use of the most prestigious poetic register of the time to attribute virtues such as courage, honor, loyalty, and compassion to indigenous warriors and heroines. [2] According to David Quint, the fact that Ercilla associated the Mapuche rebellion with heroism implied taking a stance in favor of Amerindians in the ideological debates concerning the justifications of the conquest and the legitimacy or not of the institution of the *encomienda*. Even though the idealization of Amerindian warriors was part of the glorification of the Spanish triumph over a worthy opponent and a prerequisite of the epic genre, it also rejected one of the key arguments postulated to justify the conquest, that is, the doctrine defended by Juan Ginés de Sepúlveda and the encomenderos according to which Amerindians were culturally inferior and destined to be subjugated and enslaved by superior Spaniards. In this sense, Ercilla did not need to idealize Amerindians as *ovejas mansas* (meek lambs), as had already been done by Fray Bartolomé de las Casas, "but his depiction, perhaps equally idealized, of fierce, undying [Mapuche] valor dispels the notion of a naturally servile people who deserved to be conquered." [3]

Alternatively, Elizabeth B. Davis argues that although in most cases Spanish epics tended to exclude the term "empire" and often critiqued specific aspects of imperialism, such critique was never tantamount to calling into question "the rightness of the imperial enterprise itself," and the poems' "acceptance of Hapsburg expansionism is everywhere apparent."[4] Davis adds that in sixteenth-century Spain,

> the specific role of the epic was to project an idealized image of the social group to which its writers belonged, a high-ranking group that understood its interests to be compatible with those of the monarchy and with the imperial project. It is in this sense that the epics of the imperial age lay claim to the events that they themselves depict as triumphal. Although they do not extol empire in so many words, they align themselves with imperial power, even when they seem to eschew atrocities occurring within the context of conquest.[5]

Exposing some of the contradictions that are present in the *Araucana*, Davis provides a nuanced and multilayered discussion of the different discourses and counterdiscourses used by Ercilla to represent Amerindians and to script his own subjectivity, including the discourses of nobility as service, blood, virtue, lineage, vassalage, and personal advancement. Although Davis concedes that the intersection of these conflicting threads, and ultimately Ercilla's own split subjectivity, allow for discrepant interpretations, she also underscores that the discourse of nobility as service is the dominant discourse of the poem, one that "partially conceals the writer's other discourses."[6] As evidence of her interpretation, Davis points to the abundant instances in which the narrator of the *Araucana* uses apostrophe to draw in the presence of the monarch directly into the text and the space where the action of the poem is taking place, a strategy that in turn allows Ercilla to boost his aristocratic background, postulate himself as a superior kind of Spaniard, and compensate for the poems' absence of a single well-defined Spanish hero.

Alicia de Colombí-Monguió and James Nicolopulos, on the other hand, have historicized the use of a Petrarchist/Garcilacist poetic code among poets attending *tertulias* (literary gatherings) in the viceroyalty of Peru and have made it clear that Ercilla's sophisticated representation of the amorous affairs of Tegualda and Crepino,[7] Glaura and Cariolán,[8] and Guacolda and Lautaro[9] sometimes received a cold reception and was even repudiated. The reason for this, Nicolopulos explains, is that in the colonial context, "the cultivation of Petrarchist literary practice became an instrument for codifying aesthetically the supposed cultural superiority that contemporary philosophical and legal doctrines posited as the justification for the colonizers' dominant position at the apex of the pyramid of colonial power."[10] According to Nicolopulos,

For the colonizers, at least those of literary bent, the refined and exclusive *mundus significans* encoded by Petrarchism / Garcilasism functions as a nostalgic space of communion with the distant metropolitan cultural ambit and a refuge from the potentially menacing alterity of their New World environment. Furthermore, the very exclusivity which served in the Old World to mark Petrarchist / Garcilacist poetic practices as courtly and aristocratic functioned doubly in the New World to delineate the difference between colonizer and colonized, and to justify the domination of one over the other.[11]

As a case in point of how Ercilla was taken to task by poets residing in the Spanish American colonies, Colombí-Monguió and Nicolopulos cite the response of encomendero poet Diego Dávalos y Figueroa, author of *Primera parte de la miscelanea austral* (First part of the southern miscellanea), who insists that Guacolda, the most memorable of Ercilla's indigenous female characters, "era una india como las demás" (was an Indian woman like all the others) and had this to say about the amorous episodes of the *Araucana*:

El [h]umor de que los indios más participan es la flema, en el cual pocas veces se enciende el amor . . . pues como todo esto falte en esta gente no se puede creer sean heridos de la amorosa flecha, con diferencia alguna de las bestias. Aunque sus defensores [read here Ercilla] niegan esto, atribuyéndoles mil dulzuras, que en tiernos requiebros y enamorados cantares dicen y cantan sus amadas.[12]

The type of (bodily) humor predominant amongst Amerindians is phlegm, in which love rarely ignites . . . since all these are lacking from this people you cannot believe that they are wounded by love's arrows, with any significant difference from the beasts. Although their advocates deny this, attributing to them a thousand sweetness, which in loving praise and enamored songs speak and sing their loved ones.[13]

Finally, equally valuable to my analysis are the repercussions of the depiction of the indigenous wizard Fitón as a Renaissance mage. Like the rest of Ercilla's Amerindian heroines and warriors, Fitón's depiction does not fit the parameters of the image of Amerindians disseminated by encomenderos, slave raiders, and other apologists of violent conquest; nor does it match that of the defenders of the rights of Amerindians like Bartolomé de las Casas. Rather than offering an ethnographically accurate depiction of an indigenous shaman or depicting Fitón as a discredited pagan sorcerer, the powerful indigenous mage responsible for introducing the encomium to Philip II, revealing to Ercilla the world map of Spanish possessions, and disclosing the thaumaturgic globe that displays the Spanish victories at Saint Quentin and Lepanto, is a Merlin-type sage steeped in Neoplatonist theory whose most immediate literary model and predecessor is the wizard Severo from Garcilaso de la Vega's "Eclogue II."[14] Indeed, by carefully outlining Ercilla's debt

to Garcilaso, as well as Lucan and Juan de Mena, in the key stages of the
episodes involving Fitón, Nicolopulos has convincingly shown how Spanish
American writers like Pedro de Oña and Bernardo de Balbuena reworked
Fitón's traits and went on to produce indigenous wizards like Pillalonco and
Tlascalán, thereby precisely aiming to subvert or emulate the ideological
stance encoded in Ercilla's highly literary construction of the Araucanian
wizard.[15]

The juxtaposition of Quint's, Davis's, Colombí-Monguió's, and Nicolopulos's analysis illuminates why the *Araucana* had a different reception depending on what side of the Atlantic it was read and on whether its audience
was affected, or not, by Ercilla's elaborate aestheticization of the enterprise
of conquest. Paying attention to the public response to the *Araucana* is instructing, especially since there is an acute difference particularly among
poets depending on what side of the Atlantic they are writing from. We can
find high praise for Ercilla's among writers such as Lope de Vega and Miguel de Cervantes, who never set foot in the New World and were not
personally affected by the way in which Ercilla had depicted the affairs of the
conquest. In *La dragontea* (1598), Lope de Vega wrote, "En Chile surgen,
dando a Chile espanto / Chile, de Ercilla celebrado tanto"[16] (In Chile they
suddenly appear, spreading fear through Chile / Chile, profusely celebrated
by Ercilla); and in the *Laurel de Apolo* (1630), "Don Alonso de Ercilla /
tan ricas Indias en su ingenio tiene, / que desde Chile viene / a enriquecer las
musas de Castilla, / pues del opuesto polo / trajo el oro en la frente, como
Apolo, / porque después del grave Garcilaso / fue Colón de las Indias del
Parnaso"[17] (Alonso de Ercilla / such rich Indies in his wit has, / that he
arrives from Chile / to enrich the poetic Muses of Castille, / and from the
opposite extreme of the world / he brought gold on his brow, like Apolo, /
because after the grave Garcilaso / he was a Columbus in the Indies Parnas-
sus). Miguel de Cervantes, on the other hand, in the "Canto de Calíope"
included at the end of *La Galatea* (1585) wrote, "Otro del mismo nombre
[Alonso], que de Arauco / cantó las guerras y el valor de España, / el cual los
reinos donde habita Glauco / pasó y sintió la embravecida saña, / no fue su
voz, no fue su acento rauco, / que uno y otro fue de gracia extraña, / y tal, que
Ercilla, en este hermoso asiento / merece eterno y sacro santo monumento"[18]
(Another by the same name (Alonso), who sang about the Arauco wars and
of Spanish courage, / who went to the domain where Glauco dwells / and
faced the infuriated cruelty, / neither his voice nor his tone were coarse / they
were both of an unusual grace, / and such, that Ercilla in this beautiful
dwelling / deserves a lasting and sacred monument). And later in chapter 6 of
the first part of *Don Quixote*, the priest praises the *Araucana*, together with
Juan Rufo's *La Austriada* (1584), and Cristóbal Virués's *El Monserrate*
(1587) by stating that "todos esos tres libros . . . son los mejores que, en verso
heroico, en lengua castellana están escritos, y pueden competir con los más

famosos de Italia: guárdense como las más ricas prendas de poesía que tiene España"[19] (all these three books . . . are the best that, in heroic verse, have been written in Spanish, and they can compete with the most famous ones from Italy: hold on to them as the highest poetic jewels of Spain).[20]

Certainly, the lofty portrayal of Mapuche warriors and the innovative depiction of Amerindian love notwithstanding, there are several central aspects of Ercilla's poem (particularly in part 1) that could have affronted the encomenderos' sensibility and even appeared as a direct threat to their interests. I am referring to the poem's explicit criticism of conquistadors such as Pedro de Valdivia (ca. 1500–1552) for cruelty and greed; the support of the swift measures taken by the Marquis de Cañete to control the encomendero rebellion in Peru;[21] and the unflattering depiction of Spanish colonists who escaped during the attack and destruction of the city of Concepción by Mapuche warriors.[22] Ercilla's criticism of the earlier generation of conquistadors and his validation of the authority of the monarch in the remote colonial context suggest that when trying to situate his ideological stance the more pertinent question is not whether Ercilla was in favor of or against Spain achieving a monarchy of global proportions but whether there is evidence in the *Araucana* that the manner in which that project had been carried out until then and the individuals who had carried it out were the best suited to achieve the goal and to perpetuate it. Read from this perspective, there is ample evidence that suggests the *Araucana* contains a project of reform that leaves untouched the underlying principles of imperialism and colonialism, which were inherent to the epic genre. Accordingly, in emblematic sections of his poem, Ercilla distances himself from the method of execution without rejecting the overall objectives of Spanish presence in Chile or elsewhere in the New World, including military defeat of hostile Amerindians, their subjection to the Spanish Crown, their assimilation of Spanish cultural norms, and their conversion to Christianity. The same logic of Spanish supremacy applies to Ercilla's depiction of Philip II's annexation of Portugal attached to the end of the *Araucana*. In the light of the growing transatlantic slave trade, the broader colonialist implications of Ercilla's celebration of Philip II's takeover of Portugal have yet to be fully addressed by critics.

Juan de Castellanos picked up on Ercilla's depiction of the destruction of the city of Concepción and included in his *Discurso del capitán Francisco Draque* (*The Narrative of the Expedition of Sir Francis Drake to the Indies and the Taking of Carthagena*) an episode that subverts the implications of Ercilla's portrayal of Doña Mencía de Nidos, the courageous woman who arms herself and exhorts the panic-stricken colonists at Concepción to stay and defend their city. In Castellanos's *Discurso*, the location where the threat of an attack takes place (the port of Callao near Lima); the narrator's characterization of an anonymous Spanish woman as brave; the speech she delivers to young male colonists; and even some specific lines such as "A dónde vais" (where are you going?) and "gente vil, cobarde and apocada" (low, cowardly, and fearful people) all call the attention of informed readers to sections of canto 7 of the *Araucana*.[23] The most salient aspect of Castellanos's emulation, however, is that the social group associated with military incompetence and cowardice is no longer the group condemned and emasculated in the pages of Ercilla's poem (members of the first generation of conquistadors). By invoking Ercilla's model in a context that involves English adversaries instead of Amerindians, Castellanos avoids the moralistic undertones and the outsider's perspective of Ercilla's depiction of the destruction of Concepción and calls attention to challenges faced by Spanish American colonists (particularly encomenderos) that were only marginally addressed or were altogether excluded from the pages of the *Araucana*. More pertinently, the short speech delivered by the anonymous woman in Castellanos's *Discurso* is followed by an extended harangue in which several members of the first generation of colonists take issue with royal policies affecting the administration and defense of the Spanish colonies in the New World. The voices of those colonists are the type of voices that had no outlet in Ercilla's aristocratic depiction of the campaigns of conquest, and the same type of voices that take center stage in the pages of the *Elegías* (see chapter 3).

On the other hand, although Castellanos never wrote lyric poetry as did the encomendero poet Diego Dávalos y Figueroa, he rejected vehemently the manner in which Ercilla had depicted indigenous heroines using the poetic vocabulary coined by Francesco Petrarca and popularized in the Iberian Peninsula by Garcilaso de la Vega and others.[24] Actually, decades before Dávalos y Figueroa challenged the historical accuracy of the *Araucana* and made his derogatory comments about Ercilla's Guacolda, Castellanos had postulated a poetic reform that included discarding Ercilla's version of the dominant form of amatory poetry as a language unsuited to depict the affairs related to the conquest and exploration of the New World. In this sense, the problematization of Petrarchist/Garcilacist poetic practice among poets in the New World did not have to wait until Sor Juana Inés de la Cruz brilliantly questioned its epistemological limitations to represent female subjectivity. An earlier reconfiguration of Petrarchism/Garcilacism was linked to what Adorno has called the "polemics of possession," in which the use of Petrarchist/Garcilacist poetic code to depict the affairs of the New World became a privileged site of contention. One important reason for this is because in the semantics of early modern European expansion, Petrarchism carried "not only feelings but [also] political, ethical, and juridical thought across the Atlantic from one society to another."[25] In the remainder of this introduction I refer to Ercilla's *Araucana* and Castellanos's *Elegías* to address the topic of royal and literary authority in Spanish imperial epics.

This is an idealized portrait of Alonso de Ercilla that appeared in a book entitled *Retratos de españoles ilustres con un epítome de sus vidas* (Portraits

Figure 0.1. Portrait of Alonso de Ercilla y Zúñiga from *Retratos de españoles ilustres con epítome de sus vidas* (Madrid, 1791). *Source:* Image courtesy of the Biblioteca Nacional de España.

of illustrious men of Spain with a brief summary of their lives) published by
the royal print in Madrid in 1791. Ercilla appears at the center of the composition as an elegantly dressed aristocrat, looking like a proud and determined
knight of the elite Order of Saint James, with pen in hand and in the act of
writing. The presence of the shield and the sword hanging on the back wall
expresses a sort of nostalgia for the values of an era long gone, which even
when Ercilla was alive was quickly eroding, in part because of the recent
developments in military technology and the repositioning of the nobility
within Spanish culture. Only ten years after Ercilla's death in 1594, Miguel
de Cervantes sets out to explore superbly the sharp contrast between the
changing ideologies in Spain and also the gap between reality and myth in
the pages of *Don Quixote* (1605). This having been said, the message of the
portrait is clear: Ercilla is an aristocrat, a warrior, and a poet, the embodiment
of an ideal that had been shared by the members of his social class throughout the sixteenth century and also espoused by well-known courtiers/warrior/
poets such as Juan Boscán Almogávar (1492–1542) and Garcilaso de la Vega
(1501–1536).

As a portrait created almost two centuries after Ercilla's death, this image
speaks to issues of canonicity and the emerging discipline of literary history
in the later eighteenth century. In this regard, it speaks volumes about how
writers, editors, and literary historians have interpreted the Siglo de Oro
(Spanish Golden Age of Letters) with monumentalizing gestures, which continue to be perpetuated today. This is the portrait of Ercilla that adorns one of
the most widely popular versions of the *Araucana* available to Hispanists, the
erudite Cátedra edition prepared by Isaías Lerner.[26] It is precisely as an
element of the greater discourse about Spanish Golden Age, and Early Colonial Spanish American writing in particular, that the connection between this
portrait and the manner in which Ercilla fashions his own image in the
Araucana becomes relevant to some of the issues addressed in this book.

At this point it is pertinent to point out that the 1791 portrait of Ercilla, as
well as the *Araucana*, say little or nothing about the anxieties Ercilla may
have experienced in order to gain or maintain access to the court or of the
difficulties he faced to be inducted into the Order of Saint James, which
required postulants to demonstrate their *hidalgía* (nobility). Miguel Martínez
has recently compared the trajectories of Luis de Zapata and Ercilla at the
court of Philip II and has noted that unlike Zapata, a member of the upper
nobility, at the beginning of his career the young Ercilla, "sin título, sin renta
significativa, sin señorío—que la familia pierde en 1545, en un pleito"[27]
(without a title of nobility, without significant income, without a lordship or
a state—which his family had lost in 1545, in a lawsuit) he "solicita el pasaje
a las Indias que a la larga le permitirá adquirir, gracias a su servicio militar y
tras delicado proceso de probanza . . . el hábito de Santiago"[28] (requests
permission to travel to the Indies, which in the long run will allow him to

obtain, thanks to his military service and after a sensitive process of proving his merits . . . the knighthood of Saint James). Zapata, as Martínez correctly points out, received the Gown of Saint James earlier and directly from the prince.[29] Then again, the 1791 portrait as well as Ercilla's own poem are not concerned with that and instead convey in no uncertain terms the idea that Ercilla belonged in the court and that there is a connection between Ercilla's poems and the monarch as a source of legitimacy and authority. Perhaps alluding to the retrospective quality of the *Araucana*, in the portrait the act of writing takes place far from the messy battlefields in the confines of the Arauco region, in what is now Chile, and in the more controlled space provided by one of the rooms of the palace, which is literally and symbolically the space of enunciation of the text Ercilla appears to be writing, the *Araucana*.

Although the 1791 portrait emerged in a political and literary context quite different from the one in which Ercilla lived, this particular rendering of Ercilla is far from arbitrary and is partially supported by the contours of the self-image that Ercilla carved in his own poem.[30] Ercilla strove hard to promote the fact that he was a warrior and a poet, but he endeavored even harder to promote the idea that he enjoyed an exceptionally strong bond with the court and with the sovereign. As it is well known, he suggested in the prologue to the first installment of the *Araucana* that he had started to write segments of the poem on small pieces of leather while still in the battlefield in Chile, and in key sections of his poem Ercilla develops further his profile as a warrior/poet when he describes himself in the act of writing while engaged in military campaigns.[31] For instance, the introductory section to the episode involving Bellona, the Roman goddess of war, from canto 17 from the second installment of the *Araucana*, is followed by a prophetic encomium to Philip II.[32]

Yet, throughout the *Araucana* Ercilla makes the connection between himself, the court, and Philip II even clearer, as there are abundant references to the king, and the poetic voice addresses the king directly in at least thirty-three occasions.[33] This type of bond, and particularly the use of apostrophe to invoke the presence of the king in the pages of the poem, has led Davis to conclude that in the *Araucana* "the character of Ercilla and the authorial voice appear always and everywhere connected to the figure of the monarch, and this fact lends an aura of prestige to the poet's own character that conditions the entire epic."[34] In one of the opening stanzas of the poem, in particular, Ercilla emphatically states that ultimately the source of authority that legitimizes the accounts provided in the *Araucana* is his closeness and the poem's direct connection to Philip II. Ercilla dedicated the three parts of his poem to Philip II, and the king is the intended and ideal reader of the *Araucana*, as is made evident in the following supplication:

Suplícoos, gran Felipe, que mirada
esta labor, de vos sea recibida,
que, de todo favor necesitada,
queda con dares a vos favorecida.
Es relación sin corromper sacada
de la verdad, cortada a su medida;
no despreciéis el don, aunque tan pobre,
para que autoridad mi verso cobre. [35]

I implore, great Philip (II of Spain), that thou deign to accept
upon laying your eyes on my labors
which is in need of many endorsements
is already honored by being offered to you.
It is an unblemished account tailored to the truth;
do not disdain this humble gift
so that my verses gain authority.

The word *relación* in the above-cited stanza brings to mind the *cartas de relación* (letters of relation), those documents written by explorers and con-quistadors during the age of geographic and political expansion. Those texts gained authority because they were the accounts of eyewitnesses, and as such contained references to empirical evidence that in many cases contradicted and expanded existing knowledge. Ercilla was well aware of the fact that eyewitness accounts from unknown and distant lands had revolutionized the writing of history and literature, and like many other writers of his time he increases the testimonial aspects of his poem by stressing that he is writing about events that he witnessed. But this particular type of authority is very problematic in Ercilla's writings, and this fact did not escape readers in the sixteenth century, particularly those with vested interests in the enterprise of conquest. Nowadays very few critics doubt the literary provenance of the idealized Amerindian heroes and heroines that appear in the *Araucana*, as well as the eminently literary aspects that inform Ercilla's depiction of his encounter with the wizard Fitón.[36] Nor does anybody ignore the fact that thirteen out of the fifteen cantos included in part 1 of the *Araucana* deal with events that took place before Ercilla even arrived in Chile or that Ercilla was not present at the Battles of Saint Quentin (1557) and Lepanto (1571), which are described at length in part 2 of the *Araucana*—not to mention the literary nature of Ercilla's extended defense of Cartagenian Dido in part 3 of his poem. However, the last two lines of the stanza cited above leave very little doubt as to what serves as the ultimate source of authority for the poem according to its author: "No despreciéis el don, aunque tan pobre, / para que autoridad mi verso cobre" (do not disdain this humble gift / so that my verses gain authority). The same royal endorsement that Ercilla requests in these lines had already been requested in a short dedication that precedes the opening of the poem. In both cases the powerful gaze of the monarch is enough to validate Ercilla's writing:

> *Suplico a V.M. sea servido de pasar los ojos por ella que con merced tan grande, demás de dejarla V.M. ufana, quedará autorizada y seguro de que ninguno se le atreva.* [37]

> I implore that your majesty deign to gaze at my work so that by granting me such honor not only will it be complete but also it will come to be authorized, and [I am] confident no one will dare dispute it.

In sum, and as pointed out by Davis, throughout the *Araucana* Ercilla "exhibits a confidence verging on complicity with the royal person, one that authorizes both his values and his perspective as narrator."[38] Although circumstantial, one can imagine that in addition to his service as a military officer in Chile and the increasingly popular success of the *Araucana*, this ideological affinity also played a role in Ercilla being selected to serve as censor of manuscripts that were submitted for publishing, including volume 2 of Juan de Castellanos's *Elegías*. Ercilla was commissioned to review the second volume of the *Elegías* and approved its publication by stating,

> *Yo he visto este libro, y en él no hallo cosa mal sonante ni contra buenas costumbres; y en lo que toca a la historia, la tengo por verdadera, por ver fielmente escritas muchas cosas y particularidades que yo ví y entendí en aquella tierra, al tiempo que pasé y estuve en ella: por donde infiero que va el autor muy arrimado a la verdad; y son cosas de guerras y acaecimientos que hasta ahora no las he visto escritas por otro autor, y que algunos holgarán de saberlas.* [39]

> I have seen this book and do not find anything offensive or contrary to good manners; and in regard to its subject matter I consider it to be true, [and I have found] faithfully written many things and affairs that I saw and understood in that region, during the time that I spent and lived in it: thus I infer that the author abides closely to the truth; and these are events and happenings of war that I have not seen written by any other author, and some will be pleased to learn about them.

Throughout his *Elegías* Juan de Castellanos also fashions his own image as that of or a warrior/poet, or to be more precise, as a former foot soldier and explorer who later became a priest and a writer. Castellanos would go as far as using occasionally some of the same lines employed by Ercilla to speak about his experience as a soldier/poet. Such is the case of the line "se me cayó la pluma de la mano"[40] (the quill fell from my hand) from the episode involving the goddess Bellona I alluded to earlier. This line would reappear almost word by word but in the present tense in a section of Castellanos's

Discurso that chastises English troops for iconoclasm: "La pluma se me cae de la mano / con frío temblor cuando lo escribo"[41] (the quill falls from my hand / as a cold trembling overpowers me as I attempt to write). Yet, unlike Ercilla, Castellanos could not boast in his poems any type of proximity to the king or to the court, and in at least one section of his writings he admits that neither he nor his poems are welcomed in Spain (see chapter 3). Castellanos certainly dedicated his poems to Philip II, but overall the monarch is conspicuously absent from the *Elegías*, and what we find instead is a systematic rejection of the individuals who represented royal authority on the American side of the Atlantic. Therefore, it is in the context of the relationship between the sovereign and the heroic poems produced by his subjects about the campaigns to explore and conquer the New World, and articulated so forcefully by Ercilla throughout the *Araucana*, that Castellanos's bold claim in the opening of his *Elegías* that his poems do not need any outside source of authority acquires its significance and poetic force:

> *porque las grandes cosas que yo digo*
> *su punto y su valor tienen consigo.* [42]

> because the great deeds that I speak of
> carry in themselves an intrinsic worth and significance.

Castellanos is clearly writing within the early modern paradigm of Christian and Iberian expansion, and he supports wholeheartedly the colonial enterprise, but these lines introduce a destabilizing ideological fissure that inverts the scheme of power in colonial society as they suggest that the ultimate source of authority emanates not from the metropolitan center at the court but from the colonial periphery. It is in this self-asserting critical gesture, not in the uncritical reproduction of its predecessor, as many critics would have it, that rests Castellanos's contribution to the cultural and ideological edifice of the emerging Spanish American society. Finally, a lot more could be said about the process of self-fashioning that allowed the child of humble farmers from a remote village in Andalucía to position himself not just as a local eminence in the town of Tunja but also as a preeminent authority of the narration of the events that shaped the first century of exploration and conquest of the New World as implied in the phrase "porque las grandes cosas que yo digo / su punto y su valor tienen consigo" (because the great deeds that I speak of / carry in themselves an intrinsic worth and significance).

While the setting of the idealized portrait of Ercilla is useful to consider the connection between heroic poetry, eyewitness accounts, and royal authority, the short legend at the bottom of the image is useful to explore the significance of another type of authority that also plays a pivotal role in Ercilla's poem as I shall demonstrate in chapter 2:

Don Alonso de Ercilla. Caballero de Santiago. Nació en Madrid el 7 de agosto de 1533, poeta heroico tan *dulce* como valeroso: compuso el poema *La Araucana* y falleció después del año de 159[4].[43]

Alonso de Ercilla. Knight of the Order of Saint James. Born in Madrid on August 7, 1533. Heroic poet, as sweet as courageous. Wrote the *Araucana* and died on the year 159(4).

It is noteworthy that the term *dulce* (sweet) would be chosen to describe Ercilla the soldier or the qualities of his epic poem. But it is even more revealing that in the wake of the nineteenth century the same term would continue to be emblematic of the type of poetry written by courtiers who aspired to be warriors and poets in the service of the Spanish Crown three centuries earlier. As a poetic term, the signifier *dulce* holds a great deal of currency within the love poetry written by Garcilaso de la Vega who was in turn one of the most important literary models for Ercilla (see chapter 1). Castellanos (and the encomendero poet Diego Dávalos y Figueroa when he used pejoratively the cognate term *dulzuras* to speak of Ercilla's borrowing of Garcilaso's poetic language to depict Guacolda) was quick to recognize the importance of the signifier *dulce* within the poetic language of empire as he set out to create a gendered discourse that postulated conquistadors and encomenderos, not courtiers or aristocrats, as the ideal subjects of the Spanish global monarchy. For Castellanos and the seasoned conquistadors who settled in cities such as Tunja and Santafé de Bogotá in the New Kingdom of Granada, the poetic conventions and values ascribed to Petrarchism/Garcilacism needed to be recalibrated to represent the enterprise of conquest and particularly to depict the original inhabitants of the New World. Likewise, for them Alonso de Ercilla, the author of the *Araucana* and "paje de Felipe II, jinete de don García, gentilhombre de la Compañía de Lanzas del Virrey de Perú, miembro de la Orden de Santiago, caballero de la Boca de los Principes de Hungría"[44] (page of Philip II, horseman of don García, gentleman of the Troop of Spearmen of the Viceroy of Peru, member of the Order of Saint James, knight of the Princes of Hungary), was not a comrade-in-arms or an *indiano* but a "king's man" and an outsider.[45] To this productive ideological and poetic rivalry that took place as part of the conquest of the New World by European discourses we can trace back one of the earliest expressions of Colonial Spanish American literature.[46]

NOTES

1. Diego Dávalos y Figueroa, *Primera parte de la miscelanea austral* (Lima, Peru: Antonio Ricardo, 1602), Coloquio 34, 154.
2. By making this statement I am not suggesting that Ercilla univocally offered a positive representation of Amerindians. For the nuances of Ercilla's representation of Amerindians, see

Francisco Javier Cevallos, "Don Alonso de Ercilla and the American Indian: History and Myth," *Revista de Estudios Hispánicos* 23, no. 3 (October 1989): 1–20; and Georgina Sabat de Rivers, "*La Araucana* bajo el lente actual: El noble bárbaro humillado," in *La cultura literaria en la América virreinal: Concurrencias y diferencias*, ed. José Pascual Buxó, 107–23 (Mexico City: Universidad Nacional Autónoma de México, 1996).

3. Quint, *Epic and Empire*, 171. Quint's interpretation of the *Araucana* is rooted in the notion that in the Western epic tradition it is possible to "define an opposition between epics of imperial victors and epics of the defeated" (8). For Quint, the epics written by the winners are texts that follow on the footsteps of Virgil's *Aeneid* and display a more linear, teleological, and coherent plot, and that aim to perpetuate imperial politics. Meanwhile, the epics produced by the defeated are texts that exhibit a greater affinity to Lucan's *Pharsalia* and display more random, circular, or open-ended plots, which attack or resist empire and promote less central-ized political arrangements. In regard to the *Araucana*, Quint recognizes Ercilla's debt to both Virgil and Lucan, as it is palpable in the *Araucana*'s depiction of the Battle of Lepanto (*Araucana*, canto 24, stanzas 1–95) and the episode involving the descent into the cave of the indigenous enchanter Fitón (*Araucana*, canto 23, stanzas 24–87), which imitate the *Aeneid*'s battle of Actium and the episode of the witch Ericto from book 6 of the *Pharsalia*, respectively. However, Quint places firmly the *Araucana* within the tradition of the epics of the defeated and argues that Ercilla's sympathy for the Mapuche's desire to reject Spanish colonialism and their unwavering struggle to preserve their freedom led him to superimpose Lucan's model over that of Virgil's. Accordingly, Quint establishes a connection between what he views as Ercilla's inability to bring the poem to a definite end (that is, the "inconclusiveness" of part 1, part 2, and part 3 of the poem) and the ever-resurging effort of the Mapuches to oppose the Spaniards and rise again after they had been supposedly wiped out. However, Quint acknowledges the com-plexity of Ercilla's ideological position when he writes, "Ercilla and his poem can be seen once again as divided among several ideological options depending on how they construe the posi-tion of the Spanish king as liege lord of colonist and Indian alike" (Quint, *Epic and Empire*, 172).

4. Elizabeth B. Davis, *Myth and Identity in the Epic of Imperial Spain* (Colombia: Univer-sity of Missouri Press, 2000), 12–13.

5. Ibid., 207.

6. Ibid., 20.

7. *Araucana*, canto 20, stanza 25, through canto 21, stanza 12.

8. *Araucana*, canto 27, stanza 61, through canto 28, stanza 52.

9. *Araucana*, canto 13, stanza 43–57; canto 14, stanzas 1–3, 13–18.

10. James Nicolopulos, "Reading and Responding to the Amorous Episodes of *La Araucana* in Colonial Perú," *Calíope* 4, nos. 1–2 (1998): 232.

11. Ibid. See also Alicia de Colombí-Monguió, *Petrarquismo peruano: Diego Dávalos y Figueroa y la poesía de la miscelánea austral* (London: Tamesis, 1985).

12. Diego Dávalos y Figueroa, *Primera parte de la miscelanea austral*, Coloquio 34, 154.

13. Unless otherwise noted, all translations are mine.

14. James Nicolopulos, "Pedro de Oña and Bernardo de Balbuena Read Ercilla's Fitón," *Latin American Literary Review* 26, no. 52 (July–December 1998): 100–119.

15. Ibid.

16. Lope de Vega, *La dragontea*, ed. Antonio Sánchez Jiménez (Madrid: Cátedra, 2007), 240.

17. Lope de Vega, *Laurel de Apolo con otras rimas* (Madrid: Juan González, 1630), 36.

18. Miguel de Cervantes Saavedra, *La Galatea* (Madrid: Espasa-Calpe, 1961), 191.

19. Miguel de Cervantes Saavedra, *El ingenioso hidalgo Don Quijote de la Mancha*, ed. John Jay Allen, 10th ed. (Madrid: Cátedra, 2000), 1:137–38.

20. Frank Pierce and Francisco Javier Cevallos have also reminded us of the praise assigned to the *Araucana* by contemporaries of Ercilla such as Juan Díaz Rengifo who wrote in his *Arte Poética Española*, "Bien pudiera yo tender las velas de la elocuencia en alabar las ilustres, y elegantes obras de los poetas latinos, y españoles, por las cuales viven, y vivirán hasta el fin del mundo los conquistadores de Arauco" (*Arte Poética Española* [Salamanca, Spain: Casa de Miguel Serrano de Vargas, 1592], 8). (I could easily fill the sails of eloquence to praise the

elegant and illustrious works of Latin and Spanish poets, thanks to who lives and will live until the end of the world, the conquerors of Arauco.) Pierce and Cevallos also point out that a few years later Luis Alfonso de Carvallo wrote, "Como hizo el excelente don Alonso de Ercilla, que en la historia que hizo de la rebelión de Arauco" (quoted in Pierce, *La poesía épica del Siglo de Oro*, 2nd ed. [Madrid: Editorial Gredos, 1968], 34; and Cevallos, "Don Alonso de Ercilla," 7). (As was done by the excellent Alonso de Ercilla, who wrote a history of the Arauco rebellion.) Accordingly, Cevallos points out that "any perception of anti-conquest concepts in the poem would surely have been brought to the attention of the king immediately, but the work was instead acclaimed universally upon its publication" (Cevallos, "Don Alonso de Ercilla," 7).

21. *Araucana*, canto 12, stanza 76, through canto 13, stanza 5.

22. *Araucana*, canto 7, stanzas 1–64.

23. Juan de Castellanos, *Discurso del capitán Francisco Draque*, ed. Angel González Palencia (Madrid: Instituto de Valencia de Don Juan, 1921), 29–30 (hereafter cited as *Discurso*).

24. For a lucid analysis of the complex relation between Garcilaso's and Petrarch's poetry see Navarrete, *Orphans of Petrarch*.

25. Greene, *Unrequited Conquests*, 1.

26. The same image (figure 0.1) adorns the reprint of José Toribio Medina, *Vida de Ercilla* (Mexico City: Fondo de Cultura Económica, 1948).

27. Ibid., 248–49.

28. Miguel Martínez, "Género, imprenta y espacio social: Una 'poética de la pólvora' para la épica quinientista," *Hispanic Review* 79, no. 2 (Spring 2011): 171.

29. Ibid.

30. Two possible models for the 1791 portrait are the images of Ercilla that accompanied the publication of the 1574 and 1578 editions of the *Araucana*. See Medina, *Vida de Ercilla*, 283–84.

31. Ercilla writes, "Y por el mal aparejo y poco tiempo que para escribir hay con la ocupación de la guerra, que no da lugar a ello; y así, el que pude hurtar, le gasté en este libro, el cual, porque fuese más cierto y verdadero, se hizo en la misma guerra y en los mismos pasos y sitios, escribiendo muchas veces en cuero por falta de papel, y en pedazos de cartas, algunos tan pequeños que apenas cabían seis versos, que no me costó después poco trabajo juntarlos." (See Alonso de Ercilla's poem "Prólogo," in *Araucana*, 69–70.) (And because of the lack of resources and time that the task of war allows for writing, which leaves no opportunity for that; thus, any little time I could steal, I spent in [writing] this book, which, so that it would be truthful and accurate, was made in the midst of war, and in the same locations and events, writing many times in pieces of leather owing to the lack of paper, and in small pieces of letters, some of which were so small that I could only fit six lines, and it was not an easy task to put them in order later.)

32. Ercilla writes, "Aquella noche, yo mal sosegado, / reposar un momento no podía, / o ya fuese el peligro o ya el cuidado / que de escribir entonces yo tenía. / Así imaginativo y desvelado, / revolviendo la inquieta fantasía, / quise de algunas cosas desta historia / descargar con la pluma la memoria. / En el silencio de la noche escura en medio del reposo de la gente, / queriendo proseguir en mi escritura / me sobrevino un súbito accidente / cortóme un hielo cada coyontura, / turbóseme la vista de repente, / y procurando de esforzarme en vano, se me cayó la pluma de la mano" (*Araucana*, canto 17, stanzas 34–35). (On that night, agitated, / a moment of repose I could not find, / whether from impending danger or the concern / with writing I then had. / Thus pensive and sleepless, / stirring the restless imagination, / I wanted some aspects of this story / unburdened from memory with my quill. / Amidst the silence of the dark night / whilst everyone else was at rest, / wanting to continue to write, / I was overtaken by a sudden accident / that sent chills to all my joints, / suddenly my eyesight was impaired, / and trying in vain to continue, / the quill fell from my hand).

33. Frank Pierce, *Alonso de Ercilla y Zúñiga* (Amsterdam: Rodopi, 1984), 57–58; Davis, *Myth and Identity*, 31; Isaías Lerner, "Introducción," in *La Araucana*, by Alonso de Ercilla, 9–51 (Madrid: Cátedra, 2002), 24.

34. Davis, *Myth and Identity*, 26.

35. *Araucana*, canto 1, stanza 3.

36. *Araucana*, canto 23, stanzas 24–87. For Ercilla's debt to classical and Renaissance literary sources, see Nicolopulos, "Reading and Responding"; Rolena Adorno, "Literary Production and Suppression: Reading and Writing About Amerindians in Colonial Spanish America," *Dispositio* 11, nos. 28–29 (1986): 1–25; Adorno, *Polemics of Possession*; Adorno, "The Warrior and the War Community: Constructions of the Civil Order in Mexican Conquest History," *Dispositio* 14, nos. 36–38 (1989): 225–46; Cevallos, "Don Alonso de Ercilla"; Quint, *Epic and Empire*; Beatriz Pastor Bodmer, *Discursos narrativos de la conquista* (Hanover, NH: Ediciones del Norte, 1988); and Lía Schwartz de Lerner, "Tradición literaria y heroínas indias en la *Araucana*," *Revista Iberoamericana* 38, no. 81 (October–December 1972): 615–25.

37. *Araucana*, preceding canto 1.

38. Davis, *Myth and Identity*, 27.

39. *Elegías*, 2:9. Ercilla's authorization of volume 2 of Castellanos's *Elegías* follows closely the same language and structure of the paragraph issued to authorize the publication of volume 1 of the *Araucana*.

40. *Araucana*, canto 17, stanza 35.

41. *Discurso*, 91.

42. *Elegías*, 1:60.

43. Caption on figure 0.1.

44. Jaime Concha, "El Otro Nuevo Mundo," in *Homenaje a Ercilla*, ed. Luis Muñoz G. et al., 31–82 (Concepción, Chile: Universidad de Concepción, 1969), 66–67.

45. I'm borrowing the term "king's man" to refer to Ercilla from Nicolopulos who writes, "Ercilla, raised in the court and sharing its ideological perspective, clearly saw the New World through the eyes of a 'king's man' rather than those of the adventurers in search of social mobility who filled the ranks of early conquerors and *encomendero* class." (Nicolopulos, "Reading and Responding," 234). See also Davis, *Myth and Identity*, 207.

46. On the conquest of the New World by European discourses, see Greene, *Unrequited Conquests*.

Abbreviations

Araucana   Alonso de Ercilla, *La Araucana*, ed. Isaías Lerner, 3rd ed. (Madrid: Cátedra, 2002).

Discurso   Juan de Castellanos, *Discurso del capitán Francisco Draque*, ed. Angel González Palencia (Madrid: Instituto de Valencia de Don Juan, 1921).

Elegías   Juan de Castellanos, *Elegías de varones ilustres de Indias*, 4 vols. (Bogotá, Colombia: Editorial ABC, 1955).

Chapter One

"The Great Deeds That I Speak Of / Carry in Themselves an Intrinsic Worth and Significance"

American Epic after Ercilla

Giovanni Meo Zilio is the only other critic who has embarked on a comparative analysis of the opening stanzas of Juan de Castellanos's and Alonso de Ercilla's poems. Meo Zilio makes the logical comment that Castellanos's strategy of delimiting negatively the topic of his poems is reminiscent of the strategy Ercilla uses in the first four lines of the first stanza of the *Araucana*. Meo Zilio also highlights lexical and thematic similarities between the second stanza of the *Araucana* and the tenth stanza from "Elegía I" and suggests Ercilla's poem as a possible model for Castellanos.[1] However, Meo Zilio does not comment on any aesthetically encoded messages that link the two poems or on the divergent projects laid out by each author. To illuminate how Castellanos asserts his own poetic agenda and writes himself into an emerging literary and historiographic tradition, this chapter focuses on the poetic innovations Castellanos made in the first fourteen stanzas of "Elegía I." In particular, this chapter studies the significance of the use of conquistadors and encomenderos as protagonists and the intended audience of a narrative heroic poem; the novel geographic and historiographic approach to the recounting of the exploration and conquest of the New World; and the discarding of poetic adornment in favor of realism. When read in this manner, it becomes apparent how the exordium to "Elegía I" offers a privileged window onto Castellanos's poetic practice and sharply defines the civilization-barbarism dichotomy that will pervade Spanish American literature and culture for centuries to come.

Before analyzing the exordium to "Elegía I," it is important to emphasize, although it can seem to be a tautology, that Castellanos and Ercilla embrace the conquest as necessary and uphold the legitimacy of Spanish domination. In support of this claim I can cite the fact that Spanish legislation (particularly colonial laws) and the validity of evangelization are some of the main subtexts for both poems, evident in the emphasis placed on Caupolicán's conversion to Christianity before his death by impalement at the end of the *Araucana*,[2] and in Castellanos's reiteration throughout his *Elegías* that Amerindians were barbarians under the control of the devil prior to the arrival of Europeans. In addition, both authors acknowledge that excesses have been committed while carrying out the conquest and share the presupposition that there are *good* and *bad* conquistadors. Ercilla, for example, criticizes captain Pedro de Valdivia as greedy and cruel and presents himself, more than any other Spanish character from the *Araucana*, as an ideal type of Spanish soldier. Castellanos, for his part, presents individuals such as the rebel Lope de Aguirre as a threat to the stability of the colonial regime but never indulges in the type of protagonism Ercilla ascribes to himself throughout the three parts of the *Araucana*. Instead, for Castellanos, the first generation of conquistadors who carried out exploration and became encomenderos embody the ideal type of Spanish imperial subject. This is the group that is introduced in the opening line of the *Elegías* with the blank term "mis amigos" (my friends).

It is also accurate to state that both authors are reformists but on different ends of the spectrum. Ercilla demonstrates familiarity with the reformist program outlined by Bartolomé de las Casas and makes evident that the execution of the enterprise of conquest could be improved. Castellanos, on the other hand, seeks reforms to limit the reach of the Crown's representatives, to end the policy of appointing members of the nobility to the highest posts in the administration of the American colonies, and to overturn legislation detrimental to the interests of the encomenderos.

Finally, several critics have elucidated key aspects of the opening to the *Araucana*, pointing out Ercilla's departure from Ariosto in the first two lines of the first stanza ("no las damas, amor, no gentilezas / de caballeros canto enamorados"[3] [not of ladies, love or courtesy / do I sing, nor about smitten knights]); the plural nature of the Spanish protagonists ("aquellos españoles esforzados"[4] [those vigorous Spaniards]); Ercilla's recognition of Amerindian courage ("la cerviz de Arauco no domada"[5] [the neck of untamed Amerindians]); and Ercilla's emphasis on his closeness to the monarch who is the intended recipient and ideal reader of the text ("y haberme en vuestra casa yo criado"[6] [having had the chance to be raised in your household]). Critics have also noted the importance Ercilla places in offering a true account ("es relación sin corromper sacada / de la verdad cortada a su medida"[7] [this is an unspoiled account / based on truth]) and his role as witness of some of the events he narrates ("dad orejas señor, a lo que digo / que soy de parte de ello buen testigo"[8] [heed my lord what I have to say / for I was a faithful witness to some of these events]). But much more can be said about the exordium to the first poem of the *Elegías* in the wake of the *Araucana*.

AN ALTERNATE APPROACH TO NARRATING THE CONQUEST OF THE NEW WORLD

The most obvious way in which Castellanos starts correcting Ercilla in the opening of the *Elegías* is by proposing a broader geographical scope and a different historiographical method. Castellanos introduces this change when he suggests that the affairs of the New World must to be told from the beginning (meaning since 1492) and not by narrowing them to only one single campaign. The issue of the need of a much broader geographical and historical approach comes up two times in the exordium to "Elegía I." The first time is in the last two lines of the second stanza: "pues para correr vías tan distantes / había de tomarlas mucho antes"[9] (for in order to traverse such distant paths / one ought to start from as far back as possible), and then throughout the entire fourteenth stanza when the poetic voice introduces the narration of Christopher Columbus's first journey across of the Atlantic Ocean:

> *Ya pues que cosas de Indias celebramos,*
> *para no proceder sin fundamento ,*
> *parece cosa justa que digamos*
> *algo de su primer descubrimiento:*
> *Porque de la raíz saquemos ramos*
> *que hagan al lector estar atento;*
> *pues edificio de cimiento falto*
> *mal se puede subir a lo muy alto.* [10]

> And since we celebrate the affairs of the (West) Indies
> so as not to proceed without a foundation
> it seems just to state
> something about its first discovery
> so that from the root we may obtain branches
> that will make the reader attentive;
> for a structure without a base
> cannot be raised to great heights.

In both cases the implication is that to do it otherwise amounts to falsehood, and the contrast between truth and falsehood is the thread that binds together the moral, historiographic, and poetic issues foregrounded in exordium as reiterated numerous times in phrases such as "parecióme decir la verdad pura / sin usar de ficción ni compostura" (it seemed fitting to speak the sole truth /

without the use of either fiction or style); or "porque si los discretos paran mientes, / son gustosas las verdades / y captan atención en los oyentes / mucho más que fingidas variedades"[11] (for upon reflection the prudent person will see / that truths in themselves are pleasurable / and capture the listeners' attention / much more effectively than artifice). In more substantial terms, in stanza 9 of the exordium Castellanos pledges to uphold an aesthetic standard quite different from the one adopted by Ercilla. According to Castellanos, the subject matter of his poems should serve as the sole criteria to assign their literary merit because, when writing about the conquest of the New World, poetic artifice amounts to falsehood:

> *Así que, no diré cuentos fingidos,*
> *ni me fatigará pensar ficciones*
> *a vueltas de negocios sucedidos*
> *en índicas provincias y regiones;*
> *y si para mis versos ser pulidos*
> *faltaren las debidas proporciones,*
> *querría yo que semejante falta*
> *supliese la materia, pues es alta.*[12]

> And so I shall not speak of false tales
> nor will I endeavor to devise fabrications
> surrounding the affairs that have taken place
> in the provinces and regions of the (West) Indies;
> and if my verses are lacking the required qualities
> to be considered fine poetry
> I would hope that such fault
> be remedied by the content that is of the highest order.

Castellanos anchors his account on personal experience by declaring at the beginning of his poem that he will write about events that he had witnessed: "de la verdad de cosas por mí vistas"[13] (of the truthful things I have witnessed). This is a crucial point of contention, and I will come back to it later. But for now it is sufficient to point out that the reiteration of an explicit concern with falsehood and deception in relation to what or how events should be narrated has no counterpart in the opening of the *Araucana*, nor is there in the opening of the *Araucana* something equivalent to Castellanos's self-imposed concern with purging Spanish heroic poetry of some of resources and stock conventions of the epic tradition as Castellanos does in his display of classical erudition from the fourth to sixth stanza (see appendix).

This vast and alternate approach to the events of the New World became a conundrum to which Castellanos had no practical solution, and resulted in the writing of more than 110,000 verses organized sometimes around the deeds of a particular individual and sometimes around the exploration of a specific geographic region. The profusion of verses in turn has led several critics to refer to Castellanos's writings as an anomaly or even a monstrosity.

Yet, when comparing Ercilla's and Castellanos's poetic practice, this fundamental programmatic difference must be acknowledged. Strictly speaking, Castellanos was not interested in revising, complementing, or expanding Ercilla's account of the Spanish campaigns to extinguish the resistance of the Mapuche Indians, a task embraced a decade and a half later by Pedro de Oña in his *Primera parte de Arauco Domado* (1596).[14] Instead, Castellanos offers a contending vision of the magnitude of the enterprise of conquest and proves Ercilla's account as incomplete and insufficiently narrow. This strategy was successful enough to impress Agustín de Zárate, author of the *Historia del descubrimiento y conquista del Perú* (1555),[15] and the person commissioned to evaluate the first volume of the *Elegías* and to approve it for publication. In his letter of approval Zárate is the first critic to explicitly establish a connection between the *Elegías* and the *Araucana*, and he praises both of their authors for their ability to infuse heroic poetry in *octavas reales* with so many indigenous names, a task, he noted, that had brought much recognition to the *Araucana*. But before making this assertion, Zárate recommends Castellanos's book for publication, observing that in the prolific field of texts concerning the enterprise of conquest, Castellanos's stood out because

> *Con haber tantos autores que han compuesto libros del descubrimiento y conquistas de las provincias del Perú, y de tantos y tan varios sucesos como en ella ha habido, entre los cuales se puede contar la historia que yo compuse tocante a esta materia, y otros que han trabajado en lo que toca a la Nueva España, todos estos libros quedaban defectuosos y sin principio, por no haber habido quien tomase a su cargo declarar cómo y cuándo y por quién se comenzó a descubrir tanta anchura de mar como hay así norte sur, como este oeste, desde el estrecho de Gibraltar hasta las provincias de la tierra firme donde va a parar.*[16]

With the many authors that have written books about the discovery and the conquest of the provinces of Peru, and of the numerous and varied events that have transpired there, among which we could include the volume that I wrote regarding this subject, and many others who have worked on matters concerning New Spain, all these books were flawed and lacked foundation because nobody took it upon themselves to declare how, when, and by whom the vastness of the [Atlantic] ocean was discovered as it runs north and south, east to west; from the Strait of Gibraltar to the provinces of the Tierra Firme where it ends.

In his approval of the *Elegías*, Zárate endorses the alternative historiographic approach announced in the exordium to "Elegía I" and finds fault in previous books (including his own and implicitly the *Araucana*), which narrowed their focus to a specific geographic area without providing a perspective of the early stages or of the entire scope of the enterprise. The phrase "de tantos y

tan varios sucesos" (of so many and diverse events) resonates with the metaphor Castellanos would use to match the breath of his poetic ambition with
the magnitude of the enterprise of exploration and conquest: "inexhausto
edificio"[17] (endless edifice). Of vital interest to this study is the emphasis
Zárate assigns to naming when, how, and by whom the conquest had been
carried out: "cómo, cuándo y por quién,"[18] which is at the core of Castellanos's poetic agenda. Certainly, Castellanos's concern with recognizing the
singularity of the individuals involved in the campaigns of conquest will play
a pivotal role in his innovative method to authorize his poems, taking it to the
extreme of placing the weight of his strategy on the contributions made by
explorers and soldiers typically excluded from the historical record (see
chapter 5). As implied in the previous observations made in regard to the
issue of royal and literary authority in Spanish imperial epics, it is the voice
of a common and otherwise anonymous soldier that finds an outlet and is
expressed with full force in the closing lines of the sixth stanza of the exordium to "Elegía I": "porque las grandes cosas que yo digo / su punto y su
valor tienen consigo"[19] (because the great deeds that I speak of / carry in
themselves an intrinsic worth and significance). The contrast with Ercilla
could hardly be any sharper.

However, subsequent critics have paid more attention to Zárate's comment about the meter of Castellanos's and Ercilla's poems and less attention
to Zárate's conception of essential differences between the two poets. Admit-
tedly, when Meo Zilio compares the exordium of the two poems and judges
some of the opening stanzas of the *Elegías* as weak and dull while chastising
Castellanos for taking nine stanzas to achieve what Ercilla had been able to
achieve in one,[20] he ignores this key issue and the multiple ways in which
Castellanos draws the reader in to make connections between his poems and
those of his predecessor. Far from being dull or too long, what is remarkable
is that in only fourteen stanzas Castellanos is able to challenge Ercilla and
reconfigure existing literary traditions in so many different ways: the broader
geographic and historical approach being the first, and the strategic references to his comrades-in-arms being the second.

A NEW AUDIENCE AND A NEW PROTAGONIST FOR
SPANISH HEROIC POETRY

The men that Castellanos refers to as *varones ilustres* (illustrious gentlemen)
in the title and *mis amigos* (my friends) in the fifth line of the opening stanza
("no penen mis amigos con espanto"[21] [do not be overpowered by fear my
friends]) are the same group of people avidly criticized by advocates of
reform such as Alonso de Ercilla or defenders of the rights of Amerindians
such as Fray Bartolomé de las Casas. The phrase *mis amigos* also points to

the same group of individuals whose political and economic power had been diminished by the Spanish Crown through bureaucracy and regulation in an effort to establish the Crown's authority in the newly acquired territories. By making his friends the protagonists and the implied audience of the poem and apologizing for not starting to write it earlier, Castellanos is able to present a dispersed and disenfranchised group of individuals as a homogeneous group with a single common purpose. In fact, by not providing any specific names this community immediately appears united by experience and by sharing a worldview and a common interest. In this sense, what the title and the open-ing stanza of the *Elegías* demonstrate is that heroic poetry was instrumental not only for the "pro-Castilian upper echelon of the Iberian Peninsula"[22] but also for those disenfranchised commoners who came to the New World searching for adventure, wealth, or social mobility, in their subsequent effort to refashion their own identity and imagine another type of social and politi-cal community only feasible for them on the American side of the Atlantic. The upward trajectory of Castellanos's career in the New World offers a prime example of this trend.

From another angle, if the friendship between courtiers Juan Boscán and Garcilaso de la Vega is considered the foundational event of the Spanish Renaissance, as argued by Elías L. Rivers,[23] the friendship that Castellanos refers to constantly throughout his *Elegías* should be interpreted as one of the foundational elements of Spanish American literature, which at this early stage was intricately linked to the colonialist project. By making his friends (meaning the conquistadors and encomenderos) the protagonists and the im-plied audience of the poem, readers are in effect asked to sympathize with their cause and are rendered insensitive toward the violence and suffering inflicted upon others while achieving their deeds. In this sense, the reference to friendship in lines such as "no penen mis amigos con espanto / por no lo comenzar mas de mañana"[24] (do not be overpowered with fear my friends / for not having begun [this task] earlier) is a necessary step that allows the narrator to depict the native population as barbaric and the conquest as an enterprise to bring them into civilization. Notice how in stanza 11 of the exordium Castellanos starts to weave a poetic discourse in which difference is reduced to weakness, fear, and distrust, and in which violence is intrinsi-cally embedded as part of the civilizing project carried out by Europeans in the sixteenth century:

> *Veréis pocos y ya casi perdidos*
> *sujetar increíbles muchedumbres*
> *de bárbaros crueles y atrevidos*
> *forzados a tomar nuevas costumbres,*
> *do flaqueza, temor y desconfianza*
> *afilaban los filos de la lanza.*[25]

You shall witness the few and almost defeated
subdue incredible hordes
of cruel and fearless barbarians
forced to adopt new customs
where weakness, fear, and mistrust
would sharpen the blades of the spears.

In sum, the sadness and empathy that the opening lines of "Elegía I" imbue into poetic discourse are geared toward not the destruction and the loss inflicted upon the native cultures but the tribulations, the change in fortune, and the lack of recognition given to the individuals who perpetrated it. From this angle, Ercilla's approach, particularly the fictional amorous episodes of the *Araucana*, would appear as a trivialization of the wars of conquest quite removed from the logic of the *Relación de méritos y servicios* (Relation of merits and services) and the economy of royal favor, which inform the *Elegías*. Later on in stanza 13 of the exordium, Castellanos would encapsulate the decline in social and economic standing and the unfulfilled expectations of some of the individuals who had carried out the campaigns of conquest. This downward assessment of the conquest from the perspective of the uncertainties of the moment of writing is characteristic of the *Elegías*:

> *Veréis muchos varones ir en una*
> *prosperidad que no temió caída,*
> *y en estos esta misma ser ninguna,*
> *de su primero ser desvanecida*
> *usando de sus mañas la fortuna*
> *en los inciertos cambios de esta vida;*
> *otros venir a tanta desventura*
> *que el suelo les negaba sepultura.* [26]

> You shall witness many brave men
> achieve such prosperity that feared no penalty
> and among them the said opulence be vanished
> as a result of the trickery of fortune
> in life's uncertain changes
> others to encounter such bad luck
> that even the ground refused their burial.

In his poems Castellanos does not offer a detailed or extended meditation on the meaning of friendship but makes numerous tactical references to his friends and comrades-in-arms that have crucial rhetorical functions. The one included in the first stanza of the exordium and the one in the prologue to the fourth volume of the *Elegías* are of special importance because they actively present the *Araucana* as a privileged subtext for Castellanos's writing; we should not forget that in the prologue to the *Araucana* Ercilla had also referenced his comrades-in-arms when he confessed that they urged him to submit his work to print: "ayudando a ello las importunaciones de muchos testigos que en lo más dello se hallaron"[27] (aided by the earnest requests of many witness who participated in it). Castellanos takes Ercilla's insight much further and throughout his writings he successfully develops the notion that he is writing about the experiences of his friends; that his friends gave him verbally or in writings the accounts that he is transcribing; and even that he is a close friend of well-known individuals such as historian Gonzalo Fernández de Oviedo or conquistadors Gonzalo Jiménez de Quesada and Pedro de Ursúa. The effectiveness of these references to his friends has played a significant role in critics placing the *Elegías* as an example of *verista*, or historical poetry, without exploring the intricate scaffolding that allows Castellanos to create the impression of firsthand reportage. But the abundant poetic liberties taken by Castellanos and the highly deliberate nature of his articulation of friendship indicate that such interpretation should be examined more closely (see chapter 5).

THE SIGNIFIER *DULCE*: A CALL FOR POETIC REFORM

For the purpose of elucidating the differences between Castellanos's and Ercilla's projects, it is important to recognize that by declaring that he is writing to fulfill a promise to his friends, Castellanos demonstrates familiarity with the cultural norms of the Spanish elites. Castellanos accomplishes this by stating his political and ideological loyalties rather casually and by encoding the economic and political motivations of his writing in the language of honor, duty, loyalty, and service, which were all highly aristocratic discourses skillfully employed by Ercilla in the *Araucana*.[28] Recognizing the transformation of aristocratic discourses is important, because what Castellanos actually achieves is to advance his own poetic agenda, which includes proposing a new subject for elegiac poetry and to challenge the primacy of Petrarchism/Garcilacism as the dominant poetic language of the Spanish global monarchy. The problematization of Petrarchism/Garcilacism within the *Elegías* is significant because of the central role assigned to Garcilaso's poetic practice within Ercilla's epic.

Several critics have pointed out the impact of Garcilaso in Ercilla's poetic diction and approach to the practice of poetic imitation, including José Toribio Medina (1948), Eugenio Florit (1967), Lía Schwartz de Lerner (1972), James Nicolopulos (2000), and Felipe Valencia (2015). Schwartz de Lerner, in particular, suggests that in the poetic expression in episodes such as the one involving Lautaro and Guacolda,[29] "es . . . evidente la huella de Garcilaso, tanto en la repetición de temas e imágenes de la lírica petrarquista como en reminiscencias verbales"[30] (it is . . . evident that Garcilaso is influential, in the repetition of themes and images from Petrarchist lyric as well as in verbal reminiscences). To illustrate her point, she goes on to cite several verses

from the *Araucana* and to indicate a possible source from the poetry of
Garcilaso, including a line such as "el preciso hado y dura suerte" (the
precise fate and harsh luck) spoken by Guacolda, which repeats with some
variations a verse from "Elegía I" by Garcilaso: "Oh miserables hados! ! Oh
mezquina / suerte la del estado humano, y dura, por do tantos trabajos se
camina"[31] (O miserable fate! / O wretched luck of human existence, in which
we suffer so many ordeals . . .).

Iberian Renaissance elegy, chiefly Garcilaso's, is a literary genre that
contributed to shape the amorous episodes of the *Araucana* as suggested by
Schwartz de Lerner and Luis Fernando Restrepo (2008).[32] As mentioned
earlier, given the overwhelming success of the *Araucana*, even nonspecialists
would have recognized when turning the first pages of the *Elegías* in 1589
that Castellanos must have been aware of the importance of the *Arauca-*
na when he chose to write a series of heroic poems about the campaigns of
conquest of the New World. Given the success of Garcilaso de la Vega and
his increasing ascendancy in the Spanish literary canon after Francisco
Sánchez de las Brozas's (El Brocense) annotated edition in 1574,[33] there
should not be any doubt that Castellanos must have been aware of Garcilaso's elegies when he set out to write his own series of *Elegías*. As it is well
known, the topic of Garcilaso's "Elegía II" is love and more specifically the
suffering caused by jealousy and the possibility of a betrayal. Garcilaso's
"Elegía I," on the other hand, eulogizes Don Bernardino de Toledo and offers
consolation to his older brother Don Fernando, the duke of Alba. As such,
Garcilaso's "Elegía I," in particular, meets the expectations of the genre of
Renaissance Iberian funeral elegies, which were meant to reflect "the pride
of the military aristocracy"[34] and to sing "las excelencias, virtudes y hazañas
de duques y marqueses"[35] (the distinction, virtues, and deeds of noble men).
What we find in the opening of Castellanos's *Elegías* is quite a different
topic, which aptly defamiliarizes the expectations of the genre within the
highly charged environment created after the promulgation of the New Laws.

Castellanos's *Elegías* is not about love or jealousy or about the celebration of the merits and values of the aristocracy, nor about empathizing with
the grief and providing solace to a member of the upper nobility while
offering an invective against war (see the section that begin with the line
"¡Oh miserables hados! Oh mezquina / suerte la del estado humano"[36]).
Instead, Castellanos's poems are about the unabashed celebration of the martial prowess of the conquistadors and the instrumental role they played in
carrying out the enterprise of transatlantic expansion. To this end, in stanza
11 of the exordium Castellanos augments the military aptitude of the first
generation of conquistadors by underscoring how a few of them could defy
nature and adversity to win over endless number of Amerindians. The celebration of the cult to the heroic few is as close as Castellanos would come to
agreeing with Ercilla in the exordium to "Elegía I," since a comparable

celebration of the feats of few Spaniards outnumbered by large crowds of Amerindian warriors are not uncommon in the *Araucana*.[37] But this agreement is short lived, and in the following stanza Castellanos departs again from Ercilla when he states that Spaniards conquered the New World not with the help of cannons or harquebuses (or any other type of logistic or military advantage such as horses, ships, armors, or Amerindian allies, for that matter) but with their swords and shields alone. Castellanos's unwarranted eschewal of the impact of firearms and other forms of military technology is relevant to this discussion because the asymmetries in the styles of warfare between Spaniards and Amerindians will become a central topic of consideration for Ercilla in the *Araucana*.

More to the point, one key signifier that Garcilaso de la Vega borrowed from Petrarch was the term *dulce* (sweet), a translation from the Italian *dolce* (sweet). Both words come from the Latin *dulce* (sweet, dear), which received a prominent role in Dido's disheartened speech from book 4 of Virgil's *Aeneid*. The term *dulce* is ubiquitous in Garcilaso's poetry and plays a central role in poems such as "Soneto X" ("¡Oh *dulces* prendas por mi mal halladas, / *dulces* y alegres cuando Dios quería"[38] [O sweet tokens found to my grief / dear and happy when God allowed them to be]) and "Soneto XXIII" ("coged de vuestra alegre primavera / el *dulce* fruto antes que el tiempo airado"[39] [seize the sweet fruit of your joyful spring / before irate time]). The same term reappears in the first line of "Eclogue I" ("El *dulce* lamentar de dos pastores"[40] [the sweet grieving of two shepherds]) and surfaces frequently throughout the same poem: "Se quejaba tan *dulce* y blandamente"[41] (would weep so sweet and gently); "y *dulce* primavera deseaba"[42] (and yearned for sweet spring); "Tu *dulce* habla en cuya oreja suena[43] (your dear voice in whose ear resounds); "Donde con *dulce* sueño reposaba"[44] (where in sweet sleep would rest); "le despojó su caro y *dulce* nido"[45] (destroyed his treasured and dear nest); "la *dulce* garganta"[46] (through his sweet neck); and "de allí me llevó mi *dulce* prenda"[47] (and from there she took my dear token). Likewise, the same term appears in the opening lines of Garcilaso's "Eclogue II" ("En medio del invierno está templada / el agua *dulce* desta clara fuente,"[48] [in the midst of winter lays still / the sweet water of this clear fountain]) and then reappears often in the bucolic section of the same poem: "el *dulce* murmurar deste ruido"[49] (the sweet murmur of this noise); "que con *dulce* soledad se abraza"[50] (who surrounds himself with sweet solitude); "combida a un *dulce* sueño"[51] (enticing to a sweet dream); "hinchen el aire de *dulce* armonía"[52] (may fill the air with sweet harmony); and "yo seré *dulce* más que sano amigo"[53] (I will be a dear more than a fair friend). While the significance of the term *dulce* for Garcilaso's lyric and bucolic poetry cannot be overstated, it is also pertinent to acknowledge that the same term is used in the introduction to the encomiastic section of Garcilaso's "Eclogue II" when Nemoroso gives his speech in celebration of the House of Alba.[54]

Ercilla appropriated the term *dulce* from Garcilaso and employed it in strategic lexical reminiscences throughout the *Araucana* to boost his own literary authority, particularly in the amorous fictions involving indigenous heroines such as Tegualda, Guacolda, and Glaura. The insertion of this term in the pages of the *Araucana* speaks of the fluid boundaries between genres in early modern Iberian poetry and specifically of the lyric impulse crossing into and out of the epic, as it is patent in the amorous episodes in Ercilla's poem.[55] The term *dulce* appears in the episode of Guacolda and Lautaro[56] in lines such as "*dulce* veneno" (sweet poison) and "*dulce* sueño" (sweet dream); and Guacolda as well as Tegualda and Glaura use it to refer to their husbands as "*dulce* esposo" (sweet husband) or "*dulce* amigo" (sweet friend; see chapter 2). Here we must note that the phrase "dulce amigo" could have entered the pages of the *Araucana* straight out of Garcilaso's "Elegía I," where the poetic voice uses it to refer to the bond between Don Fernando Alvares de Toledo, the duke of Alba, and Don Bernardino de Toledo, his younger brother. Incidentally, the adjective *dulce* is the same attribute that is mocked in the prologue to the fourth volume of the *Elegías* when Castellanos speaks of the excessive sweetness of Ercilla's poetry ("la dulcedumbre del verso con que D. Alonso de Ercilla celebró las guerras de Chile"[57] [the sweetness of the verse with which D. Alonso de Ercilla lauded the wars in Chile]), and the same key signifier that describes in the exordium to "Elegía I" the type of poetry Castellanos does not intend to write. Notice that in the third stanza of the exordium, the signifier *dulce* appears embedded within a conscious commentary on the manner poetry was read and written. When calling attention to this term, Castellanos is not simply rejecting specific topoi or merely discarding the use of certain terms in favor of others but drawing the attention to a worthy and authoritative literary tradition and inviting readers to adopt a different set of expectations:

> *Iré con pasos algo presurosos,*
> *sin orla de poéticos cabellos*
> *que hacen versos dulces , sonorosos*
> *a los ejercitados en leerlos.*[58]

> I shall proceed with fairly hasty steps
> without the embellishment of poetic adornments
> that make sweet and harmonious verses
> for those who are competent to read them.

What I am proposing here is that this specific term encoded strategically by Ercilla for the purpose of increasing his own literary authority offers us a unique window to perceive the intersection among literary taste, social class, and imperial aspirations. Readers familiar with the parameters set by Castellanos in the opening of the *Elegías* can interpret the reference to the *dulcedumbre* (excessive sweetness) of Ercilla's work as an ironic and disqualifying remark because he had already announced that sweetness was the one characteristic readers would not find in his poem. At least that much we can infer from his pledge that he intended to write: "sin orla de poéticos cabellos / que hacen versos *dulces*, sonorosos" (without the embellishment of poetic adornments / that make sweet and harmonious verses). In this regard, the first line, "iré con pasos algo presurosos," could be read as the very opposite of the paradigm of *sprezzatura*, a key concept for aristocrats developed in courtier manuals such as Baldassarre Castiglione's *El Cortesano*.[59] Indeed, Castellanos's blatant breaches of decorum have no equivalent in the poetry written by Ercilla or Garcilaso. In summary, the metapoetic commentary that contains the reference to the term *dulce* in the third stanza of the exordium to "Elegía I" is an explicit expression of Castellanos's call to transform the manner in which poetry was produced and consumed as part of the imperial project. That this call for reform is coming from a remote post in the periphery of the empire should not continue to go unnoticed.

CONCLUSION

Taking into account the significance of the signifier *dulce* in Garcilaso de la Vega's poetic language and the strategic use of this term by Ercilla in the *Araucana*, it should be clear that when we encounter references to *dulce* or *dulcedumbre* in Castellanos's writings (and those by Diego Dávalos de Figueroa), these references encapsulate a disdain for the use of Petrarchist/ Garcilacist poetic language by poets who had or were seeking access to the court of Philip II, and particularly the rejection of the use of such language to describe female indigenous characters in the pages of the *Araucana*. The title of the series of poems written by Juan de Castellanos (*Elegies of illustrious men of the Indies*) is not simply a euphemism that aims to silence and to obscure the unspeakable suffering and the deliberate or unintended violence that accompanied the campaigns of conquest of the New World by elevating the individuals who perpetrated that violence as heroes. But it is also part of a discourse aimed to displace Petrarchism/Garcilacism as the preferred poetic diction of empire. Accordingly, in the opening to the first of his *Elegías* Castellanos is able to steer elegiac and heroic poetry in a path different than the one charted by peninsular authors, while at the same time proposing a different group of individuals as the ideal subjects of the Spanish global monarchy and responding to the work of Alonso de Ercilla and of one of Ercilla's crucial literary models, Garcilaso de la Vega. Finally, the implications of Ercilla's favorable depiction of Amerindians heroines, his pro-aristocratic and anti-*encomendro* ideological posture, his appropriation of the language of Garcilaso de la Vega, and the narrower historiographic and geographic scope of the *Araucana* in its American subject matter must be recognized in order to understand the significance of Castellanos's emulation. These are the elements that provide logic, coherence, and poetic force to the opening stanzas of the *Elegías*.

NOTES

1. Giovanni Meo Zilio, *Estudio sobre Juan de Castellanos* (Florence, Italy: Valmartina, 1972), 69–70.
2. *Araucana*, canto 34, stanzas 14–19.
3. *Araucana*, canto 1, stanza 1.
4. *Araucana*, canto 1, stanza 2.
5. Ibid.
6. *Araucana*, canto 1, stanza 6.
7. *Araucana*, canto 1, stanza 4.
8. *Araucana*, canto 1, stanza 6.
9. *Elegías*, 1:59.
10. *Elegías*, 1:61.
11. *Elegías*, 1:59–60. Other examples include "por no darse bien las invenciones / de cosas ordenadas por sus hados, / ni los dioses de falsas religiones, / por la vía láctea congregados" (since it is not fitting / to speak of things decreed by fate / nor by the gods of false religions, / gathered around the Milky Way); "ni cantaré fingidos beneficios" (nor will I sing feigned praises); "como los que con grandes artificios / van supliendo las faltas del sujeto" (such as those that with great artifice / compensate for the limitations of their subject); and "de proceder sin mácula el hilo" (by proceeding without tainting the thread), all in *Elegías*, 1:59–61.
12. *Elegías*, 1:60.
13. Ibid.
14. Pedro de Oña, *Primera parte de Arauco Domado* (Lima, Peru: Impresso en la Ciudad delos Reyes, 1596).
15. Agustín de Zárate, *Historia del descubrimiento y conquista del Perú* (Antwerp, Belgium: Martin Nucio, 1555).
16. *Elegías*, 1:48.
17. *Elegías*, 4:133.
18. *Elegías*, 1:48.
19. *Elegías*, 1:60.
20. Meo Zilio, *Estudio sobre*, 67.
21. *Elegías*, 1:59.
22. Davis, *Myth and Identity*, 13.
23. Elías L. Rivers, *Boscán y Garcilaso: Su amistad y el Renacimiento en España* (Seville, Spain: Sibila, 2010).
24. *Elegías*, 1:59.
25. *Elegías*, 1:61.
26. *Elegías*, 1:61.
27. "Prologue," in *Araucana*, 69.
28. See Elizabeth B. Davis, "Alonso de Ercilla's Fractured Subjectivity: Internal Contradictions in *La Araucana*," in *Myth and Identity*, 20–60.
29. *Araucana*, canto 13, stanza 43, through canto 14, stanza 13.
30. Schwartz de Lerner, "Tradición literaria," 618.
31. Ibid., 619.
32. Ibid., 615–25; Luis Fernando Restrepo, "Entre el recuerdo y el imposible olvido: La épica y el trauma de la conquista," in *Épica y Colonia: Ensayos sobre el género épico en Iberoamérica (siglos XVI y XVII)*, ed. Paul Philipp Firbas, 41–59 (Lima: Fondo Editorial Universidad Nacional Mayor de San Marcos, 2008).
33. Francisco Sánchez de las Brozas, *Obras del excelente Poeta Garci Lasso de la Vega: Con anotaciones y enmiendas* (Salamanca, Spain: Pedro Lasso, 1574).

34. Julián Olivares, "Soy un fue, y un será, y un es cansado: Text and Context," *Hispanic Review* 63, no. 3 (Summer 1995): 390.

35. Ibid.; Eduardo Camacho Guizado, *La elegía funeral en la poesía española* (Madrid: Editorial Gredos, 1969), 125.

36. Garcilaso de la Vega, "Elegía I," in *Garcilaso de la Vega y sus comentaristas*, ed. Antonio Gallego Morell (Madrid: Editorial Gredos, 1972), 144–45, lines 76–93.

37. Michael Murrin, *History and Warfare in Renaissance Epic* (Chicago: University of Chicago Press, 1994), 162–67.

38. Garcilaso de la Vega, "Soneto X," in *Garcilaso de la Vega y sus comentaristas*, 112, lines 1–2.

39. Garcilaso de la Vega, "Soneto XXIII," in *Garcilaso de la Vega y sus comentaristas*, 118, lines 9–10.

40. Garcilaso de la Vega, "Eclogue I," in *Garcilaso de la Vega y sus comentaristas*, 159, line 1.

41. Ibid., 160, line 52.

42. Ibid., 162, line 104.

43. Ibid., line 127.

44. Ibid., 166, line 249.

45. Ibid., 168, line 327.

46. Ibid., line 332.

47. Ibid., line 342.

48. Garcilaso de la Vega, "Eclogue II," in *Garcilaso de la Vega y sus comentaristas*, 171, lines 1–2.

49. Ibid., line 13.

50. Ibid., 172, line 40.

51. Ibid., line 64.

52. Ibid., 173, line 69.

53. Ibid., 183, line 414.

54. Ibid., 209–10, lines 1154–68.

55. On the lyrical voices in the *Araucana* and the relationship between poetry and history, see Felipe Valencia, "Las 'muchas (aunque bárbaras)' voces líricas de *La Araucana* y la índole poética de una 'historia verdadera,'" *Revista Estudios Hispánicos* 49, no. 1 (March 2015): 147–71.

56. *Araucana*, canto 13, stanzas 43–57; canto 14, stanzas 1–3, 13–18.

57. "A los lectores" (To the readers), in *Elegías*, 4:133.

58. *Elegías*, 1:59.

59. Baldassarre Castiglione, *El Cortesano*, ed. Mario Pozzi, trans. Juan Boscán (Madrid: Cátedra, 2003).

Chapter Two

A Crisis in the Poetic Practice of *Imitatio*

An Encomendero Poet Responds to *Alonso de Ercilla's* Araucana

In this chapter I will focus on two aspects of Juan de Castellanos's emulation of Alonso de Ercilla. First, I examine the depiction of Amerindian heroines in the *Elegías* in the light of female indigenous characters from the *Araucana* such as Tegualda, Guacolda, and Glaura. And second, I analyze Castellanos's reformulation of the epic trope of the fate of the bodies of anonymous warriors who die in battle. As I shall suggest in my analysis, Castellanos undertakes a creative dialogue with the *Araucana* that aims precisely to reject the reformist program explicit in Ercilla's text, which had multiple ramifications for Spanish colonists. By elucidating the transatlantic scope of Castellanos's literary practices, this chapter aims to contribute to a better understanding of the circulation of epic tropes in the Iberian Atlantic circuit, and to our knowledge of how Renaissance literary and poetic conventions were flouted as Spain pushed its military and geographic expansion. As a point of entry to this discussion, I will comment briefly on the significance of an overt reference to Ercilla that appears in the *Elegías* and has been a persistent source of misunderstanding among critics:

> *Pero ya, vencido de persuasiones amigables, y considerando cómo se iban consumiendo con larga edad los vivos originales de donde había de sacar verdadero traslado cualquiera que tomase este cuidado, y que los que después escriben sin testigos de vista no llevan el camino tan derecho que no hallen dudosas torceduras, porque las cosas cuanto más lejanas de sus principios se cuentan, con menos certidumbre se pintan, antes de que este recurso a mí me*

faltase, puse, como dicen, faldas en cinta, y entré en este ambagioso laberinto,
cuya salida fuera menos dificultosa si los que en él me metieron se contenta-
ran con que los hilos de su tela se tejieran en prosa; pero enamorados (con
justa razón) de la dulcedumbre del verso con que D. Alonso de Ercilla celebró
las guerras de Chile, quisieron que las del Mar del Norte también se cantasen
con la misma ligadura, que es en octavas rimas; y así con ellas, por la mayor
parte, he procedido en la fábrica de este inexhausto edificio, del cual he
compuesto cuatro partes. [1]

But at last, overpowered by friendly persuasions, and taking into consideration
that live originals were being consumed by old age, [those] from whom a true
written account could be obtained by whomsoever undertook this task, and
that the path of those who later write without any eyewitnesses is not straight
enough to avoid doubtful turns, because the further [in time] things are told
from their beginnings, the less they are depicted with certainty; and before this
resource could become unavailable to me, I, as they say, girded up my loins
and entered this intricate labyrinth, whose exit would be less difficult if those
who put me there could be satisfied with the threads of its fabric being woven
in prose; but smitten (justifiably so) with the sweetness of the verse with which
D. Alonso de Ercilla lauded the wars in Chile, they wanted [the wars] on the
Northern Sea [the Atlantic Ocean] to be also sung with the same manner, that
is, in ottava rima; and thus, I have generally proceeded with it in the construction of this endless edifice, of which I have composed four parts.

This allusion to Alonso de Ercilla's *Araucana* appears in the prologue ("A
los lectores"[2] [To the readers]) that accompanies the fourth and last installment of the *Elegías* and has garnered a great deal of attention among critics
who comment on the relationship between the *Elegías* and the *Araucana*,
regardless of whether they are admirers or detractors of Castellanos's writing. Ever since the nineteenth century there has been a consensus concerning
the interpretation of this statement of authorial purpose, and most critics who
cite it, allude to it, or paraphrase it do so based upon a literal interpretation of
the passage and often as a preface to characterize Castellanos as a feverish
admirer or an epigone of Ercilla.

José María Vergara y Vergara condemns Ercilla's curt approval of the
second volume of Castellanos's poetry and scolds Ercilla for not praising
more enthusiastically the work of a fellow writer who had presumably at-
tempted to follow in his footsteps: "Don Alonso [de Ercilla] . . . no encontró
en su fecunda lengua y hábil pluma ni una palabra de elogio o de crítica sobre
el mérito literario de las *Elegías*. Ni agradeció la lisonja de la evidente
imitación de la *Araucana*; pues es indudable que Castellanos la había leído, y
más indudable que su lectura fue la que le despertó el deseo de contar en
verso las historias de estas tierras"[3] (Don Alonso [de Ercilla] . . . didn't find
even one word in his fecund tongue and skillful pen to praise or criticize the
literary merits of the *Elegías*. Nor did he express any appreciation for the

flattery in the obvious imitation of the *Araucana*; after all, it is unquestionable that Castellanos had read it and even more indisputable that it was the reading [of the *Araucana*] that awakened in him the desire to sing in verse the history of these lands). Praising the merits of Castellanos's prose and condemning the infelicities of some of his verses, Marcelino Menéndez y Pelayo writes that

> *lo más doloroso es que Castellanos había empezado por escribir su crónica en prosa, que hubiera sido tan fácil y agradable como lo es la de sus proemios, y luego, mal aconsejado por amigos que habían leído La Araucana, y le creían capaz de competir con Ercilla, gastó nada menos que diez años en la estéril tarea de reducir la prosa en verso, ingiriendo a sus tiempos muchas digresiones poéticas y comparaciones y otros colores poéticos con todo el buen orden que se requiere. Pésimo consejo, en verdad, y malhadada condescendencia la suya, puesto que así, en vez de un montón de versos casi ilegibles de seguida, hubiéramos tenido una de las mejores y más caudalosas crónicas de la conquista.* [4]

it is even sadder that Castellanos had started to write his chronicle in prose, which would have been pleasing and effortless as the prose of his prologues, and then, poorly advised by his friends who had read the *Araucana*, and reckoned he was capable of competing with Ercilla, spent no less than ten years in the barren task of translating his prose into verses, often indulging in poetic digressions, comparisons, and poetic colors without the propriety that would be expected. Terrible advise, and unfortunate submission, because that way, instead of a pile of verses almost illegible, we would have had one of the finest and more expansive chronicles of the conquest.

Manuel Alvar also criticizes the indifference of Ercilla's endorsement by stating, "Bien poca cosa para el hombre [Castellanos] que, al frente de la Cuarta Parte de las *Elegías*, vertió la prueba fiel de su devoción hacia el poeta vasco"[5] (So little toward the man [Castellanos] who at the beginning of the fourth volume of the *Elegías* left unblemished evidence of his devotion for the Basque poet). On the other hand, Mario Germán Romero introduces Castellanos's statement with the following comment: "Cuando hablamos de la influencia de Ercilla en Castellanos, no hacemos una conjetura o una afirmación gratuita. El mismo cronista se refiere a los que lo metieron (Dios los haya perdonado) en la dificultad de tejer en verso los hilos de su historia"[6] (when we speak of Ercilla's influence on Castellanos we are not guessing or making a gratuitous remark. The very own historian [Castellanos] speaks of those who put him, may God forgive them, in the arduous task of weaving in verse the threads of his history). Later Romero recalls again Castellanos's reference to Ercilla when he writes, "Hay quienes no perdonan a los que enamorados de la dulcedumbre del verso de Ercilla, metieron a Castellanos en el ambagioso laberinto de hacerle narrar la historia en verso"[7] (there are some who cannot forgive those who, smitten with the sweetness of Ercilla's poem, put Castellanos in the intricate labyrinth of having to narrate his history in verse). Likewise, Isaac J. Pardo states categorically that "la relación entre las *Elegías* y *La Araucana* la declaró Castellanos al comienzo de la *Historia del Nuevo Reino de Granada*. Indica allí cómo emprendió la versificación de la obra para dar gusto a sus amigos quienes 'enamorados' (con justa razón) de la dulcedumbre del verso con que Don Alonso de Ercilla celebró las guerras de Chile, quisieron que las del Mar del Norte también se cantasen con la misma ligadura que es en octava rima"[8] (Castellanos declared the relationship between the *Elegías* and the *Araucana* at the beginning of his *History of the New Kingdom of Granada*. There he indicates how he started the versification of his work to please his friends who "smitten" (justifiably so) with the sweetness of the verse with which D. Alonso de Ercilla lauded the wars in Chile, they wanted [the wars] on the Northern Sea [the Atlantic Ocean] to be also sung with the same manner, that is, in ottava rima). A similar approach to the relationship between the two poems resurfaced more recently in William Ospina's *Las auroras de sangre*. According to Ospina, "Fue la belleza de esa obra [the *Araucana*], y la insistencia de sus amigos, lo que decidió a Castellanos a darle a su memorial la forma de cantos escritos en octavas reales"[9] (It was the beauty of that work [the *Araucana*], and the persistence of his friends, that led Castellanos to turn his chronicle into the mold of stanzas written in *octavas reales*).

Lost in this line of inquiry is an appreciation of Castellanos's deep and abiding concern with reassessing Spain's poetic traditions in light of New World possessions. Indeed, it is surprising that none of these critics seems to wonder why a writer who is also indebted to Latin poets such as Virgil and Ovid, and to Iberian poets such as Juan de Mena, Jorge de Montemayor, and Garcilaso de la Vega, feels the need to acknowledge openly his connection to Ercilla in a prologue addressed to readers, and perhaps more importantly, to the official censors. And considering the complex relationship that exists between the *Elegías* and the *Araucana*, and the irreverence with which Castellanos appropriates and subverts some of the most memorable scenes from Ercilla's poem, why mention only that aspect of the *Elegías* that even the most untrained eye could recognize as following the trend successfully popularized in Spain by Ercilla? By taking for granted the sincerity of Castellanos, it appears that these critics aver that no other type of connection or intertextuality between the two poems is possible and believe that what is specific to Ercilla's poem and is later replicated in Castellanos's is only the use of *octavas reales*, a much too narrow reading of either text.

I doubt that the reason Castellanos decided to switch from historiography to the heroic poetry (if indeed that is what happened) was such a subjective and capricious motive. Taking into account the centrality of censorship at this time, a more plausible explanation would be to suggest that Castellanos was aware of the fact that the subject of his writing was the site of highly contested controversies and that one way in which authors could navigate sensitive topics and even avoid the constraints of official censorship was by switching from historiographic and ethnographic accounts to epic and heroic poetry, a genre that enjoyed great demand in the sixteenth century and could more easily be the beneficiary of royal endorsement. [10] Hence, by alluding to the most prestigious and popular Spanish epic of his time in the prologue, Castellanos offers the readers (and the censors) an outside reference with which to judge his work, one that conveniently situates the *Elegías* within the realm of literature, thus distancing them from controversy. [11] Yet, as we shall see from the way Castellanos depicts indigenous women and reformulates the epic topos of the fate of the bodies of soldiers who die in battle, the *Elegías* support an encomendero agenda quite different from Ercilla's.

Moreover, and contrary to what others have argued, I consider that interpreting Castellanos's reference to Ercilla literally imposes over the prologue and the rest of Castellanos's writings an immediacy and a transparency his texts do not posses and constantly strive to avoid. The allusion to Ercilla, we must note, appears embedded among highly figurative and metaphoric language, which as it turns out tends to evoke relationships and to disseminate meaning rather than to fixate it or suppress it. At least one of these metaphors in particular should serve as the telltale sign that the entire prologue should be read with a large grain of salt. Notice, for example, that before making the assertion about the *dulcedumbre* (excessive sweetness) of Ercilla's verse, Castellanos describes his own writing as a *laberinto* (labyrinth), a term loaded with political and ideological connotations ever since it was used by Juan de Mena in his *Laberinto de la Fortuna* (1444) to draw a connection between the convoluted nature of the text and the writing process and the current political situation. If Castellanos is indeed using this reference to Mena to acknowledge that he is writing within a highly contested political context, the merit of his prologue and of the reference to Ercilla in particular lies in making explicit that his poems had been commissioned by the conquistadors, but doing so in a rather casual and nonthreatening way that implies a sort of analogy between the highly aristocratic milieu of the court (center) and the Spanish colonies in the New World (periphery). Accordingly, with his reference to Ercilla, Castellanos also hints that the former conquistadors were capable of engaging in the type of patronage that coupled writing to political will in and around the court. From this we can infer that Castellanos was familiar with the indirect and courtly manner of argumentation preferred by the aristocrats who surrounded the court of the Hapsburgs. [12]

The crux of the matter is that the literal interpretation of Castellanos's allusion to the *Araucana* brings a rather low set of expectations to the reading of his poems and can only be made by denying the rhetorical function that this and other references to Ercilla serve within the prologue and within Castellanos's poetic discourse at large. Critics who take the reference to Ercilla at face value overlook the fact that almost every time Castellanos borrows from or alludes to Ercilla, he does so through an iconoclastic impulse that calls for the immediate transformation of the model or its complete rejection. Hence, asserting that Castellanos includes this reference simply to claim that he is an admirer or an epigone of Ercilla bypasses the contentiousness of the texts that participated in what Rolena Adorno has called the "polemics of possession," the cornerstones of Castellanos's ideological and literary project, and the discursive and narrative strategies he used to convey it.

A NEW DIANA FOR A NEW WORLD:
LUST AND BETRAYAL AT FUERTE DE NAVIDAD

To illustrate the extent to which Juan de Castellanos's *Elegías* diverge from the ideological and aesthetic platform that informs Alonso de Ercilla's poem, I will focus on a poem entitled "Elegía II," which was written in honor of Diego de Arana. Arana was one of the explorers who accompanied Christopher Columbus on his first journey to the New World and was left as the leader of the thirty-nine men who stayed at the Fuerte de Navidad after Columbus returned to Spain to inform the Spanish monarchs about his "discovery."[13] The second canto of "Elegía II" aims to provide readers with an explanation as to what exact motives led to the death of all of the colonists at the hands of local Indians. Castellanos's account of the incidents that took place after Columbus left the settlement at Hispaniola is quite exceptional, not only because it fuses with considerable liberty information about the historical events with allusions to Jorge de Montemayor's *Los siete libros de la Diana* and Ercilla's *Araucana*, but also because, in essence, it proposes that the colonists were killed because of an illicit love affair between a young Spanish explorer and a beautiful Indian woman who was the wife of the local Indian chieftain named Coaga Canari. Castellanos's version of the events surrounding the debacle at the Fuerte de Navidad has some of the core elements of a foundational myth that encapsulates and justifies the transfer of empire through the narration of the conflict that unraveled as a result of an illicit sexual encounter. Somewhat along the lines of classical epics such as Homer's *Iliad*, the roots of war can be traced back to a wife's betrayal of her husband and to the rage unleashed by the affronted husband. Castellanos pieces together his version of the downfall of the colonists by using a misogynistic and Eurocentric discourse that displaces any responsibility from the Spanish explorers and places the blame for the outburst of the conflict on the behavior of a lustful indigenous woman. In the end, therefore, his narrative is organized according to a series of binary oppositions that gives primacy to one side over the other and links Spanish explorers to masculinity, virtue, reason, and heroism, while linking the natives to femininity, sinfulness, irrationality, and cowardice, as conveyed in the following introductory lines:

> *Huye de la razón el amor ciego:*
> *y ciegan las lascivias de mujeres;*
> *en todos los principios indecentes*
> *los fines tienen mil inconvenientes.* [14]

> Blind love runs away from reason:
> and women's lust can impair judgment;
> where there is indecency at the outset
> the outcome has a thousand drawbacks.

Since what is of interest to us here is how Castellanos uses this story to respond to Ercilla, it is pertinent to point out that, like the indigenous heroines of the *Araucana*, the female character Castellanos creates is both the object and the emitter of Petrarchist/Garcilacist poetic discourse. In Castellanos's "Elegía II," the entire episode at the Fuerte de Navidad is narrated by an anonymous Indian who uses Petrarchist/Garcilacist language to characterize the female protagonist as an exceedingly beautiful woman capable of awakening the admiration of all who behold her. However, unlike Ercilla's use of such language, I would argue that Castellanos's has primarily an ironic function, which in the following stanzas becomes apparent from the sharp contrast created in three separate but complementary ways: first, by the merging of religious imagery with allusions to concupiscence; second, by the embellished description of the physical appearance of the indigenous maiden and the comments the narrator makes about her conduct and her character; and third, by the assignment to the protagonist of the nickname of "Diana," the name of the hunting goddess associated emblematically with chastity in Roman mythology:

> *Una señora principal había*
> *entre todos los nuestros celebrada,*
> *de la cual vuestra noble compañía*
> *era por muchas veces visitada,*
> *a quien Coaga Canari bien quería,*
> *y era del por estremo regalada:*
> *allí tenía puestos pensamientos,*
> *deleites, pasatiempos y contentos.*

> *Entre todas las cosas, la natura*
> *esta ninfa crió por más lozana;*
> *no sabré dibujaros su figura,*
> *por parecer divina más que humana;*
> *mas quiero comparar su hermosura*

al claro resplandor de la mañana
pues aunque la cubría mortal velo
no parecía cosa de este suelo.

Las gracias de las otras eran muertas
delante dones tan esclarecidos;
suspensos se quedaban por las puertas
pasando, sus cabellos esparcidos:
y aquellas proporciones descubiertas,
cadenas de potencias y sentidos;
ablandan también sus condiciones
los más endurecidos corazones.

Diana vuestra gente la llamaba,
teniéndola por cosa milagrosa,
a ella desto nunca le pesaba
ni fue de sus loores desdeñosa,
antes en gran manera se holgaba
que todas la loasen de hermosa:
enamorábanla vuestros varones
con amorosas señas y razones. [15]

There was a noteworthy woman
cherished by everyone on our side
who was visited quite often
by members of your noble troupe
she was dearly loved by Coaga Canari
who would offer her all kinds of delights:
in her he had placed his thoughts
his joys, his amusements, and his happiness.

Amongst all other things, nature
raised this nymph to be the most vivacious
I would not know how to describe her figure
because she seems more divine than human;
but I shall compare her beauty
to the bright light of dawn;
because although she was swathed on a mortal veil
she did not seem something from this world.

The graces of all other women were numb
next to such illustrious gifts;
everyone would be left mystified on their threshold
when her flowing hair went by;
and such greatness in plain sight
strings of latent faculties and aptitudes
would also soften her talents
even the toughened hearts.

> Your people called her Diana
> assuming she was a miraculous thing
> this never burdened her
> nor was she ever dismissive of their praise
> instead she very much enjoyed
> that everyone acclaimed her beauty
> your men would flatter her
> with seducing gestures and words.

In describing the physical attributes of the protagonist, the narrator appeals to some of the elements of the tradition of poetic portraits but at the same time exceeds the expectations of that tradition by suggesting that the woman is fully naked. This type of transgression is relevant because it serves to emphasize the otherness of Diana and her culture, given that such display of the human body was incompatible with the practices and the norms that allowed Spanish colonists to consolidate social hierarchies and to control sexuality legally and ecclesiastically in the emerging colonial context under the auspices of the Counter-Reformation. In this regard, Luis Fernando Restrepo has shown how Castellanos uses different strategies to represent the bodies of European and indigenous women.[16] Be that as it may, the last of these four stanzas is the most important to appreciate how Castellanos is creating an indigenous female character that is the antithesis of the ones created by Ercilla. Several critics have recognized that one of the most outstanding features of the female heroines of the *Araucana* is their chastity and irreproachable loyalty to their husbands. Here we may recall the vehemence with which Guacolda challenges Fortune and pledges to end her life in the event that the Spanish troops might put an end to the life of Lautaro.[17] We can also cite Ercilla's description of the aftermath of the Battle of Penco and the pathetic image of the devoted Tegualda looking for the corpse of Crepino to give him a proper burial. The intensity of her request is heightened by her insistence on preferring death to life without her husband.[18] In effect, at the end of the episode it is Ercilla himself who endorses the honesty of Tegualda's promise by expressing the difficulty he had in preventing her from harming herself or committing suicide.[19] Finally, we can recall the exalted joy that overcomes Glaura when she is unexpectedly reunited with her husband Cariolán, whom she thought had been killed.[20]

When read against the background of the loyalty and chastity of Ercilla's indigenous heroines, Castellanos's Diana stands out immediately, because if her physical beauty is sufficient for the narrator to elevate her to the status of a goddess, her conduct is enough for the readers to demote her to the level of a frivolous, licentious, and pernicious woman who disregards the devotion of her husband and is more concerned with the attention she inspires from her foreign admirers and with finding opportunities to succumb to her passion.

Such opportunity eventually arises after one Spanish explorer falls madly in love with her and Diana is able to arrange for an amorous encounter to take place while she is bathing nude in the company of her female friends. In his description of the place frequented by Diana, Castellanos appeals to the medieval topos of the *locus amoenus*, whose core elements (water, fountain, shadows, trees, etc.) imbue this scene with a sensuality absent from the pages of the *Araucana*. In the *Elegías*, the presence of this trope leads to the consummation of the sexual encounter, which in the overall symbolic edifice of the poem stands as a metaphor for colonization:

> *Tocada pues la ninfa de estas llamas*
> *envió mensajera diligente*
> *avisando que sola con dos damas*
> *se bañaba por aguas de una fuente*
> *cubierta con las sombras de una rama,*
> *secreta y apartada de su gente*
> *si quiere ir, mas es mejor no vella,*
> *pues nada bueno ve que ver en ella.* [21]

> And hence touched the nymph by these flames
> she sent a diligent messenger
> to inform that only in the company of two ladies
> she was bathing on the waters of a fountain
> under a canopy of shadows from the branches,
> in secrecy and away from all her people;
> thus if he wants to go, though it's better not to see her,
> since there is nothing good to see in seeing her.

Another outstanding feature of Ercilla's female indigenous characters that is subverted by Castellanos in this episode is the rhetorical strategy of referring to the beloved as the soul of the lover. Critics such as Isaac Pardo and Giovanni Meo Zilio have revealed that in the bath scene Castellanos is adhering closely to a sequence of events narrated in one of the final episodes from book 7 of Jorge de Montemayor's *Los siete libros de la Diana* (1559).[22] Indeed, after the Indian nymph becomes aware of the presence of her suitor, she reacts violently and reprimands him, and much as the knight Felis faints in front of Felismena in Montemayor's story, in Castellanos's poem the startled Spanish explorer faints in front of Diana. Likewise, just as Montemayor's Dorida throws water in the face of the knight Felis, one of Diana's female companions throws water in the face of the soldier to awaken him. One could add to Pardo and Zilio's comments about intertextuality the observation that when Diana finally starts speaking, her lament echoes not the words of Felismena but Tegualda's and Guacolda's promise to remain united to their husbands even after they are dead. This second level of intertextuality, and the correspondence between Diana's speech and the words uttered by Guacolda in the scene prior to the death of Lautaro, is accentuated by the patronym and the matronym used to refer to the male protagonist in each text respectively: Ercilla's Tegualda calls Lautaro "hijo de Pillán," and Castellanos's Diana refers to the Spanish explorer as "Hijo de Latona." Yet, while in the episode involving Tegualda Ercilla had aptly inverted the Petrarchist/Garcilacist trope of referring to the beloved as the soul of the lover, in Castellanos this trope is now transposed into a new context that aims to deprive it of any favorable connotations:

> [Diana] Decía contemplando su figura:
> hermano mío, dime, si me quieres,
> ¿Por qué quieres sin mí la sepultura,
> sabiendo que no vivo si tú mueres,
> y quedaré sin ti más sin ventura
> que cuantas han nacido de mujeres?
> recobra ya, señor, tu bello brío,
> pues ya junto tu rostro con el mío.
>
> ¿Haces eclipsi, hijo de Latona?
> ¿No oyes, alma mía, lo que digo?
> Oh ninfas de Haities y Saona!
> a cada cual de vos hago testigo
> de cómo tomaré de mi persona
> un más que crudelísimo castigo;
> maldad mía será si más aguardo,
> y con razón diréis que ya me tardo. [23]

> [Diana] She said while gazing at his figure:
> dear brother, tell me, if you love me,
> why do you seek to be buried without me?
> Knowing that I cannot go on living if you die,
> and I will be left without you with less fortune
> than all others born from women?
> Recover now, my lord, your beautiful strength,
> as I hold your face next to mine.
>
> Are you fading away, son of Latona?
> Can't you hear, my soul, what I'm saying?
> Oh, nymphs of Haities and Saona!
> I make you both witnesses
> of how I will inflict
> the cruelest punishment upon myself;
> it would be wicked of me to keep waiting
> and with reason you might say I delay.

According to Isaías Lerner, the rhetorical strategy of referring to the beloved as the soul of the lover was introduced into Spanish lyric by Garcilaso de la Vega in "Soneto XIX" and "adquiere una particular frescura en el contexto en que lo integra Ercilla; ya no se trata de la voz poética masculina en busca de su alma, sino del caso opuesto, doblemente conmovedor porque el 'cuerpo' yace literalmente sin vida y el 'alma' que habla está a punto de perder su cuerpo 'real'"[24] (acquires a particular freshness in the context in which it is integrated by Ercilla; it is no longer the male poetic voice in search of his soul but the exact opposite, which is twice as moving because the "body" literally lays lifeless and the "soul" that speaks is about to lose her "real" body). Therefore, when we interpret the exchange between Diana and the Spanish explorer from the perspective of what had been achieved by Ercilla, it becomes evident that the scene created by Castellanos is patently a parody whose goal is to dismantle what Ercilla had accomplished by using an exquisite poetic register to attribute chastity and loyalty to female indigenous characters like Tegualda, Guacolda, and Gualda.

Isaac Pardo has suggested that the idealized characterization of Amerindians found in the *Araucana* simply "passed" unchanged to the pages of the *Elegías*;[25] but Castellanos's treatment of the beloved topos suggests otherwise. Like Ercilla's female heroines, Castellanos's Diana manages to speak in Petrarchist/Garcilacist language, and presumably to do so decades before that poetic trend would gain full force among writers in the Iberian Peninsula. However, the very utterance of that language surfaces as a contradiction because her words are the ultimate confirmation of her moral turpitude and of her lack of attachment or devotion to her husband. Any reader of the *Araucana*, and particularly one who might have been reading the text in the New World, would not have missed the fact that Diana is pledging to remain united and follow into the afterlife not her husband but a foreigner with whom she is about to have an illicit sexual affair. Read in this manner, the allusion to Jorge de Montemayor also becomes very important, because it serves to reaffirm the artificiality of the poetic language that is being put on display. To put it differently, the allusion to Montemayor increases the tensions between Ercilla's and Castellanos's texts by bringing into the scene a comic release that is completely absent from the dramatically charged episodes describing the death of Lautaro and the search for Crepino's body in the aftermath of the battle at Penco. Accordingly, while the deaths of Lautaro and Crepino are very much real according to the sequence of events narrated in the *Araucana*, in Castellanos's poem the Spanish soldier merely passes out temporarily, and after one of Diana's female companions throws water on his face he quickly comes back to normal. This turn of events makes Diana's language and promises seem unnecessary and even utterly ridiculous, which is in accord with what encomendero poets such as Diego Dávalos y Figueroa will come to think of Ercilla's use of Petrarchist/Garcilacist poetic discourse to describe Amerindians.

However, the subversion of Ercilla's model is not complete until Diana goes on to make a speech in which she describes to the Spanish explorer the types of punishments her husband will impose upon them once he finds out about their dalliance. While warning her lover, Diana takes the opportunity to describe the customs and practices of her own culture but this time switching to a rhetoric similar to the one employed by the encomenderos to justify the military conquest and colonization. It is at this point that Castellanos's disavowal of Ercilla's characterization of Amerindian heroines becomes most piercing. By alluding to some of the most prestigious literary models of his time (Garcilaso de la Vega, Montemayor, and Ercilla), Castellanos cleverly sets the stage to dehumanize Amerindians and to cast them as violent, cruel, and cowardly savages who enjoy ingenious ways of torture and practice cannibalism. Diana's description of the members of her own culture as infidels not only frames the encounter between Europe and the New World as an encounter between civilization and barbarism but also justifies the conquest as a holy war and suggests that when violence is practiced by indigenous cultures it lacks any civilizing purpose:

> *Que bien sabes que rey es mi marido,*
> *el cual en guarda mía se desvela,*
> *y está de mis amores tan vencido,*
> *que hasta de los aires me recela;*
> *y al rey lo mas oculto y ascondido*
> *por mil vías y modos se revela,*
> *debajo de lo cual es lo mas cierto*
> *que será nuestro caso descubierto.*
>
> *Sabido ¿dónde piensas esconderte*
> *de flechas y flecheros violentos?*
> *O dó me defender y defenderte,*
> *si tienes de defensa los intentos?*
> *Pues el mayor amparo será muerte*
> *con varias invenciones de tormentos;*
> *porque estos que tú llamas infieles*
> *son cuanto más cobardes más crueles.*
>
> *Oh, cuán alharaquientos, cuan livianos,*
> *cuán alborotadores y apocados*
> *en las ejecuciones inhumanos!*
> *porque te llevarán por sus mercados,*
> *unas veces sin pies, otras sin manos,*
> *asido por los labios horadados,*
> *cortándote los miembros por mitades,*
> *gustando mucho destas crueldades.* [26]

You know well that my husband is a king,
who does not spare any measures to protect me,
and whose will has been so defeated by my love
that he is even suspicious of the wind;
and to the king that what is most hidden and concealed

is revealed in a thousand ways,
for which it is most certain
that our affair will be discovered.

Knowing this, where do you intend to hide
from arrows and violent archers?
Or where will you defend me and defend yourself
if it is defense what you intent to do?
for the greatest refuge will be death
by means of inventive torments;
because those that you call infidels
are crueler the more cowardly they are.

Oh, how quick, how feeble,
how unruly and vile
inhuman in their executions!
because they will take you to their markets,
sometimes without feet, other times without hands,
hanging from your pierced lips,
cutting your limbs in half,
very much enjoying these cruelties.

In summary, what Diana introduces when she attributes cannibalism to the first group of Indians that Spanish explorers encountered when they arrived in the New World is the rationale postulated over and over again by the conquistadors and encomenderos in favor of enslaving Amerindians and as justification of their own insatiable desire to colonize. As Carlos A. Jáuregui has eloquently demonstrated in his analysis of the symbolic dimensions of the trope of human sacrifice within Spanish American literature, cannibalism is understood as the preeminent cultural mark upon which encomenderos and their advocates built "el argumento principal de la apología histórica, jurídica, y filosófica de la conquista"[27] (the main historical, legal, and philosophical argument for the conquest); or the cannibal understood as the "*abracadabra* textual de la barbarie *ajena* y la excusa de la propia violencia"[28] (textual abracadabra for the savagery of others and the pretext for their own acts of violence). Thus, in at least four separate ways (nudity, lust, cannibalism, and the topos of the soul of the beloved), Castellanos transforms Ercilla's Petrarchist/Garcilacist figures in ways that undo Ercilla's monarchical, aristocratic, reformist agenda.

LA GAITANA: CANNIBALISM AND THE
EPIC TOPOS OF THE AFTERMATH OF A BATTLE

The undoing of Ercilla's literary and ideological project is further developed in the *Elegías* through Castellanos's reformulation of the epic topos of the fate of the bodies of warriors who die in battle. Throughout the bulk of Castellanos's writings there are abundant passages that attribute cannibalism to Amerindians. One of the most obvious appears in a story of captivity that is embedded within the same poem ("Elegía II") about the fate of the explorers left at the Fuerte de Navidad (see chapter 5). However, a richer episode concerning cannibalism appears in the third volume of the *Elegías* and involves a female indigenous character known as La Gaitana. The story of La Gaitana stands out for two reasons: first, because of the extent to which the narrator dwells in the most grotesque and gruesome details of cannibalism; and second, because it would appear as if Castellanos tailored the characterization of its protagonist and the most noticeable aspect of the story in order to refute some of the implications of the story of Tegualda's dramatic search for the dead body of her husband Crepino.[29]

In "Épica, Fantasma y Lamento: La retórica del duelo en *La Araucana*," Raúl Marrero-Fente analyzes the episode of Tegualda and highlights the implications of her lament within a poetic discourse that is already highly fragmented.[30] According to Marrero-Fente, by ceding the word to a member of the opposing camp, Ercilla not only affirms the heroism of the Spaniards by presenting them as capable of lending a hand to a distraught widow but also, and more importantly,

> *muestra una visión del enemigo araucano como seres humanos que sufren y que viven la guerra desde la experiencia del dolor de la muerte de sus familiares. Es precisamente la representación de estos sentimientos en el personaje de Tegualda—en especial el sentimiento del dolor humano ante la muerte por medio de la retórica del duelo—el recurso de interpelación universal que por su capacidad de apelar a todos los seres humanos crea una empatía favorable en los lectores. Ercilla crea por medio de la retórica del duelo del personaje de Tegualda una experiencia estética capaz de generar emociones contradictorias porque a la misma vez pueden originar sentimientos de pena, de dudas o de rechazo a la guerra.[31]*

shows an image of the Araucanian enemy as human beings who suffer and experience war from the perspective of grief caused by the death of their relatives. It is precisely the depiction of these emotions in the character of Tegualda—in particular the feeling of human anguish in the face of death through the rhetoric of mourning—the strategy of universal appeal that owing to its ability to move all human beings, creates empathy among readers. Through the rhetoric of mourning in the character of Tegualda, Ercilla creates an aesthetic experience capable of triggering conflicting emotions, which at the same time can prompt feelings of sorrow, doubt, or opposition to the war.

In Ercilla, therefore, the prominent role assigned to the rhetoric of mourning turns the epic trope of the fate of the bodies of anonymous soldiers into an outlet to acknowledge and deal with the suffering and the violence inflicted upon Amerindians. Even so, the recognition that the violence of war is perturbing is not equivalent to disavowing the imperial project, nor is Ercilla's epic poem less imperialistic because it makes room to depict the suffering of adversaries. Without taking away any of its literary merits, this aspect of Ercilla's poem fits in nicely within the parameters of Western epic tradition in which "en algún momento los heroes son forzados a tomar conciencia de la violencia de la guerra, una violencia [as is the case with Ercilla] que en algunos casos ellos mismos han causado"[32] (at some point heroes are forced to become aware of the violence of war, a violence that in many cases they themselves have caused). On the other hand, as with other asymmetric encounters between Ercilla and Amerindians, the exchange between Ercilla and Tegualda serves multiple other functions within the poem, which include raising Ercilla's profile not only as a warrior and as a Spaniard, as stated in Marrero-Fente's assessment, but also one could even argue as a writer, as he insists that the virtues of his literary creation (Tegualda) far exceed those of all other female Greco-Roman figures, which possibly served as models for Tegualda. Yet, after the encounter is concluded, the indigenous characters are discarded and vanish from the poem. To put it concisely, "Una vez validado el poeta, las mujeres sufrientes dejan de interesar a la economía moral de la narración y desaparecen"[33] (As soon as the poet is validated, Amerindian women disappear as they no longer interest the moral economy of the poem).

Betty Osorio and Restrepo have examined the episode of La Gaitana and highlighted the use of Christian imagery to represent this female indigenous character, at least initially, as a type of woman whose suffering resembles that of the Virgin Mary, the archetypical mother figure in Western civilization.[34] For Osorio there is a "mythical" structure in this section of Castellanos's writing that allows the narrator to transform La Gaitana from a suffering victim into a vengeful punisher, given that La Gaitana first has to passively witness the death by burning of her son and later has the chance to execute and dismember Pedro de Añasco, the Spanish soldier who had ordered her son's death. For Restrepo, on the other hand, the importance of the episode of La Gaitana rests in the reorganization of the semantic field of the female body, a strategy that "sirve primero para desautorizar a un español, Pedro de Añasco, pero luego es rearticulada para reafirmar el proyecto colonizador"[35] (first serves to disavow the Spaniard, Pedro de Añasco, but later is reconfigured to endorse the colonizing project). According to his reading, the main element of the story of La Gaitana is the fact the she is characterized as a furious woman, and within a poetic discourse in which colonization is presented as the triumph of reason over emotion, La Gaitana's uncontrollable rage triggers the invalidation of her resistance.

In my view, the key to understanding Castellanos's characterization of La Gaitana is the fact that this indigenous antiheroine appears in a poem in which references to cannibalism are not only ubiquitous but also linked to a religious sensibility that blames the devil for instigating this practice. As a result, the recurrent references to dismembering human bodies and eating human flesh that reappear throughout the eleven cantos of the "Elegía a la muerte de Don Sebastián de Benalcázar" aim to provide further evidence of the tyranny of the devil over the indigenous population, and to reinforce the notion that the violence inflicted by Spaniards upon the Amerindians is sanctified by God's endorsement as expressed by the fronstispiece that accompanied the first volume of Castellanos's writings. In this regard, I agree with Jorge Cañizares-Esguerra who places Castellanos's *Elegías* under the category of "Satanic epics," which are sixteenth- and seventeenth-century epic poems in which Christian forces fight demonic enemies. According to Cañizares-Esguerra, the *Elegías* is "organized around the premise that the 'discovery' and settlement of America pitted the forces of evil against the conquistador Christian heroes."[36] Notice, for instance, how in the following stanzas the leader of the expedition (Sebastián de Benalcázar) equates violence with evangelization and frames the confrontation with Amerindians and the colonizing effort as a descent to hell:

> *Sea pues la primera nuestra lanza*
> *que tome posesiones en la tierra,*
> *donde demás del aprovechamiento*
> *tendréis para con Dios merecimiento.*

> *Pues no cebará tanto su garganta*
> *en estas tierras de infernal abismo,*
> *dándoles mandamientos de fe santa,*
> *y el agua de católico bautismo;*
> *haremos de ciudades nueva planta*
> *en medio de este rudo barbarismo,*
> *para que vengan en conocimiento*
> *de aquel que les dio y les da sustento.* [37]

> Thus, let our spear be the first one
> that will take possession of this land,
> where in addition to the rewards [of war]
> you will receive God's favor.

> because their throats will not be stuffed as much
> in these lands of infernal abyss,
> by giving them the commandments of Holy Faith,
> and the water of Catholic baptism;
> we will establish whole new cities
> in the midst of this rough barbarism,
> so that they will come to know
> he who gave them life and now gives them sustenance.

I think that recognizing the overall context in which Castellanos introduces La Gaitana is important because otherwise readers may lose sight of the true causes for her fury, as well as the traits that link her or set her apart from Ercilla's Tegualda. Like Tegualda, La Gaitana is an Indian woman who is experiencing intense suffering and pain owing to the death of a close relative at the hands of the Spaniards. But unlike the stoic Tegualda, La Gaitana turns her intense suffering into a call for revenge against the Spaniards because of her evil and demonic nature: "¿Qué podremos decir de La Gaitana / revestida de furias infernales?"[38] (What could we say about La Gaitana / clad in infernal anger?). Within the overall scheme of Castellanos's poetic discourse, therefore, it is because of La Gaitana's affiliation with the devil that her disqualified and stubborn resistance and her calls for armed retaliation against Spaniards confirm the validity of Spanish colonialism. It is also for this reason that in Castellanos's reformulation of the epic trope involving the fate of the bodies of anonymous warriors who die in battle, there is an unvarying and total absence of empathy for the side of the Amerindians, inasmuch as they refuse to give vassalage to the Spaniards because they are minions of the devil. What we find, instead, is a self-righteous religious attitude that prevents the narrator from introducing anything that may question or undermine the necessity or the validity of the conquest as a holy war in which Christian forces battle demonic Amerindians.[39]

To set the stage for the description of the aftermath of a battle, Castellanos first comments on how on one occasion La Gaitana is said to have instigated the Indian chieftain Pigoanza to fight against the Spaniards. Chieftain Pigoanza heeded her advice, and after summoning his troops Pigoanza delivered a speech in which he enticed his troops to fight with the hope of not only defeating the Spaniards but also drinking their blood and eating the flesh of Christians.[40] The narrator then goes on to describe in detail the violent confrontation between the Christian forces and an army of Indian warriors that seems to be coming out from the depths of hell.[41] Accordingly, when the Spanish troops finally defeat Pigoanza's army, the narrator points out how the Christian soldiers attributed their victory to divine intervention.[42] Hence, after reinforcing several times that it is a Christian army that is fighting a demonic enemy, we finally arrive at the climatic scene of the episode of La Gaitana, which is highlighted in the opening stanza of the canto with the lines "pues muchas de ellas con los cuerpos muertos / usaron detestables desconciertos"[43] (for many of them abused shamefully the dead bodies). According to Castellanos, after the battle, the Amerindians, including those serving the Spaniards, proceeded to devour the bodies of the dead soldiers who were lying on the ground. One old man in particular requested permission from the Spaniards to eat one of the prisoners, and surprisingly enough, the Spanish soldiers granted his request. The old man then consumed the dead body of an entire person in one single day, only to die a day later:

A los opresos de fatal yactura
que les encaminó su propia ira,
en las entrañas de la tierra
ninguno los encubre ni retira
por dalles en la suya sepultura
los bárbaros que estaban a la mira;
porque gran cantidad desta canalla
esperaban el fin de esta batalla.

Gente de quien la nuestra se servía
en lo que suelen los subyectos siervos
amigos por la mucha cercanía,
mas en voluntad falsos y protervos;
los cuales a la carne que yacía
acudieron como voraces cuervos,
y en breves horas los campos cubiertos
quedaron libres de los muertos.

Destos de paz un bárbaro doliente
que sobre báculo se sostenía
pidió para comer un delincuente,
diciendo que con él engordaría
concediéronselo liberalmente,
y dio fin del en un tan solo día;
hinchó del vientre tanto los lugares
que luego reventó por los ijares. [44]

To those oppressed by a fatal wound
whose own ire had brought them to that point,
in the entrails of the harsh land
no one covers or takes them away
so that those barbarians that were nearby
would give them proper burial in their place
because a large part of these vile people
awaited for the end of this battle.

Even those who were serving our people
in tasks usually assigned to servants
so-called friends by their proximity,
but false and wicked in their will;
threw themselves on top of the flesh
as voracious ravens
and in only a few brief hours the grounds that had been covered
were cleared of the dead bodies.

Among these servants a sorrowful barbarian

who supported himself with a staff
asked to consume one of the rebels,
stating that it would help him gain weight;
so they freely granted him the body,
and he finished it in a single day;
his belly swelled up in so many places
that he then burst on the sides.

The telltale sign that Castellanos expects readers to establish a connection between his description of the aftermath of the battle against Pigoanza and Ercilla's description of the aftermath of the Battle of Penco is that when he reintroduces La Gaitana in the narrative, he offers a catalog of famous women that is meant to recall the opening of canto 21 from the *Araucana*.[45] Nevertheless, while Ercilla associates Tegualda with a prestigious list of noble and virtuous women, Castellanos uses a misogynistic discourse to associate his female heroine with a genealogy of the most cruel and violent women from antiquity. Among them Castellanos includes Medea, who not only killed and dismembered the body of her brother Absyrtus and scattered his remains in distant places but also stabbed to death her own children to avenge the affronts of her husband, Jason; Tulia, who went mad and ran over the dead body of her father with her chariot; Scylla, the daughter of King Nisus, who in the midst of a siege betrayed her father and her kingdom after falling in love with Minos, the commander of the enemy army; and Procne, the wife of Tereus, who is said to have murdered her own son Ilys and prepared a meal with his remains in order to avenge her husband's rape of her sister Philomela. When combined, all these references aim to prepare readers for the equally gruesome description of the appalling fate of anonymous Indian warriors who die in battle. Moreover, in a manner similar to how Ercilla invites the readers to see the actions of Tegualda as surpassing any of those of virtuous women from the past, Castellanos hints that since what is at stake (the conquest as a battle between God and the devil) is far more compelling than the circumstances that triggered the violence of women like Medea, Tulia, Scylla, and Procne ("Y si por causa débil y liviana / aun suelen concebir odios mortales"[46] [and if for a feeble and trivial reason / they readily conceive mortal hatred]), the demonic nature of La Gaitana should allow readers to place her at the pinnacle of her violent lineage. In the end, therefore, the most salient difference between the episodes of Tegualda and La Gaitana is that while Ercilla guides readers to be nauseated by the excessive acts of violence, Castellanos unapologetically redirects the attention of the readers to feel repulsion toward the acts attributed to Amerindians, and by the alleged demonic nature of the original inhabitants of the New World.

CONCLUSION

The reference to Ercilla that has been read by some critics as a compliment and as a transparent gesture of subservience and servility had in the context of the literary production of early Spanish America a clear pejorative connotation that carried with it an immense amount of animosity as well as personal and political ambition. In other words, the reference that presumably explains how Castellanos came to write his poems in *octava rima* should be cited not as proof that he had indeed *imitated* Ercilla but as evidence of a crisis in the poetic practice of *imitatio* triggered by the debates surrounding the "discovery," conquest, and colonization of the New World. Such crisis is expressed literally and figuratively in the poem about the Fuerte de Navidad in the ending assigned to its protagonist, whose suicide ironically fulfills the promises made by the loyal and chaste Amerindian heroines of the *Araucana*:

> *Con esto dimos fin a la revuelta*
> *y concluimos toda la jornada,*
> *muerta de nuestra gente la más suelta,*
> *y la que quedó viva lastimada:*
> *enterramos los nuestros, y a la vuelta*
> *a Diana hallamos ahorcada,*
> *que viendo de los vuestros la caída*
> *no quiso sin su vida tener vida.* [47]

> With this we ended our uprising
> and put an end to the day's work,
> dead some of our most poised people,
> and badly injured those who survived:
> we buried our men, and upon our return
> we found Diana hanging,
> who seeing the defeat of your people
> did not want to go on living without [the love of] her life.

To judge the merits and shortcomings of the *Elegías*, readers should also take into consideration to what extent this series of poems fails or succeeds in simultaneously pointing to and erasing the trace of Ercilla's text. Discussions in this chapter of the depictions of female indigenous characters and the epic topoi of the bodies of anonymous soldiers who die in battle have explored how Castellanos's writings resist closure, stability, and simple emulation. For this reason, the longstanding critical tendency to consider him an epigone of Ercilla appears off the mark. Rather than reading Castellanos as a credulous follower of Ercilla, the author of the *Elegías* should be recognized as the immediate antecedent and forerunner of critical responses to the *Araucana* that came out of the New World, including the one offered by Pedro de Oña (1570–1643) in his *Primera parte de Arauco Domado* (1596). [48] In the larger context of early Spanish American writing, I place Castellanos's aggressive intertextuality in the tradition of subsequent Spanish American writers who responded critically to peninsular authors such as Hernando Domínguez Camargo's engagement with Gongorismo and Sor Juana Inés de la Cruz's reconfiguration of Petrarchism.[49]

NOTES

1. *Elegías*, 4:133.
2. *Elegías*, 4:133.
3. José María Vergara y Vergara, *Historia de la literatura en Nueva Granada* (Bogotá, Colombia: Editorial ABC, 1867), 55.
4. Marcelino Menéndez y Pelayo, *Historia de la poesía Hispano-Americana*, in *Obras completas*, ed. Enrique Sánchez Reyes (Santander, Spain: Consejo Superior de Investigaciones Científicas, 1948), 27:418.
5. Manuel Alvar, *Juan de Castellanos: Tradición española y realidad americana* (Bogotá, Colombia: Instituto Caro y Cuervo, 1972), 7.
6. Mario Germán Romero, *Joan de Castellanos: Un examen de su vida y de su obra* (Bogotá, Colombia: Banco de la República, 1964), 125.
7. Mario Germán Romero, *Aspectos literarios de la obra de Don Juan de Castellanos* (Bogotá, Colombia: Editorial Kelly, 1978), 2.
8. Isaac J. Pardo, *Juan de Castellanos: Estudio de las Elegías de varones ilustres de Indias* (Caracas, Venezuela: Biblioteca de la Academia Nacional de Historia, 1991), 215–22.
9. William Ospina, *Las auroras de sangre: Juan de Castellanos y el descubrimiento poético de América* (Bogotá, Colombia: Grupo Editorial Norma, 1999), 63.
10. In making this statement I am relying on the work or Rolena Adorno who has examined the trends in censorship in the second half of the sixteenth century and its relationship to genre. See "Literary Production and Suppression."
11. On this topic, see Restrepo, *Un nuevo reino*.
12. See the chapter entitled "Poetic Theory in the Reign of Charles V," in Navarrete, *Orphans of Petrarch*, 38–72.
13. "Elegía II" is a two-canto poem included in the first installment of the *Elegías*. Castellanos mistakenly refers to Diego de Arana as Rodrigo de Arana. For alternative interpretations of this section of Castellanos's writing, see Meo Zilio's *Estudio sobre Juan de Castellanos*, 151–82. See also the section entitled "Toda su perdicion fue por amores . . . " in Romero, *Joan de Castellanos*, 298–302; and Pardo, *Juan de Castellanos*, 258–59.
14. *Elegías*, 1:136. Immediately prior to starting the narration of the episode, Castellanos would again remind readers that "toda su perdición fue por amores andar deshonestísimos caminos" (1:138; all their ruin was caused by love following stray and dishonest paths).
15. *Elegías*, 1:139–40.
16. Luis Fernando Restrepo, "Somatografía Épica Colonial: Las *Elegías de varones ilustres de Indias* de Juan de Castellanos," Hispanic issue, *Modern Language Notes* 115, no. 2 (March 2000): 253.
17. *Araucana*, canto 13, stanzas 46–47.
18. *Araucana*, canto 20, stanzas 31–32.
19. *Araucana*, canto 21, stanza 10.
20. *Araucana*, canto 28, stanza 43. The same tendency can be found in the characterization of the young Lauca (canto 32, stanzas 31–39), whose tale offers the pretext to introduce into the poem the story of the "chaste" Dido. However, an exception in the characterization of female indigenous characters from the *Araucana* can be found in Fresia, the wife of Caupolicán who denounces her husband and abandons her own son (canto 33, stanzas 73–82). In her case, as noted by Francisco Javier Cevallos, honor is more important than love. See "Don Alonso de Ercilla."

21. *Elegías*, 1:140.

22. Pardo, *Juan de Castellanos*, 214–15; Meo Zilio, *Estudio sobre Juan de Castellanos*, 162; Jorge de Montemayor, *La Diana*, ed. Juan Montero (Barcelona: Crítica, 1996), bk. 7.

23. *Elegías*, 1:141.

24. Noted by Isaías Lerner, the editor of Ercilla, *La Araucana*, 571.

25. Pardo, *Juan de Castellanos*, 222, 323.

26. *Elegías*, 1:144.

27. Carlos A. Jáuregui, *Canibalia: Canibalismo, calibanismo, antropofagia cultural y consumo en América Latina* (Madrid: Iberoamericana, 2008), 84.

28. Ibid., 88.

29. For the importance of the representation of the conduct of Amerindians during and after battles, see Adorno, "The Warrior."

30. With regard to the fragmentations of Ercilla's poetic discourse, see the chapter entitled "Alonso de Ercilla's Fractured Subjectivity," in Davis, *Myth and Identity*, 20–60.

31. Raúl Marrero-Fente, "Épica, Fantasma y Lamento: La retórica del duelo en *La Araucana*," *Revista Iberoamericana* 73, no. 218 (January–March 2007): 211–12.

32. Restrepo, "Entre el recuerdo," 46.

33. Ibid., 55.

34. Betty Osorio de Negret, "Juan de Castellanos: De la retórica a la historia," *Texto y Contexto* 17 (1991): 42; Restrepo, "Entre el recuerdo"; and Restrepo, "Somatografía Épica Colonial," 256.

35. Restrepo, "Somatografía Épica Colonial," 256.

36. Jorge Cañizares-Esguerra, *Puritan Conquistadors: Iberianizing the Atlantic, 1550–1700* (Stanford, CA: Stanford University Press, 2006), 40.

37. *Elegías*, 3:370. At least in one occasion the narrator goes as far as qualifying the weapons of the Spaniards as Christian weapons ("cristiana lanza") immediately prior to invoking Saint James as a war cry (3:418).

38. Ibid., 3:421.

39. Some of the epithets used by Castellanos to refer to Spaniards are "católico bando" (Catholic troops), "cristianos caballeros" (Christian knights), "gente Cristiana" (Christian people), "cristiana companía" (Christian troops).

40. *Elegías*, 3:425.

41. Ibid., 3:431.

42. Ibid., 3:434.

43. Ibid., 3:421.

44. Ibid., 3:434.

45. Ibid., 3:421.

46. Ibid.

47. Ibid., 1:152.

48. Oña, *Primera parte de Arauco Domado*. For the relationship between *Arauco Domado* and the *Araucana*, see Elide Pittarello, "Arauco Domado de Pedro de Oña o la vía erótica de la conquista," *Dispositio* 14, nos. 36–38 (1989): 247–70.

49. For a nuanced analysis of Domínguez Camargo and Sor Juana's poetic practices in relation to Iberian counterparts, see Kathryn Mayers, *Visions of Empire in Colonial Spanish American Ekphrastic Writing* (Lewisburg, PA: Bucknell University Press, 2012).

Chapter Three

"In This Our New Sacred Sheepfold"

Piracy, Epic, and Identity in Cantos 1 and 2 of
Discurso del Capitán Francisco Draque

The *Discurso del capitán Francisco Draque* is a five-canto heroic poem written by Juan de Castellanos soon after an English fleet sacked the port of Cartagena de Indias in 1586.[1] Francis Drake departed from Plymouth on September 14 the previous year as commander of a state-sponsored expedition that aimed to disrupt Spanish trade; he arrived at Cartagena after raiding the cities of São Tiago (Cape Verde) and Santo Domingo on the island of Hispaniola. Drake was able to stay in control of Cartagena for two months, during which he extracted a ransom of 110,000 ducats from the local authorities before sailing north across the Caribbean to capture St. Augustine, Florida. Although the financial rewards of the expedition were meager compared with the original expectations of the investors, Drake's raid on the West Indies bestowed a significant military embarrassment on Spain and soured the already strained relations between Spain and England.[2] Castellanos worked expeditiously on his poem in the months following Drake's attack and produced a text that espouses the restoration of martial values and the bravery of the conquistadores as antidotes to the mounting threat of English maritime aggressions and the emasculating effects of commerce and bureaucracy. Although Castellanos used the religious discourse of demonology to portray Drake and his troops, the end result is a far less triumphalistic depiction of the English "other" than the one Lope de Vega offered by employing a similar discourse in *La dragontea* (1598).

Castellanos did not pick up the pen or embrace the epic genre to praise Hapsburg navigational prowess, as has been suggested by Jorge Cañizares-Esguerra,[3] but to challenge the policies of Hapsburg monarchs concerning

41

the administration of the recently established viceroyalties in the New World, and above all to praise the deeds and defend the rights of the first wave of colonists.[4] Although initially individuals such as Castellanos contributed to Spain's imperial project by exploring the New World and fighting in the campaigns to conquer it, they later felt affronted by the Crown's implementation of laws aimed at limiting their political and economic power. With this tension in mind, this chapter highlights the complexities of a text that bears evidence of an internal ideological fissure that significantly shaped Spain's political and territorial expansion, and contributed to the emergence of a new type of literature. Indeed, the heroic poems written by Castellanos on behalf of the conquistadors and encomenderos represent the boldest attempt to turn one of the most prestigious vehicles of Spanish imperial discourse into a tool for the expression of colonial political concerns; the project included but was not limited to the deployment of aggressive practices of poetic imitation, the expression of a new sense of selfhood, and the demarcation of a new sense of patriotism.

THE NEW WORLD AS A NEW PLACE OF ENUNCIATION

Castellanos included the *Discurso* in the third volume of his writings, but the official censor who examined it banned its publication and ordered its removal from the *Elegías* by instructing and signing in the margin, "Desdesta estancia se debe quitar—[Pedro] Sarmiento [de Gamboa]" (henceforth must be removed—Sarmiento); and "Hasta aquí es el discurso de Draque que se ha de quitar—Sarmiento"[5] (Until here is the poem about Drake that must be removed—Sarmiento). As if anticipating such obstacles to publication, Castellanos also sent an additional copy to Melchor Pérez de Arteaga, *abad* (abbot) of Burgo Hondo in Spain, who in several ways was an ideal reader for this poem. Pérez de Arteaga had met Castellanos while working as a judge for the Real Audiencia of Santafé in the New Kingdom of Granada and had been commissioned to oversee the rebuilding of Cartagena and the reorganization of its defenses after an attack by French pirates in 1561. In the letter that accompanied the poem, moreover, Castellanos suggests that while in the New Kingdom of Granada, Pérez de Arteaga had granted him *mercedes* (favors), and out of concern for the fate of his poem, Castellanos decided to appeal to his former benefactor with the hope that Pérez de Arteaga would extend to the text the same consideration he had offered to Castellanos in the past:

> *Al tiempo que el corsario inglés Francisco Draque tomó la ciudad y puerto de Cartagena, tenía yo ocupadas las manos en la historia della; y por ser caso notable, como los demás allí acontecidos desde su primero fundador hasta la presente hora, fue forzoso ponerlo por remate: para lo cual, con la posible*

solicitud, procuré las más ciertas y verdaderas relaciones que de la costa enviaron a este Nuevo Reino, consultando así mismo muchas personas que presentes se hallaron; de las cuales unos dicen más y otros menos, según el sentimiento de cada uno, como en semejantes cosas acontece. Y así concluso, tomando lo menos sospechoso y más autorizado, trabajé tejer este discurso cuan de raíz me fue posible, con información de hombres graves que dicen conocer a ese pirata, no solamente después que comenzó a ser molesto en estas partes de Indias, pero mucho antes de pasar a ellas; e ya concluso, lo menos mal que mi pobre talento pudo, algunos me importunaron que desmembrase este nuevo suceso de su lugar, para que a solas pasase en España, adonde así él como quien lo crió es cosa notoria que no podrán hallar buena acogida, careciendo de valedor; y buscándoselo, occurrióme a la memoria quien está bien arraigado en ella por las mercedes que me hizo, gobernando este Reino y aquellas provincias de la costa, adonde, aunque no faltaron de estos acontecimientos, sobró valor en el que gobernaba para quedar libres de semejante zozobra: este es Vuestra Merced, a quien suplico sea servido, si hubiere tiempo desocupado, de leer mis vigilias, y, si tales fueren que merezcan luz, no les falte la del esclarecido entendimiento de V. M., a quien Dios nuestro Señor guarde largos años.[6]

At the time when the English corsair Francis Drake attacked the city and port of Cartagena [de Indias], I was engaged in writing the history of that city; and as it was a noteworthy event, as were all those that took place there since its foundation till the present time, I felt compelled to attached it [the poem] to complete my history. For which purpose, with all possible care I gathered the most accurate and truthful accounts I could obtain from the narratives sent to this New Kingdom from the coast; and I also consulted many individuals who were present, some who said more and some who said less in accordance with their sentiments, as is usual in such cases. Thus, taking of these the least doubtful and the best authorized, I endeavored to write this narrative from as far back as possible, with information provided by grave men who stated that they have known this pirate, not only after he began to harass these parts of the Indies but also long before that time. And after I finished it, as well as my poor talent allowed me, some individuals urged me to extract the narrative from its place and to send it separately to Spain, where it is self-evident that neither the poem nor its creator would be welcomed without a sponsor. And in searching for one, my memory recalled one who is therein well established by the rewards he granted me while governing this kingdom and the other provinces on the coast, where although such attacks were not infrequent, their then governor had enough courage to spare such misfortunes; this person is Your Excellency, whom I entreat, if you have the leisure to read the fruit of my labor, and if they should deserve to see the light, let it not lack the enlightened understanding of Your Excellency, whom the Lord our God may keep for many years.

Castellanos's letter to Pérez de Arteaga is organized around several topoi that were used widely in prologues in the sixteenth century. Some of those topoi include affected modesty: "Lo menos mal que mi pobre talento pudo"; a dedication to the reader: "Este es Vuestra Merced, a quien suplico sea servido, si hubiere tiempo desocupado, de leer mis vigilias"; and the author's request that the reader bring the text to light: "Y, si tales fueren que merezcan luz, no les falte la del esclarecido entendimiento de V. M."[7] In addition, the letter also contains several references that extend beyond the primary function of the prologue to capture the reader's attention and request his benevolence for the subject of the writing. The introductory remarks of the letter ("y por ser caso notable . . . fue forzoso ponerlo por remate") and the allusion to some anonymous individuals who pressured him to send the poem to Spain ("algunos me importunaron") make apparent that Castellanos considered it necessary to justify why he had written such a poem in the first place, and why he had decided to send it to Spain, in the second. In both instances, Castellanos appeals to justifying strategies that dilute his responsibility and suggest that he accomplished both of those tasks not of his own volition but because a set of circumstances forced him to do so.

In his letter Castellanos also concedes that there are other accounts of Drake's attacks that differ significantly from the one he offers. This topic surfaces when Castellanos details the steps he took to write the poem and fashions his own image as that of a competent, truthful, and scrupulous writer. These metatextual references are significant not only because they postulate the preeminence of Castellanos's poem in relation to other texts (most of which were official legal documents) but also because internally they establish Castellanos's exemplarity as a citizen of the New Kingdom of Granada and as a writer, two aspects that would gain increasing relevance in the most dramatic section of the poem. It is also important to recognize that by referring to the previous attacks on Cartagena and the measures taken by then judge Pérez de Arteaga, Castellanos places the threat of foreign piracy as an issue to be confronted within the realm of good and proper government, thus setting the tone for the sharp criticism he will deploy against the Crown's administrative policies in the New World, particularly concerning the security of the ports and the appointment of colonial administrators. And last but not least, in his letter Castellanos also presents his own subjectivity as that of an outsider, a person who had been born in Spain but felt there was no place for him there anymore: "En España, adonde así él [the text] como quien lo crió [Castellanos] es cosa notoria que no podrán hallar buena acogida." In addition to being an explicit reference to the polemical nature of his poem, Castellanos's characterization of himself and his text as outsiders, albeit indirectly, constitutes the first reference to the poem's place of enunciation (the New World and more specifically the New Kingdom of Granada) and the first step in delineating a cartography that shifts Europe to the periphery and the Spanish colonies to the center. It is no surprise, therefore, that the key metaphor included in the opening stanzas of the poem reassesses the location and significance of the New World in the imperial imagination:

Un caso duro, triste y espantable,
un acometimiento furibundo,
una calamidad que fue notable
en ciertos puertos deste Nuevo Mundo,
canto con ronca voz y lamentable,
que el flaco pecho de lo más profundo
envía por sus vías a la lengua.
¿Más, quién podrá sin española mengua?

Dame tú, Musa mía, tal aliento
que con verdad sincera manifieste
alguna parte de mi sentimiento
en trago tan acerbo como éste,
y aquella destrucción y asolamiento
que hizo con su luterana hueste
el Capitán inglés, dicho Francisco,
en éste nuestro recental aprisco. [8]

A hard, sad, and frightful case
a furious assault and a deplorable calamity
to some [Spanish] ports in this New World,
I sing with hoarse and woeful voice
to which my tongue sends forth
from the depths of my constricted breast
but who could sing if not to Spain's dishonor?

Give me, oh muse, such inspiration,
that I may truthfully convey
but part of what my heart does feel
in such a bitter draught as this must be
and the destruction
that with Lutheran troops at his command
the English Captain Francis [Drake]
inflicted
in this our new sacred sheepfold.

In these two stanzas, the narrative voice states the topic of the poem and requests strength from the muse to sing in a truthful manner. Interestingly enough, the narrative voice proposes to sing about not the courage or heroism of Spaniards faced with a daunting challenge but the degree of destruction caused by the enemy. The theme thus stated and the absence of a well-defined Spanish hero to rival the stature of the English adversary discloses the logic with which the poet has arranged his narrative. From the message conveyed by these two stanzas, the reader knows from the start that inasmuch as the poem refers to pirate attacks on Spanish ports, the poem will deal with defeat and not with victory. Despite the absence of a Spanish hero, however, the narrative voice is able to convey an initial sympathetic depiction of

Spanish colonists in the New World by staking out a clear place of enunciation. The poet highlights the uniqueness of the place from where he is singing by alluding to that place with the metaphor "en éste nuestro recental aprisco" (in this our new sacred sheepfold), which refers both to the New World as a whole and to the territory of the New Kingdom of Granada in particular. In this regard I share Luis Fernando Restrepo's view that the writings of Castellanos have a distinct "geographic and narrative axis, the New Kingdom of Granada (present-day Colombia), where Castellanos writes and lives."[9] Indeed, in a key section of the third canto, Castellanos again reminds readers not only of his own presence in the text but also of the place from which he is narrating: "Aqueste Nuevo Reino donde yo piso"[10] (this New Kingdom where I stand).

The term *recental* comes from the Latin *recens* and is akin to new or recent; it can be used to refer to a newborn lamb, particularly one that is born after its due date.[11] On the other hand, *aprisco* is related to the verb *apriscar* and refers to the place where shepherds gather their sheep to protect them from harsh weather.[12] In the writings of Castellanos, there is at least one example of the literal use of *aprisco* as a place of refuge for animals, but there are several instances in which he uses this noun metaphorically to refer to the Catholic Church, both as a whole and to a small portion of it.[13] Castellanos had used the term *aprisco* in this sense in his description of an initial period of harmony between Dominican and Franciscan friars and the indigenous population of Cumaná, prior to an Indian rebellion that he blames on the greed and abuses of colonist Hojeda:

> *acudieron algunos religiosos*
> *movidos de cristianas intenciones,*
> *procurando traerlos al aprisco*
> *Dominicanos y de San Francisco.*[14]

> Some religious men came
> motivated by Christian convictions
> striving to bring them to the sheepfold
> Dominicans and Franciscans.

In a similar fashion, Castellanos uses the noun *aprisco* metaphorically in the third volume of his *Elegías*: "Y comenzaron a fundar aprisco / el día del seráfico Francisco"[15] (and they started the foundation of a sheepfold / on the day of the humble Saint Francis). And he uses it later again in the same volume when he complains about the lack of effort made by local authorities in the New Kingdom of Granada to continue the exploration and colonization of the territory on behalf of the Crown of Castile.[16] Another instance of the metaphorical use of *aprisco* can be found in the second volume, "Elegía III."[17] The metaphor "en éste nuestro recental aprisco" (in this our new sacred sheepfold), therefore, has positive religious connotations that effectively present the Spanish colonists in the New World as the victims of aggression. Inherent in its meaning is the gospel analogy that presents the followers of Christ as sheep and Christ's spiritual adversaries as wolves.[18] As such, the success of this metaphor lies not only in trying to align the reader with the perspective of the narrator but also in reversing the rhetorical cornerstone of Bartolomé de las Casas's criticism of conquistadors and encomenderos. As is well known, in *A Brief Account of the Destruction of the Indies* (1552), Las Casas inverted the gospel analogy to portray Christians (Spanish colonists) as hungry wolves and the gentiles (Amerindians) as "gentle lambs." Yet, by referring to the New World as "en éste nuestro recental aprisco" (in this our new sacred sheepfold), Castellanos redeploys the gospel analogy in favor of the Spanish settlers.

The pertinence of the use of the term *aprisco* and the enduring relevance of Castellanos's metaphor among colonists from the New Kingdom of Granada can be measured by considering a similar use of the term *aprisco* later in the seventeenth century, such as in the allegorical painting entitled *Jesús divide su aprisco entre dos Franciscos* attributed to the Neogranadinan painter Gregorio Vásquez de Arce y Ceballos (1638–1711; see figure 3.1). In one of the earliest American depictions of Saint Therese of Avila, the female saint appears at the bottom left of the painting and directly to her right are Saint Francisco Solano and Saint Francis Xavier. At the very top appears the Holy Family with the infant Jesus at the center and the Virgin Mary and Saint Joseph to his right and left respectively. On the middle left of the composition, immediately below the Virgin Mary, appears Saint Sebastian wearing a green robe and a white shawl while holding an open book with the inscription "Jesús dividió su aprisco" [Jesus divided his sheepfold]. To his right is Saint Stephan holding an open book with the caption "entre uno i otro franc(isco)" [between one and the other Franciscan]. Through its use of religious iconography and the reference to the noun "aprisco" the painting allegorically presents the colonization of Nueva Granada as a religious endeavor.[19]

On the other hand, the constant and productive dialogue with the works and ideas of Bartolomé de las Casas serves as one of the organizing principles of Castellanos's writings. In a section of his *Elegías* written prior to the *Discurso*, Castellanos goes as far as overtly mocking Las Casas's rhetoric by inserting the following quotation presumably uttered by a Dominican friar (Fray Pedro de Palencia) during an Indian attack on a Spanish settlement:

> *Ovejas del obispo de Chiapa[s],*
> *ningún gusto me dan vuestros balidos,*
> *pues que por fuerza nos quitáis la capa*
> *sin darnos un vellón para vestidos;*
> *y así de lana que tan mal se hila*
> *renuncio para siempre la desquila.*[20]

Figure 3.1.   *Jesús divide su aprisco entre dos Franciscos* by Gregorio Vásquez
de Arce y Ceballos (ca. 1690). *Source:* Image courtesy of the art collection from
the Banco de la República (Colombia).

> Sheep from the Bishop of Chiapas
> I find no amusement in your bleats
> for if by force you take away our cloaks
> without offering us any fleece for clothing;
> so, from wool so poor for spinning
> I rather renounce altogether the shearing.

By mixing the jargon of animal husbandry with the language of monetary transactions and clothes manufacturing, Castellanos acknowledges the economic anxieties that fueled the encomenderos' dislike for Las Casas. In this stanza Castellanos infuses his poetic discourse with derision by employing signifiers such as *capa*, *vellón*, and *lana*, whose meanings range from sheep herding and wool processing to coinage and the accumulation of wealth. For instance, *capa* can mean the bullfighter's cape or an article of clothing but can also mean *caudal* or *hacienda* in expressions like *andar de capa caída* (to go around with a hanging cape)[21] or *sobre la capa del justo* (over the honest man's cape).[22] Likewise, *vellón* refers both to the woolen fleece obtained by shearing the sheep and to a type of coin of small denomination minted in copper. Elvira Vilches has recently argued that during the 1590s the "infamous vellón"[23] became emblematic of the anxieties generated by the difficulty to distinguish between genuine and unsound value, and the overall problem of representation surrounding the proper medium of economic exchange in Hapsburg Spain. According to Vilches, "Cooper money exposed the slippage between the commodity value of the metal and the legal value of coins."[24] Finally, *lana* means wool or profit in expressions such as "ir por lana y volver trasquilado"[25] (to go looking for wool and return sheared).[26] By playing with the multiple meanings of these signifiers, Castellanos transforms Las Casas's overtly passive *gentle lambs* into an active threat to the subsistence of the Spanish colonists. In lines such as "pues que por fuerza nos quitáis la capa," the explicit allusion to the use of force and a triple entendre allows for Las Casas's *gentle lambs* to behave more like thieves or bulls, thus increasing the menace of their economic and physical threats. Moreover, since *vellón* could also be linked to Jason and the Argonauts' search for the Golden Fleece, lines such as "renuncio para siempre la desquila" casts the conquest and colonization of the New World as an enterprise whose hardships are not sufficiently compensated. Furthermore, by revealing his displeasure for the sounds produced by the sheep ("ningún gusto me dan vuestros balidos"), the poetic voice figuratively transforms Las Casas's complaints into irrelevant and dissonant noise, hence discarding them altogether.

THE PANOPTIC VIEW: A *BAQUIANO'S* TAKE ON PIRACY

After announcing the topic of the poem and establishing a clear place of enunciation, in the first canto Castellanos tightly condenses the description of several historical events that took place over a period of approximately fifteen years. The poet begins by offering a short biographical sketch of Drake as a relative of John Hawkins (Juan de Acle) and a former page to the Duchess of Feria. Then he quickly moves on to describe some of Drake's earliest incursions into the Spanish Main; the confrontations between English and Spanish forces that took place during Drake's expedition to circumnavigate the globe (1577–1580); and the initial phase of Drake's raid on the West Indies (1585–1587). While narrating these events, Castellanos alludes to Drake's willingness to make alliances with French pirates, Amerindians, and runaway slaves, and points out the geopolitical implications of Drake's actions by describing the warm welcome his accomplishments had at the court of England and the support Drake received from Queen Elizabeth I. The recurring theme of the first canto, therefore, is the ease with which Drake and his men have been able to attack Spanish ports and vessels and successfully collect sensitive intelligence information and large amounts of wealth to take back to England. Having said this, it is important to underscore that for Castellanos, Drake's success is due not to an inherent superiority of the English over the Spaniards but to widespread administrative flaws that have boosted the confidence of individuals like Drake and have allowed heavily armed vessels to take advantage of the element of surprise and launch attacks when and where the Spaniards least expected it. Among those preventable flaws Castellanos includes the absence of a more reliable system of communication, the lack of forethought by local authorities, and the military incompetence of newly arrived merchants and bureaucrats.

Castellanos's assessment of Drake's success is revealing for two reasons. In the first place, it essentializes a distinction between two segments of the Spanish population living in the Indies and links the threat of piracy exclusively with one those segments. As such, Castellanos's assessment reveals that the group that claims ownership over the New World and asserts itself through the metaphor "en éste nuestro recental aprisco" (in this our new sacred sheepfold) does not include all Spanish colonists indiscriminately. Without a doubt, the distinction between the two segments of the Spanish population is made explicit in the aftermath of Drake's attack on the port of Callao (1579) when a distressed resident from Lima complains that in the city there are "pocos que sepan militar oficio / por carecer del uso y ejercicio"[27] (very few competent in military affairs / for lack of practice and experience) and then goes on to produce the following harangue:

> *Todos los usos son de mercaderes,*
> *letrados, escribanos, negociantes,*

convites y lascivias de mujeres,
ejercicios de lánguidos amantes;
y para los presentes menesteres,
diferentes de los que fueron antes,
de manera que las personas todas,
o los más, son de fiestas y de bodas.

Falta prevención, falta consejo,
falta a todas partes las tutelas,
y la comodidad y el aparejo
suelen al enemigo ser espuelas;
si de estas cosas trata el sabio viejo,
piensan los ignorantes ser novelas,
y el daño hecho, su respuesta para
en decir a los otros "quién pensara."

Mas el gobernador sabio y entero
a todas partes según Argos vea,
que bien hará si caso venidero
con ojos de prudencia lo tantea,
adivinando cierto paradero
de lo que puede ser antes que sea,
pues anticipación en coyuntura
no da mucho lugar a desventura.

Sea, pues, por ingleses o por Francia,
o por otras naciones extranjeras,
otro cuidado y otra vigilancia
requieren estos puertos y fronteras;
y aquellos que del Rey tienen ganancia
tomen estos negocios más de veras:
no sea todo rehenchir el jeme
y lo demás siquiera que se queme.

Por avenidas grandes o tormenta
se mudan las carreras de los ríos,
y por hacer de cosas poca cuenta
se vienen a perder los señoríos.
lo que por indios se nos representa
conozco ser notables desvaríos;
más endemoniados hechiceros
parece que nos dan malos agüeros. [28]

All we have are merchants,
lawyers, clerks, and businessmen,
banquets, drinking, and lascivious women,
the doings of languid lovers
and for the challenges at hand

very different from those that came before
everyone or at least the majority
are good for nothing but for feasts and celebrations.

Warning is lacking, as well as foresight and sound advice
while comfort and luxury serve as spurs to our enemies;
but if these truths are pointed out by wise men
ignorant people scoff at them
and after the harm is done
they tell each other "who would have thought?"

But the wise and competent administrator
should keep like Argus a close watch
for he will do good when gazing at the future with prudent eyes
foreseeing certain things before they happen
for he who can anticipate the course of things
leaves very little room for adversity.

Thus, whether [we are attacked] from France or England
or from any other foreign nation
care and stricter vigilance
are required on these ports and borders;
and those who receive rewards from the king
take their responsibilities more seriously.
Let them consider more than just to enrich their pockets
and leave the rest of it to sink and burn.

Earth tremors and storms
can change the course of rivers,
and from neglect and lack of zeal
is how kingdoms are lost or ruined.
That which is described by Amerindians I know to be false
but future woes are prophesized
by evil and demonic [Amerindian] wizards.

In the 1921 edition of the *Discurso*, González Palencia notes that such negative appraisal of the residents in Lima is in stark contrast with the views expressed by Rodrigo de Castro, cardinal of Seville, who wrote a letter to the president of the Council of the Indies regarding the threat of pirate attacks and stated that the Spanish colonists in Lima were among the most disciplined and experienced soldiers in the entire world.[29] Nina Gerassi-Navarro, on the other hand, argues that the lust of "merchants, *letrados*, and notary publics" is a "recurring theme throughout the poem and reflects Castellanos' moral critique."[30] In my opinion, however, the reference to lust in lines such as "convites y lascivias de mujeres, / exercicios de lánguidos amantes" is not necessarily a moral condemnation of lust per se but simply part of Castellanos's strategy to draw sharp differences between the old and the new settlers in order to argue that the latter are incapable of deterring the English.[31] After all, in the other instances when Castellanos mentions lust in the poem, he does not examine it in abstract terms or as a matter of principle but specifically indicates that lust is one among many traits that demonstrate the inability of those who have recently arrived to run and defend the colonies. Furthermore, Giovanni Meo Zilio points out that in several instances in the *Elegías* the author

> *se detiene complaciente y hasta complacido en la descripción naturalística de las gracias de las indias y de los juegos, mucho menos que castos, que los españoles entablan con ellas. Mas aun, en tales casos, el tono poético de la narración suele elevarse, lo cual sugiere tratarse de un tema que de por si, lejos de ser objeto de rechazo, de censura por parte del afable cura tunjano, es vivido inmediatamente como bien acepto, como materia legítima y gratamente susceptible de poetizarse.*[32]

readily dwells and even finds pleasure in the naturalistic description of the attributes of indigenous women and of the lively exchanges, far from chaste, that Spaniards initiated with them. Moreover, in such instances, the poetic tone of the narrative tends to ascend, which suggests that it is a theme that far from being objectionable or censured by the priest from Tunja, is presented as legitimate material that can readily be presented through poetry.

Given that Castellanos places the distressed colonist in front of the house of Viceroy Francisco de Toledo, and that this section of the poem appears immediately before the description of how the viceroy responded to Drake's attack, it is clear that Castellanos's main concern is not necessarily lust (sexual desire) but the examination of why kingdoms such as the viceroyalty of Peru could be lost to the enemies of Spain (colonial desire). This, and the practical issue of who are the individuals that deserve to be appointed to administer the colonies, after all, are the issues addressed in lines such as "y aquellos que del Rey tienen ganancia / tomen estos negocios más de veras" and "y por hacer de cosas poca cuenta / se vienen a perder los señoríos."

Once we establish that Castellanos is more concerned with politics than with morals, it is easier to recognize the steps that he takes to outline a political doctrine in favor of the conquistadors by offering a skewed and oversimplified assessment of the current administrative situation of the colonies. The complaint expressed by the anonymous colonist, for example, starts by aligning the first explorers with hard work, caution, abnegation, wisdom, and military experience, while simultaneously aligning newly arrived colonists with lust, lack of military experience, laziness, sleep, and meaningless celebrations. After establishing this contrast, the poetic voice goes on to suggest that administrative virtues such as caution, prudence, and foresight are lacking in the current administration ("falta prevención, falta consejo, /

falta a todas partes las tutelas"); and his plea finally reaches its peak by describing the ideal colonial administrator as Argus Panopte, a mythical creature that can stay alert at all times thanks to having one hundred eyes. Even though in book 1 of Ovid's *Metamorphoses* Juno assigns Argus Panopte the role of guardian of Jupiter's lust,[33] I would argue that by explicitly stating that "otro cuidado y otra vigilancia / requieren estos puertos y fronteras," Castellanos is clearly stripping the reference of its most immediate sexual connotations. Hence, he displaces the allusion to Argus from the context of sexual desire to colonial desire in order to suggest that the ideal colonial administrator should guard constantly not the lust of colonists but internal and external military threats. Paradoxically, while recasting the New World in the role of Io, and Hispania, as the jealous Juno, there are no characters in the poem that display the administrative zeal and the panoptic vision required to assume the role of Argus, with the exception of Castellanos (both as narrator and as a protagonist of the events). When read from this perspective, the allusion to Ovid serves to establish Castellanos himself; and the group that he represents, as the outlets that truly express Spanish colonial desire.[34]

A second conclusion we can draw from Castellanos's assessment of piracy is that Drake's aggressions, particularly the ones committed during the circumnavigation of the world (1577–1580), are solely the result of not an individual's ambition and greed but intentional provocations that justified Spain's retaliation against England. In this sense, the portrait of Drake that emerges by the end of the first canto comes closer to that of a privateer authorized by a sovereign nation to attack enemy property during a time of war than that of a sea robber trying to make a profit and recognizing no allegiance to any monarch. Castellanos's perspective surfaces clearly in his description of Drake's assault on the ship *Nuestra Señora de la Concepción* off the coast of Peru in 1579. At the time of this attack, Drake's flagship was one of the most heavily armed vessels in the Pacific Ocean, while *Nuestra Señora de la Concepción* was a merchant ship on her way to Panama, laden with silver and gold. In Castellanos's poem, Drake is favorably depicted as an alert and experienced captain ("como buen capitán, vivo y experto"[35] [as a good captain / vigilant and experienced]) sailing quickly to reach the best-suited place to engage the Spanish vessel in battle. The narrator compares the swift movements of Drake's ship to those of a dolphin and points out not only that the Spanish sailors were slow to react after realizing that a foreign vessel was approaching but also that the Spanish ship had no weapons or soldiers to defend itself. This last piece of information is useful to grasp Castellanos's point of view because, unlike Lope de Vega in *La dragontea*, Castellanos does not include it to condemn Drake for attacking an unarmed ship but to reiterate the point that at least some of the blame should rest on the Spanish side for not taking any precautions.[36]

The main difference between Castellanos's poetic version and witness accounts is his explicit references to a prevalent state of war, which transform the predatory nature of Drake's attack into a pseudo-naval battle that is over before it began owing to the inadequacy of the Spaniards to defend their cargo. As a result, at all times the actions of the English sailors are validated since they appear motivated by patriotism and honor. Notice that in Castellanos's version Drake's ship approaches the Spanish vessel defiantly displaying the flag and the military emblems of England: "flámulas, gallardetes y banderas / que por diversas partes van pendientes"[37] (pennants, banners, and flags / which are displayed is in different places). Even the lowest members of Drake's crew, whose energy and daring is exalted by Castellanos by referring to them as "jóvenes lozanos"[38] (vigorous young men), seems to be aware of the nationalistic scope of their actions as they demand Spaniards to strike sail in the name of England: "Amaina, amaina, por Inglaterra"[39] (lower the sails, lower the sails, for England). This particular verse comes straight from eyewitness accounts, yet what is unique to Castellanos's version is the suppression of the response from the Spanish sailors and the magnification of their passiveness and willingness to surrender:

> *Los nuestros no se pasan a contienda*
> *antes están turbados y sin bríos*
> *como faltase, pues, quien lo defienda,*
> *ocupan los contrarios el navío;*
> *pide Francisco Draque su hacienda*
> *diciendo: "Dame luego lo que es mío";*
> *porque llevar pillaje quien más puede*
> *el derecho de guerra lo concede.*[40]

> Our troops do not engage in battle
> instead they are dispirited and confused
> and since there was no one to defend it
> the [English] enemies take control of the vessel;
> and Captain Francis Drake inquires about his share
> saying: "give me then what is mine";
> for war prescribes the victor has by right
> all spoils that he can lay his hands on.

In the second half of this stanza, Drake's and the narrator's voice are in unison in explaining that as the winner of the battle Drake is entitled to seize the ship's cargo based on the right of the victor to take possession of the spoils of war, thus clarifying how the word "pillage" is being used in this section of the poem. In addition, in Castellanos's description of the aftermath of the assault, Drake situates his attack in the larger context of confrontations between Spain and rival European nations. He states that he has taken possession of *Nuestra Señora de la Concepción*'s cargo as retaliation for what Philip II (through his representatives) had taken from John Hawkins at the port of San Juan de Ulúa back in 1568, a time when Spain and England were supposedly not at war. Moreover, Drake challenges the legitimacy of Spain's sovereignty over the New World based on the bulls of donation issued by Pope Alexander VI in 1493:

> *Quépanos parte, pues, de la ganancia.*
> *y no perdamos estas ocasiones,*
> *que también son acá hijos de Eva*
> *para gozar lo que esta tierra lleva.*
>
> *Pues que tenéis tan buen entendimiento*
> *hace[d] me de esta duda satisfecho:*
> *¿Adán mandó por algún testamento*
> *a solos españoles el provecho?*
> *la cláusula mostrad y ordenamiento;*
> *haré renunciación de mi derecho,*
> *porque de lo contrario de esto fuere*
> *habrá de llevar más quien más pudiere.* [41]

Let us then have our share of the rewards
and not waste [time] in occasions such as this,
that we are also children of Eve
and deserve to enjoy the wealth of this land.

And as you are said to have such enlightened minds
please free me from this doubt,
did Adam leave a will and testament
whereby he entrusted these lands to Spain alone?
If so, show me the deed and the decree
and I will renounce to all my claims
because if the opposite is true, "he who can, takes all."

My point is that nowhere in this section, or in any other section of the poem, does Castellanos actually refute Drake's line of reasoning. Castellanos certainly refers to Drake as a pirate, a corsair, a thief, and a tyrant, but he also shows tremendous admiration for the boldness of Drake's actions and repeatedly comes close to endorsing some of those actions by suggesting that Drake acted as any astute and diligent commander should when carrying out a mission, whereas Spanish colonists and sailors acted as if they had forgotten they were at war. Likewise, Castellanos includes sporadic references to Drake's boastfulness and hints that Drake is a cocksure and arrogant individual, but the sections in which Castellanos magnifies Drake's stature and foreshadows the attacks Drake will conduct in the future far outweigh the negative assessments.

THE ENGLISH *OTHER* AS A HEROIC DEMON

The second canto deals with the first half of Drake's expedition to the West Indies (1585–1586), starting with brief references to the English incursions in Bayona (Galicia), the Canary Islands, and the Cape Verde Islands, and culminating with a detailed description of the devastating effects of Drake's attack on Hispaniola. In accord with the criticism of merchants and colonial administrators postulated in the first canto, Castellanos stresses the vulnerability of the port of Santo Domingo owing to the lack of ammunition, fortifications, and properly trained soldiers. He specifically criticizes the performance of Cristóbal de Ovalle, president of the Real Audiencia, who allegedly received news of the imminent attack but ignored the warning and imprisoned a Portuguese man who had sailed from São Tiago to Hispaniola to alert the residents. Unlike the first canto, however, in the second canto Castellanos places far greater emphasis on the religious aspects of the antagonism between Catholic Spain and Protestant England and gives free rein to demonizing Drake and his troops. The narrator uses numerous epithets to convey the godless and evil nature of the enemies and vehemently condemns Martin Luther for presumably leading an entire nation (England) to the depths of hell.[42] Castellanos's use of the discourse of demonology adds a new layer to the already complex characterization of Drake, especially since in the previous canto Castellanos had dismissed as unfounded the rumor that Drake's success was due to the fact that he was hosting some sort of demon. In this canto, however, the ubiquitous conflict underlying Castellanos's narrative acquires the tone of a religious war against a demonic enemy, and the main differences between the English and Spaniards are predicated on their adherence or disdain for the Catholic faith.

A second rhetorical move that allows Castellanos to increase the urgency of Drake's threat and advance his criticism of newer colonists and bureaucrats is the use of biblical references. In the second canto the weight of Castellanos's poetic discourse is carried by a biblical allusion, which likens the circumstances surrounding the attack on Santo Domingo to God's foretold destruction of the city of Nineveh in the book of Jonah from the Old Testament. Thus the violence inflicted by the English upon the Spaniards appears as a punishment allowed by God for the iniquities committed by the colonists, and an opportunity for devout Christians to gain salvation.[43] Concomitantly, the narrator introduces the warning delivered by the Portuguese messenger to local authorities in the form of a prophetic announcement that condemns their faults as "vices" worthy of divine punishment. Notice in the following stanza the striking similarities between the messenger's speech and the complaints included in the harangue voiced by the local veteran after Drake's attack on the port of Callao seven years earlier:

!O corazones ya poco robustos!
¡O presumpción de más que flaco buelo!
¿Pensais que sois tan sanctos y tan justos
que no merezcais más duro flagelo?
¿Todos tienen que ser lascivos gustos
sin temer punición del alto cielo;
saraos han de ser todos y fiestas,
requiebros y pisadas deshonestas? [44]

O hearts grown soft and sunk in lassitude!
O vain and shallow arrogance!
Is it that you think yourselves so holy and just
that you do not deserve a more severe punishment?
Must all revolve around lascivious doings
without fear of chastisement from heaven,
must all be dance and celebration,
vainglory and dishonest gestures?

In his *Noticias historiales* (1625), Fray Pedro Simón (1574–1628) also included a description of Drake's 1586 attack on Santo Domingo and used a reference to the second book of Maccabees to argue that the assault had been God's punishment against his chosen people for straying from the righteous path. [45] However, Fray Pedro Simón's version shifts the emphasis of Castellanos's narrative by spreading the blame to all Spaniards who had been residents of Hispaniola, and singles out the utter decimation of the local indigenous population as their greatest sin, as opposed to lust, laziness, lack of prudence, and military incompetence. According to Fray Pedro Simón, all that was lost or destroyed during the attack had been violently taken from the Indians by the ancestors of the current residents, and as such Drake's assault had been God's judgment on their descendants. [46]

In the second canto Drake steps up to the role of general and commander of a large military operation and personally supervises the execution of an attack that is carried out with efficiency and precision. The night before the assault, Drake gathers his troops and delivers a speech outlining the strategy for a simultaneous naval and ground attack, and subsequently orders eight hundred of his men to disembark two leagues north of Santo Domingo and start advancing slowly toward the city. Drake's speech deserves attention not only because it establishes a sense of camaraderie, order, and readiness that is lacking on the Spanish counterpart but also because Drake emerges as a confident and perceptive commander who can balance the concern for his troops with the resolve to deal with practical issues such as desertion. Given the stark discrepancy between the narrator's adamant denunciation of the English as demonic heretics and the more favorable traits that emerge from the words attributed to Drake, it is equally pertinent to highlight that there are several key issues mentioned in Drake's speech that erase any sense of foreignness from his words and reconcile Drake's point of view with that of the narrator. For example, at a time when Santo Domingo's economic and administrative preeminence among Spanish colonies had eroded, both Drake and Castellanos exaggerate the financial rewards of the attack and share the view that Santo Domingo still constituted the principal seat of Spanish government in the New World: "la tierra destas partes fundamento"[47] (the bedrock of this part of the world), according to Drake, and "la matriz del indio suelo"[48] (the womb of the Spanish Indies), according to Castellanos. In addition, Drake, like Castellanos, shows disdain for individuals profiting from commerce and assures his followers of an easy victory, taking for granted that the residents of Santo Domingo were mostly merchants with little or no military experience. In short, the speech delivered by Drake adds to the exaltation of martial values and military life and contributes to the discrediting of the current residents of Santo Domingo. To borrow from a similar phrase coined by Elizabeth Wright, it would be as if the English explorer and privateer were speaking with a Spanish accent.[49]

The overlapping between Drake's and Castellanos's perspectives also occurs in the opposite direction when the narrator, like a ventriloquist repeating the words previously uttered by his own dummy, expresses slightly modified versions of the same arguments uttered by Drake earlier. An example of this occurs when Castellanos points out to readers that the residents of Santo Domingo were not prepared to defend what was in essence a frontier territory ("faltaban las industrias y maneras / que se suelen tener en las fronteras"[50] [lacking was the industry and caution / typically found in frontiers]), and subsequently issues an argument like the one pronounced by Drake after his attack on the ship *Nuestra Señora de la Concepción*. However, instead of asking for a deed signed by Adam that would guarantee Spain's right to the New World, Castellanos alludes to a deed signed by God that would guarantee that the Spanish possessions across the Atlantic would never be attacked by any of Spain's rivals:

> De guerra la ciudad muy olvidada,
> cuantos en ella son, mal advertidos,
> como si para ser asegurada
> de casos en el mundo sucedidos,
> tuvieran una cédula firmada
> de Dios para no ser jamás rompidos;
> como quiera que en tierras como estas
> siempre deben estar defensas prestas.[51]

> Of war the city had forgotten,
> its citizens poorly advised,
> as if they were insured
> from the type harm that often happens in the world
> all was as if they possessed a deed signed by God

that forever spared them from any threat
whereas lands such as this
must always be quick to employ defensive measures.

This stanza not only reveals a deep-seated siege mentality on the part of Castellanos but also serves the rhetorical function of postulating the need of a warrior class that would be willing to defend any threat to Spanish sovereignty. Indeed, the narrator's complaint takes for granted that Spain's primacy over the New World would be contested and that, as such, sovereignty over the colonies had to be anchored on military strength and decisive military victories.

Be that as it may, when the English ground forces reach the outskirts of Santo Domingo, their unexpected presence immediately causes pandemonium. The widespread reaction among local residents ranges from pusillanimity to consternation, and women rush to abandon the city, leaving their belongings behind. There is no sustained opposition to the attack, and even though a small group of men, whose names are individually recorded by Castellanos, makes an effort to face the incoming forces, the inadequacy of their weapons is no match for the strength of the English firepower. Drake's troops sweep through the city like a violent storm, leveling buildings, burning ships, pillaging everything in their path, and placing the English flag at the top of the cathedral. The narrator augments the dramatic efficacy of his descriptions by limiting the number of markers that indicate the progression of time, thus creating the impression that several of the events narrated take place at the same time. In addition, Castellanos describes with vivid details how, while ransacking and destroying a monastery, the English troops capture, ridicule, and hang two elderly Dominican friars and later proceed to desecrate religious statues and paintings. Although the specific names of the friars are not mentioned, the narrator illustrates how the friars patiently endure the abuses committed against them and march willingly to their deaths, gaining strength and inspiration from Christian martyrs and saints who had died under similar circumstances.

A scene describing the execution of the two Dominican friars also appears in two English sources dealing with Drake's attack on Santo Domingo, albeit not staging it as an episode of Christian martyrdom, nor depicting the behavior of the English as acts of random and unnecessary violence, but showing it as retaliation against Spaniards for murdering a black boy who was serving as messenger for Drake.[52] Irene A. Wright has argued that the story describing the execution of the two friars is apocryphal, given that the documents sent to Spain by local authorities after the attack make no mention of any such incident.[53] True or not, within Castellanos's poetic discourse the scene serves a pivotal purpose because it is out of empathy for the suffering of the friars and outrage for the desecration of religious images that the narrator feels compelled to insert himself in the middle of the action and to launch his sternest condemnation of the English:

> *!O fiera crueldad, furor insano,*
> *nefando crimen, infernal motivo!*
> *la pluma se me cae de la mano*
> *con un frío temblor cuando lo escrivo.*
> *Aquel Juez, immenso, soberano,*
> *llueva sobre vosotros fuego bivo,*
> *y a todos os abrase y os consuma*
> *sin que quede de vos hueso ni pluma.* [54]

> O furious cruelty, insane rage!
> Evil crime and demonic act!
> My pen falls from my hand
> as a cold trembling overpowers me as I attempt to write it.
> May that sovereign and all encompassing judge
> send fire upon you
> so you are all consumed by flames
> until no trace of you is left.

In this stanza the narrator is able to call attention simultaneously to the abhorrent nature of the acts he is describing and to his own emotional distress through the alliteration of the phoneme /f/ in words such as "fiera," "furor," "nefando," and "infernal," which are distributed across the first two lines. The simultaneity evoked through alliteration and the exclusion of any verbs from the same two verses foster the impression of direct approximation to the action and heighten the sense that events are actually taking place as they unfold across the page. By the same token, the narrator synchronizes further the time and place of the attack with the time and place of narration by introducing a metatextual reference whose two verbs are both conjugated in the present indicative: "la pluma se me cae de la mano / con un frío temblor cuando lo escribo." Even though Castellanos did not witness the events and he wrote his poem months after Drake's attack on Santo Domingo, these strategies allow him to establish a concrete presence within his own narrative and to delineate a subject position whose piety and fervor matches the sacrifice made by the two Dominican friars. In effect, the correspondence between the scene describing the friars' execution and the scene describing the narrator's reaction is also manifested in the fact that each scene discloses the reverse side of the same economy of salvation. After all, the friars' expectations for heavenly reward ("Al coro celestial ambos anhelan / donde reina la bondad que ellos estiman"[55] [they were yearning for the heavenly chorus / where the goodness that they cherish reigns]) go hand in hand with the narrator's expectations for heavenly vengeance, and the same deity that privileges and rewards the conduct of the friars is summoned by the narrator to annihilate the enemies of the Spaniards. However, the main difference be-

tween the two responses described in this section of the poem is that while
the pious passivity of the friars sublimates the violence inflicted by the English into a form of religious mysticism, the narrator's angered diatribe appears as the proper outlet for the expression of the frustration of Spaniards in
dealing with Drake and as a call that summons them to take action.

After thirty-one days of occupation and the payment of a ransom, the
narrator closes the second canto describing the untimely arrival of a judge
sent from Spain to conduct an inquiry about the attack and assign responsibility to the persons responsible for the losses. In addition, the narrator
predicts that the attack on Cartagena will replicate the one in Santo Domingo:

> *Y quiero ya contaros otro tanto*
> *de los de la ciudad de Cartagena,*
> *donde veréis en el futuro canto*
> *pusilanimidad no menos llena;*
> *y haremos principio de jornada*
> *desde este Nuevo Reino de Granada.* [56]

> And I would like to tell you more
> about what transpired at the city of Cartagena
> you will find in the next canto
> no less fear and pusillanimity
> and we shall begin this new section
> from this, the New Kingdom of Granada.

I have cited these lines not only because they disclose Castellanos's interpretation of what had taken place in Cartagena as early as the end of the second
canto ("donde veréis en el futuro canto / pusilanimidad no menos llena") but
also because from a structural point of view they provide a rather artificial
connection between the events narrated in the first two cantos and the events
Castellanos will narrate in the third. Within the same stanza Castellanos
practically contradicts himself by first stating his anxiety to start describing
the attack on Cartagena and then switching altogether the direction of his
poetic discourse to clarify that he will do so by first talking about the New
Kingdom of Granada. As it turns out, the events Castellanos will narrate in
canto 3 have little or no bearing at all on the actual fall of Cartagena, and
readers interested in that event could go on to the fourth canto. Ironically, it
is in the third canto that Castellanos will construct the poem's locus of
enunciation (the New Kingdom of Granada) as a stronghold of Spanish military prowess and a repository of the values that he claims are absent from the
rest of the colonies. It is also in canto 3 that Castellanos articulates more
forcefully a foundational myth that lionizes the conquistadors in general and
the encomendero class from the New Kingdom of Granada in particular.

CONCLUSION

It should be clear that Castellanos's *Discurso* is a text that portrays the recent maritime history of Spain in the New World as a progression of unpunished affronts by the English and a series of administrative misjudgments on the part of the Spanish Crown and its representatives. To gauge the significance of employing the epic genre to produce this assessment, we need only to remember that while Castellanos emphasized the vulnerabilities of Spanish ports in the New World, courtiers such as Alonso de Ercilla were praising Hapsburg naval dominance and the consolidation of Spanish imperial aspirations by narrating the Battle of Lepanto[57] as a reenactment of the epic battle of Actium inscribed on the Shield of Aeneas described by Virgil in book 8 of the *Aeneid*.[58]

In his dramatization of the rivalries among the Spanish population residing in the colonies, Castellanos clearly favors the side of the conquistadors and encomenderos. He assumes readers would conclude that if more members of that group were appointed as governors and administrators, problems such as piracy would not arise or would be dealt with appropriately. At face value this argument suggests that Castellanos viewed piracy not only as a result of Spain's monopoly over intercontinental trade or of England's effort to get a share of the wealth coming from the Indies but also and primarily as a side effect of the Spanish Crown's policy of appointing favorites, nobles, or university-trained bureaucrats to the most covetous posts in the administration of the New World. Accordingly, at the root of Castellanos's assessment of English piracy vis-à-vis colonial politics is the conviction that by not rewarding the deeds and merits of the first wave of colonists, Philip II was forfeiting his prudence, which was the emblematic attribute of monarchs in the sixteenth century. And prudence, combined with an unwavering "spirit of conquest," is the main quality that Castellanos and the rest of the colonists from Nueva Granada display in canto 3 in their desire to defend the territory they had usurped from the Muiscas.[59]

This is not to suggest that Castellanos did not attribute any negative traits to Drake as a literary character, which he did, particularly greed, but to highlight the fact that at a time when Drake was still a very controversial figure in England, he selectively excluded the least favorable incidents in Drake's career. Castellanos chiseled his description of the English enemy in order to exaggerate Drake's talent as a military commander and undermine the abilities of the Spanish administrators who were running the colonies despite their lack of previous military experience. Given that the first two cantos summarize Drake's ventures prior to the attack on Cartagena, it is surprising that Castellanos makes only a passing, but favorable, reference to Drake's participation in John Hawkins's attack on San Juan de Ulúa in 1568. During this attack Drake allegedly abandoned his superior and peers and returned separately to England. According to Harry Kelsey, the charge of desertion "haunted Drake for the rest of his life, for John Hawkins was forced to abandon a hundred of [his] men on the Mexican coast, and most of them never saw England again."[60] Neither is there any mention of the command problems that arose during the expedition to circumnavigate the world or of Drake's display of sheer ruthlessness by trying and executing onetime friend Thomas Doughty for supposedly attempting to incite mutiny among the crew. Nor is there any reference to the multiple problems regarding logistics, discipline, and command that arose during Drake's raid on the Caribbean (1585–1587), some of which can be traced back to Drake's "lack of talent for planning and conducting an extended military or naval campaign."[61]

Instead, what we find in Castellanos's poem is a very ambiguous and often openly sympathetic characterization of Drake that in accord with the ethos of the Counter-Reformation depicts Drake as a heretical and greedy Lutheran demon. Yet Castellanos also presents Drake as a loyal servant to the queen of England, a successful commoner who was able to ascend the social ladder, a well-spoken and courteous captain who could show mercy on his adversaries, and above all an exemplary military commander who could flawlessly conduct both naval and ground attacks. In my view, Castellanos tailored Drake's depiction to indicate, first, that despite the arbitration of Rome and the promulgation of papal bulls legitimizing Spanish possession over American territories, the control over the resources and sovereignty over that land was ultimately to be decided by military might. Second, in order to secure that victory, the Spanish Crown needed to summon support from the same group of individuals that it was systematically alienating by excluding them from the administration of the colonies.

Finally, the metaphor "en éste nuestro recental aprisco" (in this our new sacred sheepfold) discloses a fondness for the New World that is seldom found in the writings of sixteenth-century Spanish authors. The use of this metaphor suggests that, contrary to the trends and attitudes of contemporary Spanish writers and intellectuals who never set foot in America, by 1586 there were Spanish writers who had found a new *patria* in the New World and were beginning to reshape their loyalties and subjectivities.[62] In this regard it is instructive that in a crucial section of the poem Castellanos boosts his authority to give advice to the president of the Real Audiencia by explicitly declaring that he was in fact a *natural* of Nueva Granada:

> *Si para resguardarlo no hay olvido,*
> *aqueste reino, por natural juro,*
> *a ninguno podrá ser ofendido.*[63]

> If defensive measures are adopted without delay,
> I am certain, as one of its citizens, that this Kingdom
> can never be assaulted by our enemies.

By inscribing such a clear sense of local pride across his text, Castellanos anticipated a tradition whose continuity would immediately be assured by the first generation of local *criollo* writers that emerged in the New Kingdom of Granada in the seventeenth century. To be sure, it would not have been hard for the first descendants of the conquistadors to establish a link between the political impulse that sustained verses such as "en éste nuestro recental aprisco" (in this our new sacred sheepfold) and their own reappropriation of the American territory made explicit in lines such as "Esta, de nuestra América pupila"[64] (This, our American pupil), as it would be expressed half a century later in the writings of the most distinguished Baroque writer from New Granada, Hernando Domínguez Camargo (1606–1656).[65] As such, the most productive way to read Castellanos's *Discurso* is as one of the earliest testimonies of the emergence of a new type of personal and collective consciousness that would in turn serve as the paradigm for the development of a new type of literature.

In 1998 Georgina Sabat de Rivers included Domínguez Camargo's line "Esta, de nuestra América pupila" as an epigraph to a dossier devoted by the journal *Caliope* to Colonial Spanish American poetry. While explaining the epigraph, Sabat de Rivers invited readers to place Domínguez Camargo next to José Martí, given that "en el verso del santafereño hay también intención política: América, representada por la ciudad costera de Cartagena de Indias (tema del poema de donde se toma el verso), aventaja y reemplaza a Europa"[66] (there is also a political intention in Domínguez Camargo's poem: America, embodied by the coastal city of Cartagena de Indias [which is the theme of the poem from which we borrow this line], displaces and surpasses Europe). Incidentally, in the opening paragraph of his essay "Nuestra América" (Our America), Martí reminded readers of the contributions made by Castellanos:

> *Lo que quede de aldea en América ha de despertar. Estos tiempos no son para acostarse con el pañuelo en la cabeza, sino con las armas de almohada, como los varones de Juan de Castellanos: las armas del juicio, que vencen las otras. Trincheras de ideas valen más que trincheras de piedra.*[67]

> What remains of the village in America must rouse itself. These are not the times for sleeping in a nightcap, but with weapons for a pillow, like the warriors of Juan de Castellanos: weapons of the mind, which conquer all others. Barricades of ideas are worth more than barricades of stones.

Martí here is doing a critical reading of the *Elegías*. He first introduces a reference to Castellanos and subsequently corrects him. Yet, by doing so, Martí also reminded the readers of "Nuestra América" of the link between Juan de Castellanos, heroic poetry, and a nascent Spanish American literature.

NOTES

1. The *Discurso*, by Juan de Castellanos, contains 715 stanzas written in *octavas reales*, with the exception of a short section written in *tercetos* that appears in the third canto. All references to the *Discurso* are to the edition edited by Angel González Palencia (Madrid: Instituto de Valencia de Don Juan, 1921).

2. The expedition lost approximately 25 percent of the money pledged by the investors. See Harry Kelsey, *Sir Francis Drake: The Queen's Pirate* (New Haven, CT: Yale University Press, 1998), 281–83. See also Geoffrey Parker, "David or Goliath? Philip II and His World in the 1580s," in *Spain, Europe and the Atlantic World: Essays in Honour of John H. Elliott*, ed. Richard L. Kagan and Geoffrey Parker, 245–66 (Cambridge: Cambridge University Press, 2002), 264. For analysis of the modes of exchange and circulation between Spain and England during this period, see the essays in *Material and Symbolic Circulation between Spain and England, 1554–1604*, ed. Anne J. Cruz (Aldershot, UK: Ashgate, 2008).

3. Cañizares-Esguerra, *Puritan Conquistadors*, 39.

4. Cañizares-Esguerra does not examine the *Discurso* but offers a bold typological and allegorical interpretation of the frontispiece of the first volume of Castellanos's *Elegías* (1589). Although I agree with his brilliant interpretation of the frontispiece, I have found no evidence that the actual poems written by Castellanos wholeheartedly embrace Hapsburg imperial agenda or Hapsburg navigational prowess. In addition, I highly doubt that Castellanos had much to do with the decision behind what the frontispiece was and probably didn't get to see it until he had the printed book in his hands.

5. *Discurso*, viii.

6. *Discurso*, xv.

7. See Ernst Robert Curtius, *European Literature and the Latin Middle Ages* (New York: Pantheon, 1952), 82–89; and Alberto Porqueras Mayo, *El Prólogo como género literario: Su estudio en el Siglo de Oro español* (Madrid: Consejo Superior de Investigaciones Científicas, 1957), 140–44.

8. *Discurso*, 1–2.

9. Luis Fernando Restrepo, "Sacred and Imperial Topographies in Juan de Castellanos' *Elegías de varones ilustres de Indias*," in *Mapping Colonial Spanish America: Places and Commonplaces of Identity, Culture, and Experience*, ed. Santa Arias and Mariselle Meléndez, 84–101 (Lewisburg, PA: Bucknell University Press, 2002), 84.

10. *Discurso*, 128.

11. *Diccionario de Autoridades* (Madrid: Editorial Gredos, 1969), 3:513.

12. Aprisco: "El cercado o la estancia donde recogen los pastores su ganado . . . y todo lugar donde se abriga el ganado y se repara del viento y frío y las inclemencias del cielo" (Sebastián de Covarrubias Horozco, *Tesoro de la lengua castellana o española* [Madrid: Iberoamericana, 2006], 192; The fenced area or small farm where shepherds gather their sheep . . . and all other places that shelter animals and protect them from wind, cold temperature, and inclement weather).

13. "Y así por las cabañas y el aprisco / do pastan los ganados de esta gente" ("Relación de las cosas del Cabo de la Vela," in *Elegías*, 2:273; As well as in the shelters and the sheepfold / where their animals graze).

14. *Elegías*, 1:563.

15. "Elegía a la muerte de Sebastián de Benalcázar," in *Elegías*, vol. 1, canto 1, 325.

16. "Elogio de Gaspar de Rodas," in *Elegías*, vol. 3, canto 4, 699.

17. "Elegía III," in *Elegías*, vol. 2, canto 4, 250.

18. "Behold, I send you forth as sheep among wolves." See Matthew 10:16 and Luke 10:3.

19. I'm indebted to Jaime Borja and Juan Antonio Sánchez Hernández for providing information about this painting.

20. *Elegías*, 2:644.

21. Figuratively, to be crestfallen or down in the mouth.

22. This saying contains an allusion to the gospel passage describing Roman soldiers casting lots over Jesus's garments.

23. Elvira Vilches, *New World Gold: Cultural Anxiety and Monetary Disorder in Early Modern Spain* (Chicago: University of Chicago Press, 2010), 223.

24. Ibid., 212. In her analysis of *A Treatise on the Alteration of Money*, Vilches points out that for its author (the Jesuit Juan de Mariana), the vellón "destroyed the foundation of trade and, worse, undermined the confidence in money needed to assure its role as a medium of exchange" (ibid., 236). I'm indebted to Elizabeth Wright for suggesting this reference.

25. See Covarrubias Horozco, *Tesoro*, 1164.

26. Figuratively, to get more than you bargain for.

27. *Discurso*, 32.

28. Ibid., 33–34.

29. Ibid., lxxxv.

30. Nina Gerassi-Navarro, *Pirate Novels: Fictions of Nation Building in Spanish America* (Durham, NC: Duke University Press, 1999), 41.

31. The impact of the rivalry between new and old colonists in Spanish epic poetry has also been studied by José Durand; see "El chapetón Ercilla y la honra araucana," *Filología* 10 (1964): 113–34.

32. Meo Zilio, *Estudio sobre Juan de Castellanos*, 154.

33. Ovid, *Metamorphoses*, trans. Charles Martin (New York: Norton, 2004).

34. References to Argus Panopte are frequent in Renaissance and Baroque texts but for the most part are made to evoke "the figure of Argus in hyperbolic comparisons with a jealous man's possessiveness" (Steven Wagschal, *The Literature of Jealousy in the Age of Cervantes* [Colombia: University of Missouri Press, 2006], 60). An example of that trend would be the comparison of Felipo de Carrizales, the protagonist of Cervantes's "El celoso extremeño" (The jealous extremaduran), with Argus Panopte, which has clear sexual references. See Miguel de Cervantes Saavedra, "El celoso extremeño," in *The Complete Exemplary Novels*, ed. Barry Ife and Jonathan Thacker, 337–89 (Oxford, UK: Oxbow Books, 2013).

35. *Discurso*, 39.

36. Lope de Vega, *La dragontea* (Valencia, Spain: Pedro Patricio Mey, 1598). Lope's poem is about the last and least successful campaign of an *old* and *diminished* Drake, about the destruction of his fleet, and about his subsequent death after capturing the trading town of Nombre de Dios, near Panama. By and large, Lope avoids in his depiction of Drake the commercial aspects of the rivalry between Spain and England and instead magnifies the providential mission of Spain as a defender of the faith. As such, *La dragontea* is a poem that embraces imperial ideology and whose ultimate goal is to praise the might of the Spanish forces and their definite triumph over its adversaries, particularly the English. For a nuanced interpretation of *La dragontea*, see Elizabeth Wright's *Pilgrimage to Patronage: Lope de Vega and the Court of Phillip III, 1598–1621* (Lewisburg, PA: Bucknell University Press, 2001). For another poetic depiction of Drake's attack of the ship *Nuestra Señora de la Concepción*, see canto 8 of *Armas antárticas* (1609) by Juan de Miramontes Zuázola; repr., ed. Paul Philipp Firbas (Lima, Peru: Pontificia Universidad Católica del Perú, 2006).

37. *Discurso*, 40.

38. Ibid.

39. Ibid.

40. Ibid., 41.

41. Ibid., 42.

42. *Discurso*, 93. Also note in *Discurso* "profanos" (59; blasphemous), "gentes malas" (70; bad people), "ejército maligno" (73; evil army), "ministros del infierno" (78; ministers of hell), "bestias fieras" (79; cruel beasts), "basiliscos fieros" (81; fierce basilisks), "luteranos infernales" (85; Lutherans from hell), "miembros del demonio" (86; allies of the devil), "pérfida nación, ciega maligna" (88; deceitful, blind, and evil nation), "protervas gentes" (perverse people), "abominables delincuentes" (abominable delinquents), "sacrílegos sin Dios" (sacrilegious and godless people), "canalla vil" (90; vile scoundrels), "capitán cruel" (cruel captain), "insensato" (senseless), "ladrón traidor, hereje, furibundo" (92; thief, traitor, furious heretic), "hijo de perdición y hombre perdido" (child of sin and tainted man), "ciega nación desventurada" (blind and luckless nation), "contagiosa pestilencia" (93; contagious pestilence), "furiosísima demencia" (furious madness), "pérfida canalla" (95; deceitful scoundrel), "gente

fementida" (97; false people), and "ladrón hereje fementido" (102; heretical and deceitful thief).

43. The words used by Castellanos are "flagelo," "punición," and "castigo" (scourge, chastisement, punishment).

44. *Discurso*, 62.

45. Fray Pedro Simón dedicated the entire sixth chapter of his book to Francis Drake's pursuits in the New World. See *Noticias historiales de las conquistas de Tierra Firme en las Indias Occidentales* (Bogotá, Colombia: Biblioteca de Autores Colombianos, 1953), vols. 7 and 8.

46. Ibid., 7:270.

47. *Discurso*, 70.

48. Ibid., 97.

49. Wright studies the cultural affinities that explain elite Spaniards' admiration for Drake and proposes that for individuals seeking upward mobility, Drake served as "the very model of the early-modern Atlantic subject." See "From Drake to Draque: A Spanish Hero with an English Accent," in *Material and Symbolic Circulation between Spain and England, 1554–1604*, ed. Anne J. Cruz, 29–38 (Aldershot, UK: Ashgate, 2008).

50. *Discurso*, 65.

51. Ibid.

52. See "A Summary and True Discourse of Sir Frances Drakes West Indian Voyage" and "The *Primrose* Journal," in Francis Drake, *Sir Francis Drake's West Indian Voyage*, ed. Mary Frear Keeler, 179–209, 210–78 (London: Hakluyt Society, 1981).

53. Irene A. Wright, ed. and trans., *Further English Voyages to Spanish America, 1583–1594* (London: Hakluyt Society, 1951), xxxvii.

54. *Discurso*, 91.

55. Ibid., 90.

56. Ibid., 102.

57. *Araucana*, canto 23, stanzas 83–95.

58. On Ercilla's depiction of the Battle of Lepanto, see Nicolopulos, *Poetics of Empire*, 214; see also Karina Galperin, "The Dido Episode in Ercilla's *La Araucana* and the Critique of Empire," *Hispanic Review* 77, no. 1 (Winter 2009): 31–67, 69–70.

59. Prudence and patronage are themes that will resonate in subsequent epics such as Lope de Vega's *La dragontea*. As has been shown by Elizabeth Wright, implicit in *La dragontea* "is a criticism of the way the crown networks of patronage failed to properly compensate Spaniards who served the king in the Americas, a fault that, in the poet/chronicler's estimation, allowed Drake to make dangerous inroads in Spanish America." See Elizabeth Wright, "El enemigo en un espejo de príncipes: Lope de Vega y la creación del Francis Drake español," *Cuadernos de Historia Moderna* 26 (2001): 115–30.

60. Kelsey, *Sir Francis Drake*, 39.

61. Ibid., 394.

62. In making this statement I am by no means suggesting that Castellanos advocated any type of independence or separation from Spain, which will be anachronistic. However, historians such as D. A. Brading have traced some aspects of what is commonly referred to as "creole consciousness" to the requests for the extension or the permanent allocation of the *encomiendas*, which flooded the Crown around the same time that Castellanos's poem was written. Some of those petitions make arguments very similar to the one Castellanos makes in the *Discurso*, and by and large Castellanos's writings are imbued with the same "anguish, nostalgia and resentment" that Brading recognizes in those requests. See the chapter entitled "Creole Patriots," in *The First America: The Spanish Monarchy, Creole Patriots, and the Liberal State, 1492–1867* (New York: Cambridge University Press, 1991).

63. *Discurso*, 116.

64. Hernando Domínguez Camargo, *Obras* (Caracas, Venezuela: Biblioteca Ayacucho, 1986), 381.

65. In 1657 Domínguez Camargo became rector of the Cathedral of Tunja, the same post held by Castellanos for more than thirty years. With regard to Domínguez Camargo's knowledge of Castellanos's writings, Meo Zilio writes, "Es dable suponer que Camargo en sus años

mozos, en la casa de probación de los jesuitas, ubicada en aquel mismo pueblo de Tunja del que Castellanos fue Beneficiado, se haya empapado del poema de su antecesor, publicado en su primera parte unas décadas antes [1589] y seguramente poseído por la biblioteca de aquel colegio. Mas aún, si tenemos en cuenta que el poema del alanicense es la primera obra literaria del Nuevo Reino, no podemos dejar de suponer que fuese archiconocido en Tunja por aquellos años, a pesar de que su continuador lo ignora altivamente desde lo alto de su trono gongorino" (*Estudio sobre Juan de Castellanos*, 139; It is plausible to assume that in his youth Domínguez Camargo, who attended the Jesuit school in Tunja, the same town in which Castellanos served as a Beneficed priest, would have been familiar with the poem of his predecessor, published a few decades earlier [1589] and most likely owned by the library of that school. In addition, if we take into account that Castellanos's poem is the first major literary work from the New Kingdom of Granada, it follows that the poem would be well known in Tunja at the beginning of the seventeenth century, although Domínguez Camargo seems to disdain it in his quest to affiliate with the poetic language of Góngora).

66. Georgina Sabat de Rivers, "Introducción, Esta, de nuestra América pupila: Estudios de poesía colonial," *Calíope: Journal of the Society for Renaissance and Baroque Hispanic Poetry* 4, nos. 1–2 (1998): 8. For a recent assessment of Domínguez Camargo's poem, see Juan Vitulli, "Blanco pequeño de ambos mundos: Una lectura del 'Agasajo' de Hernando Domínguez Camargo," *Calíope: Journal of the Society for Renaissance and Baroque Hispanic Poetry* 18, no. 2 (2013): 139–60.

67. José Martí, "Nuestra América," in *Obras completas*, 6:15–23 (Havana: Editorial Nacional de Cuba, 1963), 15.

Chapter Four

Poetic Emulation and the
Performance of Power in Canto 3 of
Discurso del Capitán Francisco Draque

There are three salient and intimately connected changes that take place in canto 3 of the *Discurso del capitán Francisco Draque* in relation to the previous two cantos (see chapter 3). Juan de Castellanos turns his attention, and that of the readers, to the internal situation of the New Kingdom of Granada proper, an area that was approximately three hundred miles away from the port of Cartagena de Indias and was never the target of Francis Drake's attacks either during the 1585–1586 expedition to the West Indies or in any other expedition.[1] Concomitantly, Castellanos reorganizes the parameters of the narrative sequence. Thus, if up until that point the action of the poem has advanced according to the progression of Drake's attacks, in canto 3 the narrator focuses exclusively on the events that unraveled as letters, dispatches, and rumors about the attacks on Santo Domingo and Cartagena reached the cities of Santafé de Bogotá and Tunja, the political and administrative center of the New Kingdom of Granada. By doing this, Castellanos is able to take issue with the limitations imposed by the system of communication and to imbue his description of the internal situation with the sense of awe and disbelief caused by the magnitude of those attacks. The title of canto 3, "Donde se cuenta la confusión y sospecha que causaron las preñadas nuevas . . ." (which narrates the confusion and suspicion produced by the woeful news), and several of its opening stanzas speak of the consternation that vague or exaggerated reports about Drake's attacks caused among the local Spanish population. However, the most important change that takes place in this canto is that the authority of the poetic voice increases considerably as it switches from the secondhand reportage of events that occurred elsewhere (i.e., Panama, the port of Callao, Lima, Santo Domingo, or Cartagena) to the first-person testimony of a privileged eyewitness. In other words, since Castellanos is describing no longer what he has learned secondhand but his own actions and those of other local colonists, in canto 3 he ceases to be merely a narrator and emerges as one of the principal protagonists of his own poem. The authority gained by switching from narrating recent historical events to providing an eyewitness account is nowhere more evident than in the synecdoche through which the versification of a letter Castellanos sent to Judge Francisco Guillén Chaparro, president of the High Royal Court of Santafé, occupies the centerpiece of canto 3 (and of the entire poem) and speaks for him.

In this chapter, I offer an analysis of the two highpoints of canto 3 of *Discurso del capitán Francisco Draque*: (1) the information included in the letter Castellanos sent to the president of the High Royal Court; (2) and the description of a military parade of former conquistadors preparing to defend the New Kingdom of Granada. In my analysis, I pay special attention to the way in which Castellanos constructs New Granada as a stronghold of military prowess, while problematizing the function of writing in the colonial context and using heroic poetry to boost the political authority of the local encomendero class. My analysis is informed by the notion that in early modern societies power was intimately connected to display and that Colonial Spanish America, in particular, was a highly ritualized society in which public ceremonies played a major role in the symbolic representation of power and in the concrete exercise of monarchical authority. Alejandro Cañeque's study of the viceroy's public persona as a living image of the majesty of the monarch has shown that "pomp and pageantry, spectacle and splendor [were] treated as integral parts of the political process and the structure of colonial power."[2] Taking into consideration that precedence and protocol were essential to what Cañeque calls the "geometry of [Colonial Spanish America] power," I will examine the political message encoded in the versification of the letter and the description of the military parade to show how Castellanos uses these sections of his poem to contest the authority of the president of the High Royal Court and to criticize Philip's II liberality, that is, the monarch's obligation to be generous with his subjects and to reward the service of worthy vassals, which was a key political principle within the existing economy of service and favors.[3] More precisely, by using the parade as an allegory of the New Kingdom of Granada as a political body, I will argue that while on the surface the political body appears healthy, harmonious, and hierarchical, upon closer scrutiny, the said body appears out of sorts because it has not one but two heads competing for preeminence. My analysis will also show how the practice of poetic emulation continues to inform Castellanos's writing, as his catalog of local militias and his description of the military parade are designed to outdo the parade of

Amerindian warriors from canto 21 of the *Araucana*. In that regard, this chapter shows how the ancient epic topoi of a catalog of warriors and a military parade acquired new meaning in Colonial Spanish America, given the symbolic capital of public spectacle and etiquette to validate or contest political authority.[4]

JUAN DE CASTELLANOS'S LETTER TO THE PRESIDENT OF THE HIGH ROYAL COURT OF SANTAFÉ DE BOGOTÁ

The textual authority canto 3 ascribes to Castellanos is so evident that one might say, in what is perhaps the most dramatic section of the poem, the infamous English antihero, Francis Drake, is relegated to the background of the action while the narrator moves to the forefront and temporarily takes over the role of protagonist. Castellanos places himself in the middle of the action at a junction when contradictory reports have led local colonists to suspect that Drake's upcoming attack is not just upon the port of Cartagena de Indias but also upon the entire Spanish Main and on the New Kingdom of Granada in particular. According to the more recent information that arrives to the cities of Santafé de Bogotá and Tunja, the English have sent ships around the Strait of Magellan in order to conduct a simultaneous attack on the Atlantic and the Pacific coasts, and there is an army of twenty thousand English troops who have taken control of the ports and are ready to build fortifications and to move up the mountains until they reach and destroy that kingdom:

Pero la mala nueva no embargante
que no salía bien de entre los dientes,
después pasó su voz tan adelante
que hacía temblar a los oyentes,
diciendo ser ejército pujante
y sobre veinte mil los combatientes;
y que, pues tanto número venía,
era por ganar esta monarquía .

Y que tenían de marinos puertos
los más acomodados y mejores
para permanecer después de muertos
todos los españoles moradores,
y así, por los caminos descubiertos,
de lo de más adentro ser señores;
y que entraron también por el Estrecho
otros del mar del Sur al mismo hecho.[5]

But nonetheless the melancholy news
that at the lips found an uneasy vent,

in little time so publicly was heard
that every hearer trembled.
It was said that [Drake's forces were] a formidable army
with twenty thousand men and more
and that this mighty army he designed
to become master of this monarchy.

Moreover that he had of seaboard ports,
the best and most prosperous well prepared,
enough to remain once all the Spanish settlers were dead;
and thus, through roads that had been discovered he would make his way [to the highlands]
and that reinforcements through the Strait [of Magellan]
had come from the South Sea to the same end.

Castellanos offers no substantive evidence in support of these claims, and it is obvious that he is indulging in hyperbole. The reasons port cities such as Santo Domingo, Havana, and Cartagena de Indias quickly became recurrent military targets are self-evident, but it is not clear exactly what military advantages or economic rewards the English might have gained by launching a large-scale invasion to a remote and difficult-to-access post on the highlands of the Andes. In spite of their imprecisions, however, these two stanzas go a long way in terms of situating the New Kingdom of Granada within the imperial global cartography, which is, after all, one of the main thrusts of this poem.

By introducing an allusion to the Strait of Magellan, a key fixture in Ercilla's *Araucana*, Castellanos is invoking a location that by the second half of the sixteenth century, had come to represent "colonial desire, the impulse to empire, [and] the drive to both apprehend the world and to posses it," as Ricardo Padrón has elucidated.[6] But if references to the Strait of Magellan, and particularly to its closure, play a pivotal role in the metageography of Ercilla's poem and in the formulation of a countercartography of empire that condemns conquistadorial brutality as argued by Padrón, in the stanza cited above, Castellanos situates control over the strait in the context of emerging geopolitical rivalries between Spain and England and reminds readers that the Strait of Magellan remained open. On the other hand, by referring to the New Kingdom of Granada as "esta monarchía" (this monarchy), Castellanos captures the sentiments of the local Spanish residents who aspired that New Granada would become a viceroyalty on equal footing with the viceroyalties of New Spain and Peru. This was something for which New Granada would have to wait another 150 years until the administrative reorganization brought about by the implementation of the Bourbon Reforms, precisely at the time when Spanish monarchs had begun to treat their Spanish American possessions less like satellite kingdoms and more like actual colonies. In any event, to make matters worse, the news of an English invasion also reaches the Amerindian population and raises the possibility of a general indigenous uprising.[7]

It's when faced with the possibility of an external and internal attack that Castellanos assumes the role of protagonist and decides to write a letter to the president of the Real Audiencia with advice on how best to secure the territory. As alluded to earlier, Castellanos's letter to Judge Guillén Chaparro is by no means the only letter mentioned in this canto. Prior to turning the contents of the letter into verses, the narrator has built anticipation by referring to several other letters that either have reached New Granada or could have been sent there from adjacent cities. In a matter of a few stanzas, Castellanos's poetic discourse crisscrosses the (textual) territory of the New Granada in several directions to include references to letters sent from Spain with information about Drake's upcoming expedition: "por cartas enviadas de la corte, / del potente pirata, que venía"[8] (through letters sent from the court / about the powerful pirate that was heading this way); a letter the governor of Venezuela never sent to the High Royal Court in Santafé de Bogotá: "pues al Audiencia no se lo escribía / el que es gobernador en Venezuela"[9] (since the High Court did not receive a written report / from the governor of Venezuela); letters that were never sent to New Granada from the island of Hispaniola by way of Cabo de la Vela: "siendo de la Hespañola tan vecinos / y siempre frecuentados los caminos"[10] (being that Hispaniola and Cabo de la Vela are so close / and the paths between them so well tread); a letter sent to Antonio Joven, *corregidor* (chief magistrate) of Tunja, by Baltasar Soler, a resident in Venezuela;[11] a letter that arrived from the town of Mompox with information about the fall of Cartagena: "de Mompox escribieron ser tomada / la próspera ciudad de Cartagena"[12] (from Mompox we received a missive about the siege / of the prosperous city of Cartagena); a letter that should have been sent by the governor of Cartagena: "El Gobernador Bustos no escribía, / debiendo ser su carta la primera"[13] (Governor Bustos did not write to us / though his letter should have been the first to arrive); and finally, a detailed report sent by Lucas de Espinosa from the town of Mompox, where colonists from Cartagena had taken refuge to escape Drake's attack.[14]

The abundant references to all this correspondence (or in some cases to the lack thereof) and to the exasperation that spread among the local colonists due to rumors, delays, and miscommunication suggest that on some level Castellanos believed the New Kingdom of Granada did not react more promptly to the threat of a naval attack on Cartagena de Indias because the neighboring administrative centers did not inform them in a more timely fashion. Read in this manner, canto 3 of the *Discurso* offers not necessarily a description of the prompt reaction from colonists from cities such as Santafé de Bogotá and Tunja, as has been suggested by other critics, but rather alibies explaining the lack of a more timely response. However, if rumors and delays lessened the impact of all this correspondence and led local colonists to extrapolate the magnitude of the threat, Castellanos suggests that at least his own letter accomplished its intended goal by commenting that Judge Guillén Chaparro responded favorably to his advice and wrote back to inform him of the measures the High Royal Court had already taken to secure the territory:

Vido mi carta y, aunque mal compuesta,
como sabio varón y comedido,
vino muy comedida la respuesta;
y dijo que tenía proveído
pues mandaba tener su gente presta
a las justicias de cualquier partido,
haciendo lista de armas y de gente,
y que diesen avisos brevemente. [15]

Having read my letter, although poorly written
as a wise and cautious man
he sent me his prudent reply;
stating that he had already provided all the means to defend [the kingdom],
requiring that the authorities make a list of the weapons and the men that were available,
and to send warnings without delay.

Since the amicable exchange recalled in this stanza is the only instance in the *Discurso* when the perspectives of local colonists and representatives of the Spanish Crown come together into (almost) perfect alignment, it appears that Castellanos is suggesting that the security of the colonies would improve significantly if more administrators were as receptive as Judge Guillén Chaparro to the input offered by *baquianos* (knowledgeable and skillful veterans). This is especially the case if we take into account that in his letter to the judge Castellanos characterizes himself as a *baquiano* and justifies sending his unsolicited military advice with claims to his previous experience: "pues muchas veces como *baquiano* / he visto pesadísimas reyertas"[16] (because as a knowledgeable and skillful veteran / I have had to face difficult and violent fights).

I would argue, nonetheless, that by making metatextual references to a letter he sent to the president of the High Royal Court and then transcribing the contents of the letter in the poem, Castellanos is not only drawing attention to the performance of judge Guillén Chaparro but also problematizing the position of writers in the colonial setting and the relationship of the genre of epic and heroic poetry to the dominant imperial ideology. In effect, by versifying what he had written to the highest-ranking official of the High Royal Court, Castellanos not only reveals the contents of the letter but also unveils the social and political function of that form of writing by mimicking some of its conventions.[17] By doing so, Castellanos creates a more ambiguous discourse that simultaneously offers a *mise en abyme* of those writing practices and exposes the encomiastic function of epic poetry. To be sure, once transformed into *tercetos* (tercets) and embedded into the discourse of the poem, Castellanos's letter to Guillén Chaparro starts serving completely new rhetorical and ideological functions, and its contents have to be interpreted in relation to what is expressed or silenced in the rest of the poem. In this sense, the most immediate effect of versifying the letter is to enhance the ironic aspects of this section of the *Discurso* by inserting the letter in a context that leads readers to interpret it in a manner quite different to that of its first recipient. The transcription of letters for dramatic and ironic purposes was a literary recourse widely used in the sixteenth and seventeenth centuries.[18] To put it succinctly, if Judge Guillén Chaparro had the chance to read the private letter originally addressed to him in the context of a poem whose intended audience (Abad Melchor Pérez de Arteaga, and possibly the members of the Council of the Indies and the monarch) was on the other side of the Atlantic, his response would have been less amicable than the one described by Castellanos in the afore-cited stanza. I shall illustrate this hypothesis by way of three separate examples that show how Castellanos's military advice and unrequested flattery serve to enhance the poet's position (and that of the group he represents) and to question the performance and credentials of the president of the High Royal Court.

Castellanos introduces the letter into poetic discourse by way of recalling the initial act of writing it and by confessing the apprehension he experienced for overstepping the administrative prerogatives of the president of the High Royal Court of Santafé de Bogotá:

> *Tanto que yo, debajo buen intento,*
> *por tener algún curso y experiencia*
> *de cuanto mal y cuanto perdimiento*
> *suele causar la mucha negligencia,*
> *tomé (no sin temor) atrevimiento*
> *de dar alguna voz en el Audiencia*
> *al que tenía vez de Presidente;*
> *y lo que le escribí, fue lo siguiente.*[19]

> So much did this appear that I, who have,
> from sore firsthand experience attained
> a certain knowledge of the bitter fruits
> that spring from seeds of negligence;
> with good intent (though with some fear) I took the liberty,
> of sending my advice to the person who was then president of the High Court
> and what I wrote is this that follows.

The line "tomé (no sin temor) atrevimiento" not only foregrounds the connection between writing, politics, and power but also positions Castellanos as vulnerable to the authority of Guillén Chaparro and cautions readers that due to such a disadvantage, he might not have been at liberty to express openly any disapproval of the judge's authority. It goes without saying that Castellanos's letter lacks the accusatory tone of the bitter tirades launched by *baquia-*

nos against merchants, administrators, and newly arrived colonists in cantos
1 and 2 and discussed in the previous chapter. This time he conveys his
criticism amid a mixture of affected modesty, submissiveness, and condes-
cension. In fact, in at least two instances throughout the letter, Castellanos
goes out of his way to maintain a conciliatory tone and to indicate that the
warnings and recommendations outlined in his letter should be interpreted
not as an indictment of Guillén Chaparro's leadership but as the result of his
own local pride and religious zeal. [20]

Nonetheless, readers cannot avoid making note of the ambivalence of
Castellanos's disclaimers because, in his letter and throughout the rest of
canto 3, he makes several narrative choices that put into question Guillén
Chaparro's credentials as a military commander and seek to undermine the
judge's authority to lead. Indeed, the dwarfing of Guillén Chaparro's authority begins precisely in the introductory remarks of the letter in which Castellanos appears to be paying lip service to the judge by apologizing in advance
for not writing exclusively to praise his virtues, and subsequently pledges to
make up for this lapse in an indeterminate future:

> *Señor doctor Chaparro: si mi rima*
> *en os loar cumpliera su deseo,*
> *ninguna fuera de mayor estima,*
>
> *y no hiciéramos encuentro feo;*
> *pues si buenos merecen alabanza,*
> *era la vuestra principal empleo.*
>
> *Tiempo podrá venir de más bonanza*
> *para que, fuera de estas confusiones,*
> *paguemos con enmienda la tardanza.* [21]

> Doctor [Francisco Guillén] Chaparro: if these verses
> could fulfill their goal by praising you
> none other would be more highly esteemed by me.
>
> And we would not have such awkward encounter
> for if good men merit praise
> in you alone they would deserve to be employed.
>
> A more prosperous or fitting time will come
> when unhindered by all this chaos
> I will reward you dearly for the delay.

The problem with choosing to postpone the occasion when he will use his
writing to praise the deeds and virtues of Guillén Chaparro is that Castellanos
dedicates a disproportionately large section of canto 3 to showcasing the
merits of those individuals who gained control of the territory of the New

Kingdom of Granada in the first place and expressing his utmost respect and admiration for them. As a matter of fact, almost the entire canto 3, with the exception of the introductory stanzas and the transcribed text of the letter, is devoted to this task. It is particularly telling that immediately before evading praising the merits of Guillén Chaparro, Castellanos had already started to praise Antonio Joven, a former soldier who participated in the campaigns of conquest and was serving as *corregidor* (chief magistrate) of the city of Tunja. In the first of the following two stanzas Castellanos comments on the diligence displayed by Joven when preparing for the defense of the New Kingdom of Granada, and in the second, Castellanos attests to the courage and prudence Joven would display if he were to reach Cartagena prior to Drake's arrival:

> *Antonio Joven, pues, hombre rompido,*
> *lleno de toda buena suficiencia*
> *de cualquiera recado recibido,*
> *daba prestos avisos a la Audiencia*
> *y procuró de estar apercibido*
> *con viva y admirable diligencia,*
> *buscando necesarias municiones*
> *para las venideras ocasiones. . . .* [22]

> Antonio Joven, a bold and determined man
> capable for so many different tasks
> any news that reached him
> he would swiftly inform the court.
> And he strove to remain alert
> with lively and admirable diligence
> preparing all necessary weapons
> to face the impending battle. . . .

> *Pero, caso supuesto que pudiera [Antonio Joven]*
> *ir a los puertos antes del aprieto,*
> *de su valor se cree que hiciera*
> *y de su buen gobierno gran efecto;*
> *ánimo fuerte no le falleciera*
> *ni prontitud de capitán discreto,*
> *sin faltar en ardides importantes*
> *que demandan negocios semejantes.* [23]

> But in the event that he [Antonio Joven] could reach
> the port prior to Drake's attack,
> I'm confident he would make great use of his intelligence, skills, and expertise.
> A brave disposition will not fail him
> or the readiness of a great captain
> nor the necessary cunning to face this type of situation.

Castellanos further undermines the authority of the president of the Real Audiencia and enhances his own textual authority and that of the local encomenderos by discarding as impractical the option of sending troops to assist in the defense of Cartagena de Indias and clarifying (not just to Guillén Chaparro but also to the readers of the poem in the Iberian Peninsula) that his main concern is how best to protect the territory of the New Kingdom of Granada proper.[24] Castellanos's clarification is necessary because it establishes that even though local colonists had temporarily assumed that the English forces were large enough to launch an invasion of the Spanish Main, Castellanos and the former conquistadors were confident that they could still repel their assault if the correct defensive measures were taken. By making explicit the purpose of his letter and particularly his confidence that the colonists from the New Kingdom of Granada could deter the English threat, therefore, Castellanos is indicating to readers that from a narrative and thematic point of view, his letter to Judge Guillén Chaparro serves as a counterpoint to the speeches delivered by Francis Drake elsewhere in the poem, particularly the one Drake delivered before his assault upon Santo Domingo. Indeed, the sort of speech attributed to Drake and Castellanos's letter to Guillén Chaparro provides indispensable tools for interpreting their respective goals and the implications of their actions. Accordingly, each of these two sections of the poem addresses directly the issue of exerting force to gain or retain control of a particular territory. However, if in his speech Drake (the poem's antihero) makes explicit the desire to dominate by typifying his attack on Hispaniola as the rape of a woman ("vais a gozar ciudad que está doncella / de todo belicoso rompimiento"[25] [you will enjoy a city that is still a virgin / of the breakings and destruction of war]), in his own letter, Castellanos plows over Guillén Chaparro's preeminence and emerges as the true Spanish hero of the poem by taking the initiative and assuming the responsibility for asserting the local colonists' desire to resist any type of intrusion. Like his counterpart, Castellanos also sexualizes the colonial space by insisting on the need to shut all the entrances where the New Kingdom of Granada could be penetrated and by replacing the vulnerability conveyed in the original metaphor he had used to refer to New Granada in the exordium of the poem ("en éste nuestro recental aprisco"[26] [in this our new sacred sheepfold]) with a new metaphor that attributes more martial characteristics to the same territory: "Es todo él (the New Kingdom of Granada) inexpugnable muro"[27] (the entire [New Kingdom of Granada] is an insurmountable wall).

However, the most interesting manner in which Castellanos diminishes the stature of Judge Guillén Chaparro is by disclosing to readers that the president of the High Royal Court lacks any type of military experience. Castellanos reveals this information on two separate occasions when he records the names of the troops assembled to defend the New Kingdom of

Granada. The first time, he does so explicitly to accentuate a void or an absence around the judge's apparent deficiency:

> *El General [en Santafé de Bogotá] ser quiso*
> *aquel por quien entonces se regía*
> *aqueste Nuevo Reino donde piso,*
> *que el cargo justamente merecía,*
> *pues suplican las letras y el aviso*
> *el uso que de guerra no tenía;*
> *y de este cargo se quedó vacío*
> *el capitán Antonio de Berrío.*[28]

> The post of General [in Santafé de Bogotá]
> was taken by he who was governing at the time
> this New Kingdom where I stand,
> a position he justly deserved because his education and readiness
> compensate for his lack of experience in war;
> and this post [of general] was diverted from
> Captain Antonio de Berrío.

Castellanos devotes six lines of this stanza to point out that Judge Guillén Chaparro took on the role of commander of the local militias in Santafé de Bogotá owing to his responsibility as administrator. But since the name of the judge is nowhere found throughout the stanza, on a symbolic level the president of the Real Audiencia is actually absent. When Castellanos clarifies that he is referring to the highest-ranking official at New Granada, Judge Guillén Chaparro continues to remain absent while the poet brings his own presence into the text by reminding readers, once again, of the poem's place of enunciation: "aqueste Nuevo Reino donde [yo] piso."[29] Likewise, when Castellanos acknowledges that Judge Guillén Chaparro is at the top of the military hierarchy, he does so in a way that reminds readers that the judge has education and wit but no expertise in military affairs: "pues suplican las letras y el aviso / el uso que de guerra no tenía."[30] Consequently, even though the judge is the first to appear or to be named and stands at the pinnacle of the hierarchy of military and administrative power, readers cannot help but notice his deficiencies, especially in light of the surplus of merits, experience, and services Castellanos will attribute to local colonists such as Captain Juan de Montalvo, *corregidor* Antonio Joven, and many others elsewhere in the same canto. It is also revealing that in a poem where there are several speeches by anonymous bystanders and where Castellanos cedes the word to Francis Drake on several occasions, there is never an intervention by Guillén Chaparro except to endorse the suggestions made by Castellanos. When read from this perspective, it is clear that Guillén Chaparro's symbolic absence from two key stanzas of this canto and the reference to his lack of military competence are intended to signal that the preeminence of administrators like him was far from absolute and is constantly being challenged by local colonists.

THE BATON OF ENCOMENDERO AUTHORITY

The second time Castellanos brings up the judge's lack of military experience, he does it through a pun built around the significance of horses in sixteenth-century warfare and the symbolism of the baton as an expression of political and military authority.[31] As he had done earlier, Castellanos's new strategy continues to destabilize the hierarchy of power by proposing an alternative order that gives preeminence to local colonists over functionaries sent from Spain by the Crown. Notice that the last person to be mentioned in the following stanza is Antonio Joven, the same colonist whose merits Castellanos started to praise while deferring the praise of judge Guillén Chaparro:

> *En un caballo blanco regalado*
> *salió Guillén Chaparro bien guarnido,*
> *en Santafé, con el bastón dorado,*
> *que por su dignidad le era debido.*
> *Antonio Joven iba de brocado,*
> *en Tunja lo mejor de su partido;*
> *y el día que se hizo la tal muestra*
> *también tuvo bastón su mano diestra.*[32]

> On an elegant and zesty white horse
> nicely attired [Judge] Guillén Chaparro came out
> in Santafé, with the golden staff
> befitting to his high rank.
> In Tunja Antonio Joven was wearing a rich burnished silk fabric
> accompanied with the best [men] from his realm;
> and on the day of the parade
> a staff he was also holding with his skilled hand.

Horses were an essential component of the Spanish style of warfare ever since the Middle Ages and as such played decisive roles in the campaigns to expel the Moors from the Iberian Peninsula, as well as during the exploration and conquest of the New World. In his letter to the president of the High Royal Court, Castellanos builds upon the importance of horses as military assets to persuade readers of the risk of an indigenous uprising by pointing out that Amerindians have become great horsemen and are not afraid of horses as they had been in the past.[33] However, if the allusion to Amerindians' aptitude to ride horses is included to boost the imminence of their threat, the reference to Judge Guillén Chaparro riding on a horse ("En un caballo blanco regalado") aims to puncture the judge's stature because it is a pun built upon the expression "caballo de regalo," which was another form of saying battle horse ("caballo de batalla"). But how could the judge have a battle horse if he had never participated in a battle? Within the same stanza Castellanos also challenges Guillén Chaparro's preeminence by saving his last remarks to highlight the military experience of a former conquistador. In the last four lines of the stanza, the *corregidor* Antonio Joven appears elegantly dressed and holding a baton of authority while participating in the respective parade in the neighboring town of Tunja. Interestingly enough, Castellanos hints that unlike the judge, Joven is holding a baton not because that privilege has been conferred upon him by the prerogatives of his office ("que por su dignidad era debido") but because he has earned it with his experience: "Antonio Joven iba de brocado / en Tunja lo mejor de su partido; / y el día que se hizo la tal muestra / también tuvo bastón su mano diestra." Although the narrator concedes that Guillén Chaparro is carrying a golden staff as a symbol of his authority, it is only when speaking of the *corregidor* that Castellanos highlights that Antonio Joven is actually holding the baton with his hand: "también tuvo bastón su mano diestra." This wording, especially in juxtaposition to what has been said or omitted about the judge, brings to mind the figurative meaning of the phrase "empuñar el bastón" (to grab the baton), which means to take charge or command ("asumir el mando"). This is important because, by giving equal attention to the elegant attire of the two individuals Castellanos levels the symbolic field and suggests that they are equally worthy, by reserving his last comments for Joven, and by focusing on the act of holding the staff with his hands, Castellanos situates the encomenderos as the individuals who are or should be in command.

The last two lines of the stanza cited above are especially important because they serve to confirm Alonso de Ercilla's parade of Amerindian warriors from canto 21 of the *Araucana* as a privileged subtext of this section of Castellanos's poem. In the opening stanza of the parade of Araucanian warriors, Ercilla uses the same rhyme between the words *muestra* and *diestra* to refer to the baton of authority Chieftain Pillilco was holding while marching in the parade:

> *Era el primero que empezó la muestra*
> *el cacique Pillilco, el cual armado*
> *iba de fuertes armas en la diestra*
> *un gran bastón de acero barreado.* [34]

And the first to march in the parade
was chieftain Pillilco,
wearing a heavy armor
while holding in his right hand
a great staff barred with steel.

Through his allusion to this specific section of Ercilla's parade, Castellanos is cleverly taking the baton away from the hands of chieftain Pillilco and putting it in the hands of the former conquistador turned encomendero: "y el día que se hizo la tal muestra / también tuvo bastón su mano diestra."[35] By doing this Castellanos is restoring the textual authority conquistadors and encomenderos were denied in the pages of Ercilla's poem. In terms of the local scheme of power in New Granada, moreover, Castellanos's strategy allows him to attribute the same or more preeminence to the *corregidor* and the encomendero class from Tunja than the royal official that had been sent as president of the High Royal Court of Santafé de Bogotá.

THE EMULATION OF ERCILLA'S PARADE OF AMERINDIAN WARRIORS: LIBERALITY AND THE ECONOMY OF FAVOR

The narration of the preparations taken by the colonists from the New Kingdom of Granada to defend their territory provides Castellanos with ample opportunity to emulate the ordered and meticulous description of the parade of Araucanian heroes included in the second volume of the *Araucana*. Here we recall that in canto 21 of his poem Ercilla had offered two adjacent descriptions of the preparations taken by the Spanish and the Araucanian troops prior to the battle of Andalicán. Most of what Ercilla had to say about the Spanish side is included in the following two stanzas, which, much as Castellanos will do later in his own version, aestheticizes warfare and transforms the violent confrontations involving the events of the conquest into a sort of exciting sporting contest. I cite first Ercilla's and then Castellanos's amplification:

> *¿Quién pudiera pintar el gran contento,*
> *el alborozo de una y otra parte,*
> *el ordenado alarde, el movimiento,*
> *el ronco estruendo del furioso Marte,*
> *tanta bandera descogida al viento,*
> *tanto pendón, divisa y estandarte,*
> *trompas, clarines, voces, apellidos,*
> *relinchos de caballos y bufidos?*[36]

> Who could render the great excitement,
> the joy in each and every side
> the ordered display, the movement,
> the hoarse uproar of furious Mars,
> so many flags waving in the wind,
> so many banners, ribbons, and standards,
> trumpets, boasts, and clamors
> the neighing and snorting stallions?

* * *

Ya, pues, en aquel sitio recogidos
tantos soldados, armas, municiones
todos los instrumentos prevenidos,
hechas las necesarias provisiones,
fueron por igual orden repartidos
los lugares, cuarteles y escuadrones,
para que en el rebato y voz primera
cada cual acudiese a su bandera. [37]

And then, on that site gathered
so many soldiers, arms, and ammunitions
all instruments prepared
[and] stocked all required provisions
and in similar order were divided
squadrons, posts, and barracks,
so that upon the first call for alarm
each will respond and join his troops under their respective standard.

The most significant line from Castellanos's stanzas is "y acude cada cual a su bandera," which is a reformulation of Ercilla's "cada cual acudiese a su bandera" cited above. This type of intertextuality signals to informed readers to interpret the parade of conquistadors and encomenderos from the New Kingdom of Granada with an eye to what Ercilla had accomplished earlier:

Estando, pues, los pechos inclinados
al bélico furor que en todos arde
llegáronse los días disputados
en que se tiene que hacer alarde;
andan unos y otros negociados,
cualquiera brevedad se hace tarde,
aquí y allí la gala reverbera
y acude cada cual a su bandera.

Ya las bastardas trompas dan clamores
que mueven corazones y con ellas
suenan incitativos atambores
volando van sulfúreas centellas;
llenos están los altos miradores
de bellas damas, dueñas y doncellas;
extiéndense las séricas banderas
y pónense por orden las hileras.

Pasan con ordenados movimientos,
a los unos y otros acudiendo
la gran solicitud de los sargentos
que las hileras iban componiendo;
ay de los arcabuces violentos
retumbo furioso, son horrendo;

continuando salitrosas cargas
entre la selva de las picas largas. [38]

And while they were all leaning forward
from the warlike furor ignited in their chests
the time arrives to flaunt their military might
there is a bustling among them all
and every small delay seems excessive
here and there the elegant attires shine forth/ and each one runs to their respective standard.

Then the roar of brazen trumpets
stirs hearts and with them
the rumble of the drums
and the sulfurous flares fill the air
and the balconies and windows fill with
beautiful ladies and maidens
the shiny flags undulate wide open
and the troops orderly take their place.

They march in precise and well-ordered fashion
and all men respond promptly
to the diligence of the sergeants
who give shape to each and every row
the furious tremor of violent harquebuses, a horrible tune
and the firing continues amongst a jungle of longs pikes.

Ercilla's brief description of the excitement and anticipation that overtook the Spanish troops is followed by a more elaborate and individualized description of the parade of Araucanian warlords marching in front of Caupolicán's gaze. One by one, Ercilla introduces each warrior by his name and then describes his weapon and highlights his athleticism and skills. Thus we see Chieftain Pillilco, the strong Leucotón, the arrogant Rengo, the robust Tulcomara, the conceited Caniotaro and the talcamávidas, the young Milla-lermo, the proud Mareande, Lepomande, Lemolemo, Gualemo, Talcaguano, Tomé, Andalicán, the young Orompello, Ongolmo, the elegant Elicura, the illustrious and wise successor of Ainavillo, the eager Cayocupil, Purén, Lincoya, Peycaví, the grave and saddened Caniomangue, and the proud Tucapel. Ercilla concludes his parade by likening Caupolicán's greatness as a warrior to that of Mars, the Greek god of war, and depicting the Araucanian chieftain holding a baton of authority:

> *El gran Caupolicán, con la otra parte*
> *y el resto del ejército araucano,*
> *más encendido que el airado Marte*
> *iba con un bastón corto en la mano*
> *bajo de cuya sombra y estandarte*
> *venía el valiente Curgo y Mareguano,*

y el grave y elocuente Colocolo,
Millo, Teguán, Lambecho y Guampicolo.[39]

The great Caupolicán, on the other hand,
with the remainder of the Araucanian army,
more inflamed than Mars, the spiteful,
proceeded carrying a short staff in his hand;
and beneath his shadow and standard
came the courageous Curgo and Mareguano,
and the grave and eloquent Colocolo,
Millo, Teguán, Lambecho, and Guampicolo.

It bears mentioning that halfway through his description of the parade of Araucanian warriors Ercilla inserts a digression to narrate a tale that explains the origin of the armor worn by Gualemo. According to Ercilla, Gualemo's father is said to have fought and killed an enormous sea creature ("caballo marino" [sea horse], "marino monstruo" [sea monster], or "monstruo devoraz" [voracious monster]) that had fallen in love with his wife and tried to steal her and to take her deep into the ocean. Although the episode has a clear literary provenance, as pointed out by Isaías Lerner, it confirms and reinforces the traits that Ercilla attributes to the majority of the warriors marching in the parade, particularly those of physical strength, courage, loyalty, and heroism, all of which Gualemo's father demonstrated while recovering his wife. In sum, canto 21 contains some of the most favorable depictions of Araucanian warriors to be found in the *Araucana*, and such favorable representations go hand in hand with Ercilla's plan to produce a poem that celebrated the achievements of Spain while correcting the excesses of the wars and proposing an alternative method of conquest. At the end of canto 21, Ercilla's call for reform is conveyed in the words attributed to Don García Hurtado de Mendoza, under whose command Ercilla had served in Chile:

Lo que yo os pido de mi parte y digo
es que en estas batallas y revueltas,
aunque os haya ofendido el enemigo,
jamás vos le ofendáis a espaldas vueltas;
antes le defended como al amigo
si, volviéndose a vos las armas sueltas,
rehuyere el morir en la batalla,
pues es más dar la vida que quitarla.

Poned a todo en la razón la mira,
por quien las armas siempre habéis tomado,
que pasando los términos la ira
pierde fuerza el derecho ya violado.
Pues cuando la razón no frena y tira
el ímpetu y furor demasiado,
el rigor excesivo en el castigo

justifica la causa al enemigo. [40]

> What I request and command you to do
> is that during skirmishes and battles,
> even if the enemy has betrayed you
> never harm them after they have turned their backs;
> instead, if they face you and surrender their weapons,
> and renounce to die in battle
> then defend them as you would defend a friend
> because it is a greater deed to preserve a life than to take it.

> Let everything be guided by reason
> which is what has led you to take up arms,
> because when wrath overtakes us
> the law that has already been violated is weakened.
> Since when reason does not restrain maddened impulse and rage
> excessive punishments
> legitimize the cause of the enemy.

Castellanos, on the other hand, does not offer a parade of Amerindian warriors, nor does he grant similar protagonism to Amerindians in this or any other section of the *Discurso* or elsewhere in his heroic poems. Quite the contrary, his emulation of the *Araucana* is designed not only to refute Ercilla's proposition to reform Spanish conduct in war but also to symbolically erase the indigenous legacy from the New Kingdom of Granada and to cast indigenous presence as a threat to the very subsistence of that kingdom. Certainly, in a section of his letter to Judge Guillén Chaparro, Castellanos had used the typical rhetoric of the encomenderos to describe Amerindians as dangerous, disloyal, and deceitful: "son para las virtudes incapaces, / pero para maldad, si ven su día, / ninguno hay más prontos y sagaces"[41] (they are inept for any type of virtue / but for wrongdoing, if they have a chance / none more eager and astute). Here, however, we see that Castellanos also expands, transforms, and subverts some of the same core elements Ercilla had used to construct his parade to create rather a catalog of heroic conquistadors and then to describe an ostentatious display of nonindigenous military prowess that takes place simultaneously in all the towns that constitute the New Kingdom òf Granada. Among key elements present in both texts we can cite the sense of order, discipline, and hierarchy; the description of weapons; references to the clothing worn by the warriors; and the blood ties that link some of the individuals who participate in the parade. Using a catalog of warriors and the description of a military parade to create an allegory of the political body of the New Kingdom of Granada is particularly efficient since Castellanos typically represents the New Kingdom of Granada in terms of not an *urbs* (a city) but *civitas* (a community of citizens that share laws and a common purpose) or as a human conglomerate.[42]

Prior to writing the *Discurso*, Castellanos had used a similar strategy to lionize conquistadors and encomenderos in canto 6 of "Elegía XIV" from the first volume of his *Elegías*. On that occasion, he described the preparations taken by the colonists from the New Kingdom of Granada to respond to the threat posed by Lope de Aguirre's rebellion. In particular, Castellanos used a catalog of names and the description of the readiness of the troops to contrast the loyalty and discipline of local colonists with the acts of treason and the violence unleashed by Lope de Aguirre and his followers. [43] The catalog of warriors from canto 6 of "Elegía XIV" is meaningful to our analysis of canto 3 from the *Discurso* because at the time of Lope de Aguirre's rebellion, the president of the High Royal Court of Santafé was Judge Melchor Pérez de Arteaga, the same individual Castellanos had chosen as an alternative recipient of his poem in order to avoid the constraints of censorship. As someone deeply acquainted with the internal politics of the New Kingdom of Granada, Pérez de Arteaga was an ideal reader to recognize not only the political overtones I have outlined thus far but also the pervasive sense of disappointment that permeates the catalog and the description of the parade Castellanos inserted in canto 3 of the *Discurso*. To be sure, the colonists from cities such as Santafé, Tunja, and others appear once again as obedient and loyal subjects eager to serve the king. But one of the main messages conveyed through their description is that they never received the recognition and rewards they deserved or expected, given the services they had provided to the Crown during the campaigns of exploration and conquest.

Moving on to the section of the catalog that describes the troops enlisted, Castellanos is clearly interested is transmitting a sense of order and hierarchy. This is palpable by his choosing to start the catalog with the description of the organization of the militias in the city of Santafé de Bogotá, which was the seat of the High Royal Court, and then continuing to describe what happened in places such as Tunja, Vélez, Pamplona, Mérida, San Cristóbal, and Muso. Similarly, a sense of hierarchy can also be perceived in the catalog starting with the highest military commander and then advancing to officers of lower rank: "General," "Maese de campo" (chief of staff), "capitanes" (captains), "jinetes" (horsemen), "piqueros" (pikemen), "arcabuzeros" (harquebusiers), "rodeleros" (swordsmen), and so forth, until finally ending his description with references to the specific military formation: "escuadras breves y sumarias" [44] (small and tight squadrons). The hierarchical arrangement of the catalog proves useful for the author of the *Elegías* inasmuch as it allows him to convey a sense of discipline, compliance, and order within an administrative unit that for the most part had been associated with chaos ever since it was founded in 1538 and well until the end of the sixteenth century.

However, I would argue that there is also another order or guiding principle, if you will, that underlines Castellanos's poetic discourse, one that actually makes it possible for Castellanos to continue to undermine the authority of Guillén Chaparro and transcend the very sense of discipline that characterizes the hierarchical parade described by Ercilla. This underlying arrangement does not follow necessarily a vertical scheme but functions instead according to references to deficiency and surplus or lack and excess that are embedded throughout the poetic discourse and transform a mere list of names into something approaching the epic sublime.

The opposition between deficiency and surplus is established poignantly in the verses devoted to Captain Juan de Montalvo: "sobróle merescer, faltó ventura / para tener la vida más segura"[45] (he possessed ample merits, but lacked the fortune / to have a less uncertain life). Castellanos refers to Montalvo (and later to several other colonists) with the epithet *descubridor* (discoverer), a term Ercilla had employed in the same canto in which he describes the battle of Andalicán. However, Ercilla used that noun strictly limiting its meaning to the currency it had within military jargon. As such, for Ercilla *descubridores* are those soldiers who scout the territory and lead the troops: "nuestro[s] descubridores, que la tierra / iban corriendo por el largo llano"[46] (our discoverers, / who would go down the plains scouting the territory). Castellanos, instead, transforms *descubridor* into a euphemistic title that means scout or troop guide but is also in alignment with the motto of Hapsburg Spain: *Plus Ultra* (further beyond). By using this term, therefore, Castellanos not only avoids using the always controversial *conquistador* but also conveys the notion that to discover, to explore, to conquer, and to colonize are the highest forms of service a vassal could provide to his king. According to Castellanos, the injustice being committed against individuals such as Captain Juan de Montalvo is accentuated by the fact that even in their old age ("honrado viejo venerado calvo"[47] [honest gentleman, respected elder]) these *descubridores* continue to show eagerness to serve the Spanish Crown, despite having received insufficient compensation from the monarch.

After completing the catalog of troops from Santafé de Bogotá, Castellanos goes on to describe the diligence of the colonists from Tunja to enlist in the troops. In this section Castellanos continues to present the local colonists as outstanding paladins ready to engage in individual combat. Castellanos has nothing but praise for each one of them and serves as guarantor that all of these individuals are prudent, trustworthy, loyal, courageous, experienced, disciplined, and honorable vassals who have already served the king in the past and are ready to continue serving the monarchy. If we read that particular section of canto 3 with an eye to the catalog offered by Ercilla, at least one aspect in particular stands out: the references to the type of bonds that link some of the warriors included on the list. In his parade of Amerindian warriors, Ercilla had also pointed out that some of the men were related to each other (e.g., Mareande and Lepomande are cousins) and that some warriors had taken the place that once was occupied by their father (Caniomange, for instance, has taken the place once held by his father). Accordingly, the inclusion of these types of family connections allowed Ercilla to introduce the anecdote of Guacol, Gualemo's father. In his catalog of heroes from Tunja, Castellanos enhances the impression of realism precisely by avoiding such literary anecdotes. However, the mention of genealogical connections is also pivotal for Castellanos to go beyond what Ercilla had accomplished. Castellanos does that by introducing references that enhance the historicity of his account and portray colonists from the New Kingdom of Granada as the true heirs of the knights who had fought in the campaigns to expel the Moors from the Iberian Peninsula. In this sense, the allusion to the House of Lara ("manifestando la prosapia clara / de los ilustres Manriques de Lara"[48] [manifesting the unblemished lineage of the illustrious Manriques de Lara]) is of particular importance, not only because it suggests that the local colonists have an ascendancy as illustrious as that of one of the most distinguished noble families of Spain, but also because it allows Castellanos to reach past Ercilla and to connect his parade of Spanish colonists with the catalog of nobles and great men from antiquity included by Jorge Manrique (1440–1479) in his *Coplas a la muerte de su padre* (Stanzas about the death of his father).[49] As such, Castellanos's use of genealogical references is an essential part of the reconfiguration of the former territory of the Muiscas into a kingdom organized according to the codes of *limpieza de sangre* (purity of blood), faith, and military service.

In the rest of the description of the organization of the militias from Tunja, Castellanos will continue to exploit the opposition between deficiency and excess as almost every single individual who enters the catalog is introduced by his proper name and often with references to his surpassing merits. When read from the perspective of the interplay between lack and excess or between deficiency and surplus, Castellanos's poetic discourse appears more as a highly rhetorical *relación de méritos y servicios* (relation of merits and services) crafted on behalf of conquistadors and encomenderos than an objective description of an actual parade. However, the important thing to notice is that the sense of discipline and structure that characterizes Ercilla's description of Araucanian heroes is here reconstituted to postulate an alternative hierarchy that presents the New Kingdom of Granada as a homogeneous chivalric utopia. Likewise, it is also imperative to notice that Castellanos's emulation of Ercilla is key to transform the more abstract or unspecified community invoked in the opening of the *Elegías* ("no penen mis amigos con espanto"[50] [do not be overpowered with fear my friends]) into a concrete social group embedded in a specific historical and social context. As such, Castellanos's appropriation of Ercilla's parade of Araucanian heroes goes beyond what the model had offered because in Castellanos's hands the description of the military parade results in the textual and symbolic construction of an entire kingdom. It is in this sense that subsequent authors have returned to the pages of the *Elegías* to trace back the genealogy of the New Kingdom of Granada.

Finally, it is also important to point out that both of their catalogs, Ercilla's and Castellanos's, pay particular attention to the description of the attire of some of the warriors. In the *Araucana* the references to clothing serve at best to enhance the physical strength of the warriors and highlight their complete communion with nature, and at worst to reinforce the utter otherness of the Araucanians. Such is the case of the description of Tulcomara, whose ferocity is likened to the tiger he had killed and whose skin he is now wearing. Notice that in this stanza Ercilla uses the same adjective to describe Tulcomara and the tiger:

> *Tras él con fiero término seguía*
> *el áspero y robusto Tulcomara,*
> *que vestido en lugar de arnés, traía*
> *la piel de un fiero tigre que matara,*
> *cuya espantosa boca le ceñía*
> *por la frente y quijadas la ancha cara,*
> *con dos espesas órdenes de dientes*
> *blancos, agudos, lisos y lucientes.* [51]

> Behind him [Rengo] with a fiery disposition there appeared
> the harsh and athletic Tulcomara,
> robed in lieu of a breastplate
> with the skin of a ferocious tiger he had killed
> whose menacing snout he had draped
> round about his jaws and forehead with two thick rows of sharp,
> white, smooth, and glistening, fangs.

The description of the attire is also indispensable for Castellanos but for a different reason. For Castellanos the reference to the clothing worn by the warriors during the parade attempts to convey their inner worth and to link local colonists with the attributes that Spaniards associated with personal worth, refinement, culture, civilization, and ultimately the majesty of the king. As a result, the aging soldiers appear arrayed in refined and expensive clothes typically associated with noble warriors riding into battle and somewhat incongruent to recent developments in gunpowder weapons and the increasing tactical protagonism of infantry forces. It is evident that the dazzling colors and the luminosity of the description is meant to attest in the eyes and the minds of the readers the type of people who had conquered and were now residing in the New Kingdom of Granada:

> *Al lado va la hoja fina*
> *que muchas tienen guarnición dorada;*
> *sale (como piedra cristalina)*
> *fulgente resplandor de la celada;*
> *ostentase la malla jacerina,*

la rica vestidura perfilada,
la bordadura, la librea nueva,
muestra del corazón del que la lleva.

Ceban la vista trajes variados,
telas de seda fina diferentes,
las calzas y jubones recamados,
capeletes con plumas eminentes
la mayor parte de ellos estampados
con perlas y esmeraldas excelentes;
aumentan capitanes su decoro
con ricas joyas y cadenas de oro. [52]

The fine blade goes on the side
many have a golden handle;
a dazzling brightness (like crystal-like gemstone)
shines out of their helmet;
boasting the impenetrable mesh,
the rich garments shown,
the embroidery, the new livery,
displays the heart of those who wear it.

Varied suits delight the gaze,
different fabrics of fine silk,
embroidered breeches and vests
hats with elegant feathers
most of them bedecked
with excellent pearls and emeralds;
captains increase their decorum
with rich jewels and golden chains.

On the most fundamental level, this and all other descriptions of the parade are geared toward awakening the reader's admiration for each of the individuals that are singled out. Admiration had already been invited by mentioning their willingness to answer the call to defend the port of Cartagena de Indias and to protect the entire New Kingdom of Granada. Here, however, admiration is invited more concretely for the services they had already provided to the monarch during the early phase of exploration. Following this line of reasoning, the actual weapons they could use to repel the naval attack are secondary or marginal. Within a symbolic economy of ostentation that allows Castellanos to connect Castilian ideas of aristocracy and honor to early modern empire building, what matters is for readers to recognize the magnificence and splendor of the king's majesty transposed to the New World in the bodies, demeanor, and attires of the colonists. The abundant references to the incandescent luminosity of their swords and clothing, and the overall magnificence of the parade, invite readers to see the presence of the monarch in this public spectacle. Furthermore, if in the political vocabulary of the time the king was often referred to as the sun, the light emanating from the weapons and the clothing of the encomenderos invites readers to establish a direct connection between the colonists, sovereignty, and the majesty of the monarch. In the last analysis, what is legible in their performance and display is their desire to remind readers of their merits and deep loyalty to the monarch even while their honor has been injured by the breach in the economy of favor. It must be stated that the recognition and rewards are not necessarily limited to the financial realm, and that the references to precious metals and other commodities extracted from the New World (pearls, emeralds, gold, etc.) that adorn their clothing cannot serve as guarantee that the financial situation of the aging soldiers was far from precarious.

Perhaps the most interesting irony of the description of the parade of paladins from cities such as Santafé de Bogotá and Tunja is that while disregarding the dramatic potential of the fall of Cartagena de Indias, Castellanos arranges the sequence of events so that from a dramatic point of view, the climax of the poem corresponds with events where no actual military confrontation takes place. By doing so, Castellanos presents the eagerness of the Spanish colonists from the New Kingdom of Granada to defend their territory and to march into battle not as something completed in the past but as something that continues to linger in the present and projects into the future.

CONCLUSION

Castellanos's appropriation of the parade of Araucanian heroes from canto 21 of the *Araucana* is not the type of imitation that wants the previous text to speak or to make it relevant but instead an emulation that aims to allude to the precedent with enough force in order to silence it. If cantos 1 and 2 of *Discurso del capitán Francisco Draque* use poetic discourse to map imperial weaknesses, canto 3 establishes the lineage of a New Kingdom shaped by the reorganization of the Muisca population and the unfulfilled expectations of the Spanish colonists who took control of the Muisca territory. The catalog of names and the parade of troops must be interpreted in terms of the topic of the political body and the manner in which the symbolism of the said body was understood in the Spanish American viceroyalties. Cañeque has shown in other contexts that "the recurring visual public spectacles—processions and official events—asserted and affirmed the trope of the body as central to the political practices of New Spain."[53] Here too, the parade of encomenderos aims to convey to the reader the sense that the New Kingdom of Granada is a harmonious and hierarchized political body. Yet, on a closer examination, and unlike the texts studied by Cañeque, the very ordering of the bodies and the underlying arrangement of the sequence destabilizes the hierarchy of power by displacing the official representative of the Crown to a subordinate position and placing the political authority on the hands of the *corregidor* and the local colonists. If the parade represents the social and political body of the New Kingdom of Granada, this is an anomalous body with two heads, one that belongs to judge Guillén Chaparro, the official representative of the Crown, and another belonging to the *corregidor* Antonio Joven and the former conquistadors and encomenderos. As such, Castellanos's poem grants the conquistadors and encomenderos from New Granada a textual authority they did not always enjoy in the social fabric. The precarious nature of the encomenderos' status is confirmed when we consider that the original manuscript of the text that presents their point of view (Castellanos's poem about Drake) was banned from publication and destroyed by Pedro Sarmiento de Gamboa in his capacity as a member of a very efficient and rational bureaucracy put in place to carry out and protect not the interests of the encomenderos but the administrative and political priorities of the Spanish Crown.

Whether accurate or not, Castellanos's remark that after the military parade, order and peace were fully restored among the native population in New Granada is cognizant of the notion that rituals and public displays of power had an ordering force.[54] Evidence of the use of the same logic can be found in other sections of the *Elegías*. Above all, Castellanos's description of the dismembering and public display of the remains of rebel Lope de Aguirre confirms the use of the same symbolic grammar but in the realm of punishment for treason against the monarch. Unless readers are conversant with the significance of this type of symbolism and with the performative aspect of displays of power and authority, they would be at a loss as to why Castellanos needs to end the first volume of his *Elegías* with such an extensive account of Pedro de Ursúa's failed expedition and the terrible fate encountered by Lope de Aguirre, his daughter, and his followers ("Elegía XIV"). In my view, it is within a context in which the issue of rebellion was prevalent and in which the colonists from New Granada had repeatedly been accused of disobeying the New Laws, embezzling royal funds, and mistreating the indigenous population that it makes sense for Castellanos to juxtapose the validation of monarchical authority and the public punishment of Lope de Aguirre (canto 7) with the exemplary conduct of the colonists from New Granada to respond to the threat of rebellion (canto 6). In other words, the narration of one of the most disastrous Spanish expeditions in the sixteenth century fits in as a proper ending to the first volume of the *Elegías* because it allows Castellanos to appeal to the symbolism of power and authority to boast, as he does elsewhere in the *Elegías*, that the conquistadors and encomenderos are the model subjects of the Spanish empire. Such is the message spelled out in the description of the parade of militias preparing to defend the kingdom of New Granada and in the first of three warnings that announce to Captain Pedro de Ursúa while he is deep into the Amazon jungle the upcoming doom of his expedition:

Mirad, señor, que no tratáis ahora
con los del Nuevo Reino de Granada,
donde toda bondad y virtud mora,
y es gente cuerda, noble y asentada;
y que con vos lleváis gente traidora
a vueltas de la bien intencionada
que sin temor de Dios ni miedo vuestro
han de soltar las riendas y el cabestro. [55]

Behold, my lord, that you are not dealing
with men from the New Kingdom of Granada,
where kindness and virtue dwell
for they are all reasonable, noble, and agreeable people;
those around you now are traitors
and they don't hold the best intentions
and without fear of God or you
they are bound to let loose the reins.

NOTES

1. The term Nueva Granada (New Granada) started to be used at the end of the sixteenth century, and its geographic area did not include regions on the Atlantic coast, including Cartagena. See Alvaro Félix Bolaños, *Barbarie y canibalismo en la retórica colonial: Los indios Pijaos de Fray Pedro Simón* (Bogotá, Colombia: Centro de Estudios de la Realidad Colombiana, 1994), 26.

2. Alejandro Cañeque, *The King's Living Image: The Culture and Politics of Viceregal Power in Colonial Mexico* (New York: Routledge, 2004), 119. Although the New Kingdom of Granada did not become a viceroyalty until the eighteenth century, the symbolism of power outlined by Cañeque is useful as a category of analysis, as it was something common to the validation of royal authority across the vast domains of the Spanish imperial monarchy and not exclusive of the viceroyalty of New Spain in the sixteenth and seventeenth centuries. What is unique in this case, as I hope to make clear, is that while in the viceroyalties of New Spain and Peru there existed a greater distance between the viceroy or the president of the Real Audiencia and the local *corregidores* (chief magistrates), owing in part to the larger number of functionaries and the size of the bureaucratic edifice, in New Granada the lack of such administrative apparatus brought to the forefront the tensions between the president of the Real Audiencia and the *corregidor*, both of whom represented different aspects of the authority and functions of the monarch.

3. Ibid., 159.

4. Although I have benefited enormously from the ideas presented by Cañeque in *The King's Living Image*, the analysis presented in this chapter complements and expands his findings by focusing on the symbolism of the staff or baton of authority, which was not the focus of Cañeque's pioneering study.

5. *Discurso*, 105.

6. Ricardo Padrón, "Between Scylla and Charybdis," in *The Spacious Word: Cartography, Literature, and Empire in Early Modern Spain*, 185–230 (Chicago: University of Chicago Press, 2004), 195.

7. "Mas con las estampidas y los truenos / que daban de tan terribles males / por este Nuevo Reino, sus terrenos / que tienen cantidad de naturales, / no se mostraban con intentos buenos, / así ladinos como los bozales; / y por verlos andar tan inquietos / no presumíamos buenos efectos" (*Discurso*, 111; But by the tremor and pandemonium caused by these reports, / which did so terrify all the inhabitants of this New Kingdom of Granada, / which large numbers

has of Indians / these [Indians] now began to murmur, both the ones that had been baptized and those that were not; / and from seeing so much unrest / we gathered they were planning a revolt).

8. *Discurso*, 104.

9. Ibid., 105.

10. Ibid.

11. Ibid., 107.

12. Ibid., 108.

13. Ibid., 110.

14. Ibid.

15. Ibid., 125.

16. Ibid., 123.

17. On the topic of mimicry in colonial discourse, see Homi Bhabha, "Of Mimicry and Man: The Ambivalence of Colonial Discourse," in *Tensions of Empire: Colonial Cultures in a Bourgeois World*, ed. Frederick Cooper and Ann Laura Stoler, 152–60 (Berkeley: University of California Press, 1997).

18. As an example, we can cite the letters written from Diana to Sireno (17–18); Ismenia to Selvagia (50); Selvagia to Ismenia (51); Don Felis to Felismena (106); Felismena to Don Felis (107); Celia to Don Felis (119); and Anselmo's letter, all of which appear in Jorge de Montemayor's *La Diana* (1558); as well as the letter from Don Quixote de la Mancha to Dulcinea del Toboso in the first volume of Cervantes's *Don Quixote* (Cervantes Saavedra, *El ingenioso*).

19. *Discurso*, 111.

20. "Esto digo debajo de buen celo / y no porque de vos conozca falta, / pues sois de buenas partes el modelo" (ibid., 119; This I write out good zeal alone / and not because in you I find any faults / for you are the model of all good qualities). "De estos avisos no recibáis pena, / ni lo tengáis a mal, pues sé deciros / ser enviados con voluntad buena / y ninguno mejor para serviros" (ibid., 124; Do not be saddened by my advise / nor considered it a recrimination / for with all certainty I can declare that I am sending them with the best intentions / and no one better than I to serve you).

21. *Discurso*, 112.

22. Ibid., 107.

23. Ibid., 108.

24. "No para dar socorros [to Cartagena] digo esto / que sería notorio desvarío, / mas porque vele cada cual su puesto. / Mal pueden ir soldados por el río / con armas y bastantes alimentos, / por carecer de todo buen avío. / Otro camino llevan mis intentos / y es que del Nuevo Reino las entradas / estén con los posibles munimentos" (ibid., 113; I'm not stating we should send assistance [to Cartagena] / which will make no sense, / but that each [man] should guard his post. / Hardly can soldiers take the river way / with weapons and enough supplies / for it lacks proper planning and rewards. / My intent is quite different / and it is that all paths to this New Kingdom of Granada / be guarded with the best defensive measures).

25. *Discurso*, 70.

26. Ibid., 2.

27. Ibid., 116.

28. Ibid., 128.

29. Ibid.

30. Ibid.

31. In my analysis of the political significance of references to the baton held by the *corregidor* from the city of Tunja I am guided by the instructions included in Jerónimo Castillo de Bobadilla's manual for good government for local magistrates (*Política para corregidores y señores de vasallos, en tiempo de paz y de Guerra* [Madrid: Luis Sanchez, 1597; repr., Madrid: Imprenta Real de la Gazeta, 1775]), which states that the *corregidor* is an image (*simulacro*) of the king and that his staff ("vara, que trae en las manos" [the staff he carries in his hands]) is a representation (the words used by Bobadilla are *figura* [figure], *efigie* [effigy], and *simulacro* [simulacrum]) of the royal scepter. This understanding of the staff as an indisputable sign of royal sovereignty and authority was shared by Spanish colonists from New Granada and quickly understood by the local indigenous population, sometimes using it to defend their own

interests in disputes against the encomenderos. In particular, when *mestizo* indigenous chieftain Don Diego de Torres was accused and persecuted by the Real Audiencia of Santafé, he proceeded to bury the staff in his home province of Turmequé, prior to traveling to Spain to present his complaints and seek the protection of Philip II. Accordingly, while retelling the vicissitudes of Don Diego de Torres's ordeal, historian Ulises Rojas makes key references to the staff handed to the president of the Real Audiencia upon arriving to Santafé de Bogotá (*El beneficiado Don Juan de Castellanos, cronista de Colombia y Venezuela* [Tunja, Colombia: Biblioteca de Autores Boyacenses, 1958], 36), to the staff carried by the local *alcaldes* (33), as well as the staff carried by individuals demanding tributes from the natives in the province of Tunja (57). Likewise, in his account of the aforementioned expedition of Pedro de Ursúa and Lope de Aguirre's subsequent rebellion, Castellanos hones in on the symbolism of the staff, namely, after the leader of the expedition has been murdered and Don Fernando is chosen as king in the middle of the Amazon jungle. Explicitly, when the soldier Valcazar is appointed *justicia mayor* (chief justice of the expedition) and handed the staff in the name of king don Fernando ("la vara le presentan publicando / que se la daban por don Fernando" [they offered him the staff of authority / announcing that they were doing so in the name of don Fernando]), Valcazar discloses his loyalty to the Philip II by stating, "'La vara tomo yo por don Felipe, mi rey y mi señor a quien Dios guarde'; / mas el varón fiel, leal y fuerte / después pagó con gloriosa muerte" (*Elegías*, 1:642; "I accept the baton in the name of Philip II, my king and lord, may God protect him"; / but the loyal, steadfast, and stout gentleman / later paid with heroic death).

32. *Discurso*, 143.

33. "Sabed, señor, que ya pasó solía [*sic*] / cuando se desmembraba con temblores / cualquier indio que caballo veía; / ajenos estáis ya de estos temores / del estasis y frígido recelo / que ponían caballos corredores, / pues juntaban el rostro con el suelo cuando, corriendo con furor, asoman, / cubierto de armas el sudado pelo. / Ellos ahora son los que los toman, / les ponen los cabestros y collera / y los que los amansan y los doman. / En ellos andan, pasan la carrera, / como si fuesen diestros andaluces / de aquellos de Jerez de la Frontera" (*Discurso*, 122; Know, my lord, that it is long gone / the time when most Indians would be shaken / at the sight of a horse; / they no longer experience such fear / nor the frigid and numbing distrust / that running steeds would cause / as they used to place their face on the ground / when horses suddenly appeared / their sweat-drenched flanks covered with arms. / Indians are now the ones that go out and catch, / harness, tame, and break horses. / They go around riding them / as if they were practiced riders from Andalucía / such as those from Jerez de la Frontera).

34. *Araucana*, canto 21, stanza 28.

35. *Discurso*, 143.

36. *Araucana*, canto 21, stanza 19.

37. Ibid., canto 21, stanza 26.

38. *Discurso*, 142.

39. *Araucana*, canto 21, stanza 48.

40. *Araucana*, canto 21, stanzas 55–56.

41. *Discurso*, 120.

42. In this regard, I agree with Rodolfo M. Guzmán who has pointed out that "El prolífico catálogo de capitanes, adelantados gobernadores, corregidores, religiosos, soldados, y demás personalidades destacadas que discurren a los largo de las *Elegías*, ciertamente corresponde a los temas de la ciudad [or the entire kingdom] entendida como *civitas*" ("City, Writing, and Identity: Emergence and Consolidation of the Creole in Santafe de Bogotá [1586–1808]" [PhD diss., John Hopkins University, 2002], 48; The prolific catalog of captains, military commanders-in-chief, governors, chief magistrates, soldiers, clerics, and other distinguished individuals that appear throughout the *Elegías* certainly corresponds with the theme of the city [or the entire kingdom] understood as *civitas*). For an analysis of Castellanos's depiction of the New Kingdom Granada from the perspective of topography, space, and geography, see Restrepo, "Sacred and Imperial Topographies."

43. *Elegías*, 1:664–69.

44. *Discurso*, 125–44.

45. *Discurso*, 129.

46. *Araucana*, canto 22, stanza 8.

47. *Discurso*, 129.

48. *Discurso*, 131.

49. Jorge Manrique, *Coplas a la muerte de su padre* (Madrid, 1799).

50. *Elegías*, 1:61.

51. *Araucana*, canto 21, stanza 30.

52. *Discurso*, 143.

53. Cañeque, *King's Living Image*, 8.

54. At the end of canto 3 Castellanos writes, "Estas preparaciones de instrumentos / y aquel hervor de salitrosos truenos / abatió por ventura pensamientos / de los que presumían no ser buenos; pues de indios, a la sazón atentos, / todos los pueblos estuvieron llenos, / quedándose pacífica la tierra / sin conocerse manifiesta Guerra" (*Discurso*, 144; All these preparations of arms / and the intensity of the weapon's thunder / trounced the intentions / of those who were seeking to do us harm / because each town was full of astute Indians; / leaving the land peaceful / without fulfilling the threat of impending war).

55. *Elegías*, 1:63. As it is the case of the military parade I analyze in this chapter, the reference to horsemanship in the last line of this stanza ("soltar las riendas y el cabestro") acquires meaning through the intersection between restrain, loyalty, and the horse as a symbol of royal authority.

Chapter Five

Captivity, Authority, and Friendship in the Writings of Juan de Castellanos

In "Elegía II" from the first installment of his *Elegías*, Juan de Castellanos interpolated the tale of the abduction and three-year imprisonment of a Spanish soldier named Juan de Salas at the hands of a tribe of Carib Amerindians. In the two stanzas cited below, Castellanos introduces the story and starts to weave an intricate discursive web that strives for self-authorization by declaring that what he is about to narrate is a true story ("quiero tartar de cosa cierta"), by linking the narration of these events to his worth as a writer ("sin con buenos alguna cosa valgo") and by presenting the protagonist as a comrade-in-arms he had met during his youth ("y en medio de los tiros y las valas / en mocedad fue compañero nuestro"):

> *Y pues quiero tratar de cosa cierta,*
> *si con buenos alguna cosa valgo,*
> *no te pese lector que me divierta,*
> *para que deste pueda decir algo;*
> *pues casi nos estamos en la puerta*
> *y de las dichas islas no me salgo;*
> *recogeréme bien en el estilo,*
> *y volveré después a nuestro hilo.*

> *Este que padeció fortunas malas*
> *y el hado por allí le fue siniestro*
> *sabrán que se llamaba Juan de Salas,*
> *antiguo capitán, soldado diestro;*
> *y en medio de los tiros y las balas*
> *en mocedad fue compañero nuestro,*
> *ejercitándonos por tierra y agua*
> *en las crueles de Cubagua.* [1]

101

> And since I want to address something true,
> if I am worth anything to those who are worthy,
> do not be burdened reader if I divert myself,
> so I can say something about this topic;
> since we are near the entrance
> and from said islands I do not depart;
> I will do my best to follow the style,
> and then return to the main thread.
>
> The one who suffered adverse fortunes
> and to whom destiny was sinister
> you will know his name was Juan de Salas,
> experienced captain, skilled soldier;
> and in the midst of gunshots and bullets
> as a youth he was our partner,
> laboring hard in land and sea
> in the cruel ones of Cubagua.

By pledging to pay careful attention to the conventions of literary style ("recogereme bien en el estilo"), moreover, Castellanos accentuates the aesthetic aspects of this tale, thus promising to deliver the type of pleasurable experience associated with reading the tale of a Christian who has been taken captive in an exotic and foreign land. Although we can only speculate on how contemporary Iberian readers reacted to this particular episode of the *Elegías*, Castellanos's success in producing a pleasurable story can be gauged by the more recent assessment of a critic who stated that the story of Juan de Salas's captivity "es un cuento de relieve, de lo más hermoso"[2] (is a lovely and engrossing tale). The critic, however, does not disclose what specific aspects of this tale he finds pleasing or enthralling.

Since no information about Juan de Salas has surfaced elsewhere and Castellanos acknowledges up front that what he is about to narrate is essentially a story of misfortune, at least one question emerges from reading the introductory stanzas, namely, why should the mishaps of an individual who has been excluded from the historical record be included as a preamble to the narration of Christopher Columbus's second journey of exploration and among the deeds of those that Castellanos refers to as the *illustrious men of the Indies*? As it turns out, Juan de Salas's story is emblematic of Castellanos's literary and ideological agenda for a number of reasons. Certainly, Juan de Salas's tale not only provides Castellanos with the opportunity to insert the first lengthy mythologizing descriptions of Amerindian societies and of the type of individuals who set out to conquer them but also offers the earliest example of the use of several narrative strategies that Castellanos will employ often throughout his writings, such as the use of a digression to illustrate specific aspects of the larger narrative thread, the inclusion of autobiographical references to lend verisimilitude to his account, and the use of metanarrative references to establish a dialogue with readers. Through these strategies, Castellanos justifies putting on hold the narration of events related to Christopher Columbus's second journey across the Atlantic and switches instead to describing the ordeal faced by Juan de Salas some sixty years later, at a time when Castellanos himself had already arrived in the New World and was presumably involved in campaigns of exploration and conquest.[3]

In this chapter I shall read the story of Juan de Salas as an extended metaphor that allows Castellanos to effectively advance three overlapping goals. First of all, the narration of Salas's experience is useful to present the exploration and conquest of the New World as a redeeming act endorsed by God to save the Amerindians; second, this story is essential to portray conquistadors and explorers as the ideal subjects of the expanding Spanish global empire; and third, by inserting this tale at the beginning of his *Elegías*, Castellanos anchors his authority as narrator on the type of knowledge acquired through firsthand experience and prolonged residency in the New World. Very recently, Lisa Voigt has brilliantly argued that in the early modern period Iberian writers used stories of captivity to underline "the value of the captive's cross-cultural experience" and to postulate the "superiority of experimental knowledge" over classical knowledge, hence anticipating "generic transformations . . . associated with what would come to be known as the Scientific Revolution and the 'rise of the novel': the privileging of experimental authority and the proliferation of prose fiction claiming to be both true and entertaining."[4] This chapter builds on Voigt's insights and demonstrates that Castellanos recognized the value of captives and their narratives, as well as the captive's role in the production of knowledge and imperial expansion. However, my analysis adds a new layer to the use of early modern captivity narratives among Spanish American colonists by showing how Castellanos used this genre to identify the protagonist with the New World over his initial place of origin in the Iberian Peninsula, thus confirming a new site of enunciation for Spanish heroic poetry and assigning a new function to the discourse on captivity. At a time when Iberian authors were starting to attribute degenerative properties to prolonged residency in the New World and conquistadors turned encomenderos were facing harsh criticism from multiple fronts, the story of Juan de Salas unequivocally celebrates military conquest and presents the New World as a territory blessed by the implantation of Christianity and the site of an uncorrupt Spanish identity. When read in this manner, Juan de Salas's story offers the conquistadors' response to authors who used narratives of shipwreck and captivity to propose more benign methods of colonization and of spreading the gospel, particularly Fray Bartolomé de las Casas (1484–1566) and Alvar Núñez Cabeza de Vaca (1488–1558). It bears mentioning the connection between Juan de Salas's tale and nonliterary texts about captivity written by Las Casas and

Cabeza de Vaca not only to highlight the fluid circulation of among genres that accompanied transatlantic imperial expansion but also to avoid conceptualizing the emergence of captivity tales in Spanish America as the result of a unidirectional scheme of influence that supposedly ran from the Iberian center to the colonial periphery. Like the majority of Spaniards in the second half of the sixteenth century, Castellanos was well aware of the pressing urgency of the phenomenon of captivity among Moors and Turks, and prior to his death he bequeathed a small portion of his state to the liberation of Spanish captives at North Africa.[5] Hence, it's not surprising that he would rely on the familiarity of Iberian readers with the phenomenon of Barbary captivity to convey to them the alterity of the New World. However, since the study of captivity in Spanish Golden Age has been traditionally associated with the works of Antonio de Sosa and Miguel de Cervantes, my analysis will underscore that the most notable features of Juan de Salas's tale respond and engage fiercely with texts about captivity and shipwreck written from and about the New World. This type of analysis in turn would allow us to include the *Elegías* among the earliest literary texts produced in the New World that could have had an impact in the depiction of the historical phenomenon of Barbary captivity by Iberian authors.[6]

Giovanni Meo Zilio has suggested that when writing "Elegía II," the poem in which the story of Juan de Salas appears, Castellanos's main concern was the accurate rendering of historical events. According to Meo Zilio, in sections of the tale of Juan de Salas, Castellanos "se limita a presentar lo real, con rápida y enérgica pincelada de poeta, con discreción y recato de historiador imparcial"[7] (narrows his scope to depict only what is real, with the fast and spirited stroke of the poet, with the discretion and modesty of an unbiased historian). As evidence of Castellanos's historical impartiality, Meo Zilio cites the fact that the narrator begins the first canto of "Elegía II" with invocations to Clio and Melponeme, the Greek muses of history and tragedy respectively. In reaching this conclusion Meo Zilio overlooks the fact that references to Clio and Melponeme could be added or removed without necessarily diminishing or intrinsically enhancing the factual merits of a poem. In fact, at the end of the exordium to the first poem of his *Elegías*, "Elegía I," Castellanos underscored the artificiality of this type of formula by invoking the guidance of the Virgin Mary and explicitly rejecting the assistance of Calliope and Clio while calling attention repeatedly to the factual elements of his writing. In the context of the increasing religious fervor of the Counter-Reformation, Castellanos's rejection of Greek muses and his professed devotion to the Virgin Mary at the start of the *Elegías* seems a logical and prudent choice:

> *!Oh musa celestial! Sacra María,*
> *a quien el alto cielo reverencia,*
> *favorecedme vos, Señora mía,*

> *con soplo del dador de toda ciencia,*
> *para que con socorro de tal guía,*
> *proceda con bastante suficiencia;*
> *pues como vos seáis presidio mío*
> *no quiero más Calíope ni Clío.* [8]

Oh, celestial muse! Sacred Mary,
whom the heaven up high reveres.
Favor me, my lady,
with the spirit of the one who gives all wisdom,
so that with the aid of such guide
I can excel in this task
for as long as you are my guardian
I do not want any more Calíope or Clío.

If in the digression about Juan de Salas the invocation to Clio and Melponeme can be cited as proof of anything, it is mainly of obliquely postulating
Castellanos's conviction that deeds such as the crossing of the Atlantic and
the exploration and colonization of the New World were tantamount if not
superior to the deeds accomplished by the Greeks and the Romans while
carrying out their imperial expansions. The same conviction that the modern
Spaniards were surpassing the deeds of ancient Greeks is also expressed in
the encomiastic poems written in Latin and Spanish by Castellanos's friends
and included as a preamble to the first volume of the *Elegías*. [9] Concomitantly, what is made apparent by the allusion to Clio and Melponeme (other than
plotting the events as a tragedy) is not a commitment to historical accuracy
but an expression of the belief that the exchange between Europeans and the
inhabitants of the New World was in essence an encounter between civilization and barbarism, which is part of the blueprint of epic poetry as demonstrated at length by David Quint. Castellanos shared wholeheartedly such a
view of the exploration and conquest of the New World, and when he introduces the tale of Juan de Salas he explicitly states that his goal in retelling
this story is to illustrate the savagery of Carib Indians:

> *Esta ferocidad que se recita,*
> *porque no la juzguéis por desvarío,*
> *la certidumbre de ella nos incita*
> *a deciros de un amigo mío,*
> *vecino de la isla Margarita*
> *a quien tomaron éstos [Caribs Amerindians] un navío,*
> *todos sus hombres muertos y captivos,*
> *pues él y otro no más quedaron vivos.* [10]

This fierceness that is narrated,
so that you do not judge it illusory,
the certainty of it urges me
to tell you about a friend of mine,

resident of the Margarita Island
to whom these [Caribs Amerindians] took a vessel,
all of his men dead or captive,
only himself and another man were left alive.

This stanza reduces the ambiguity of the poetic discourse and begins to narrow the possibility that readers might interpret the initial phase of the exploration and conquest of the New World as anything other than an armed confrontation instigated by the brutish and ferocious Amerindians against the chivalric Christian knights that Providence had chosen to civilize them. The line "esta ferocidad que se recita" refers to the statements made in the two previous stanzas in which the narrator describes Caribs as bellicose and cruel tribes whose cultural and social inferiority when compared to Spaniards is illustrated by their custom of cannibalism: "Son tan bravos, feroces y tan diestros / que hacen poca cuenta de los nuestros," and "todos ellos comen carne humana / mejor que la de puercos y venados; / acometen con más atrevimiento / que tigre que a la caza va hambriento"[11] (All of them prefer to eat human flesh / instead of swine or deer; / and they attack with more daring / that a hungry tiger in pursuit of his prey).

By asserting that the story of Juan de Salas is intended to illustrate the ferocity of cannibalistic Amerindians, the narrator postulates by default that their cultural and social aberrations are to be interpreted in reference to the virtues displayed by Spaniards, particularly to the extent that those virtues are embodied by Juan de Salas. It is for this reason that the narrator goes a great distance to characterize the protagonist as a courageous, loyal, generous, pious, and well-spoken Christian, while vehemently demonizing Amerindians and referring to them as "esta caribe gente, vil, sangrienta" (these Carib people, despicable, bloody), "abominable pestilencia" (despicable nuisance), "salvajes inhumanos" (inhuman savages), "bestiales gentes y naciones" (bestial people and nations), "gentes malas" (evil people), "infieles" (infidels), "bestias tan crueles" (beasts capable of such cruelty), "gentes llenas de cien mil maldades" (people filled with a thousand evil purposes), "gentes fieras" (beastly people), and "vulgo bestial y tan horrendo" (such beastly and horrendous multitudes).[12] The stark differences the narrator attributes to the two groups are also reinforced through the spatial categories used to refer to the islands that form the Caribbean archipelago. Hence, the territory that is still under control of the Caribs is described as "infames islas" (abominable islands), "tierras de costumbres inhumanas" (lands of inhuman practices), and "islas peligrosas" (dangerous islands),[13] while the territory where Spaniards have been able to establish settlements is described as "pueblos de cristianos" (Christian towns) and "tierras de cristianos" (Christian lands).[14] It would be to "tierras de cristianos" that Juan de Salas will make his return upon regaining his freedom. However, if we look past Castellanos's impenitent effort to separate Spaniards and Amerindians into opposing and hostile camps, there is more to be found in this story than the mere postulation of cultural oppositions. As we have seen throughout this book, cultural oppositions are rampant across the *Elegías* but by themselves are insufficient to explain how a brief vignette about misfortune functions as a metaphor for the entire enterprise of transatlantic expansion or as a fitting synecdoche for the bulk of Castellanos's voluminous writing. Rather than taking the references to Clio and Melponeme as confirmation of any type of impartiality or historical accuracy, I propose to explore the issue of authority in relation to the friendship between narrator and protagonist, which is informed by classical ideas of the friend as another self. With the caveat that Castellanos does not construct a theoretical or abstract formulation of friendship and that the type of companionship he refers to as friendship is based primarily on a shared experience in a concrete historical context and a concrete geographic location in the New World: "Y en medio de los tiros y las balas / en mocedad fue compañero nuestro / ejercitándonos por tierra y agua / en las crueles de Cubagua"[15] (And in the midst of gunshots and bullets / in younger years he was our companion / and we would endeavor in land and sea / in the cruel ones of Cubagua).

On the surface, the story of Juan de Salas's abduction, imprisonment, and escape fits the mold of an early modern Christian narrative of captivity. The story is organized around the itinerary of involuntary separation and return, and in its conception of the protagonist, plot, language, theme, and narrative structure the tale displays some of the same features of captivity narratives that circulated in the Iberian Peninsula during the sixteenth and seventeenth centuries. Captivity stories dealt primarily with the tribulations endured by Christians who were abducted by Barbary corsairs and kept as prisoners until ransomed or sold to the highest bidder in the slave markets of Algiers, Tunis, or Constantinople. Such narratives were often narrated in the first person, appeared embedded within larger narratives, and were typically organized around key episodes that included the initial abduction of the Christian; the description of the physical and spiritual ordeals endured while kept as a prisoner or as a slave; the attempts to escape; the requests for ransoms; the miraculous intercession of God or the Virgin Mary, which usually resulted in the liberation of the captives; the journey home; and the reunification of the former captives with their families. Additional elements that could heighten the intrigue of this basic plot arrangement would include the description of raging storms, the development of complicated love stories, and the description of the temptations that sometimes lured captives to renounce Christianity and convert to Islam. Without a doubt, the literary genre of captivity tales was connected to the oral and written depositions that former captives gave to local authorities or ministers of the Spanish Inquisition, but its literary roots can also be traced to Byzantine novels. Within the tradition of epic and heroic poetry, the relevance of captivity goes as far back as the story of

Chryseis and Briseis, the two female captives at the center of the dispute between Agamemnon and Achilles in book 1 of Homer's *Iliad*.[16]

When read from the perspective of the parameters of the narratives described above, it's clear that Castellanos had in mind these sensationalist stories that described Barbary captivity when he decided to include the story of colonist Juan de Salas in the second poem of his *Elegías*. The tale begins with the imprisonment of Salas after an armada of Carib Amerindians launches an attack on the port of Guayana on the island of Borinquen (present-day Puerto Rico) and proceeds to raid the vessel where Salas had been sleeping. Salas's first reaction is to run for his life, but eventually he puts up a fight until most of his companions are dead and he is left with no other option but to turn himself in. After three years' captivity, Salas's experience inside an Amerindian tribe reaches its climax with the description of his dramatic escape one night when his captors have passed out after engaging in a decadent ritual involving heavy drinking, debauchery, and cannibalism. The tale concludes with the successful return of Juan de Salas to his community and the reunification with his distraught mother, who is a resident on the island of Margarita. While narrating this story, Castellanos deliberately draws the attention of the readers to captivity narratives by using the epithet *cautivo* (captive) to refer to Salas and by having the Caribs refer to their prisoners in the same way. As it was characteristic of Iberian captivity stories, the protagonist and his mother are portrayed as exemplary pious Christians and the narrator gives a great deal of consideration to the role played by God and the Virgin Mary in the protagonist's ability to remain alive and to regain his freedom.

While the main events in the plot allow us link the story of Juan de Salas to other Iberian captivity narratives, the advantages of inserting this tale early on in a volume of heroic poems about the early exploration of the New World are to be found in the interstices where Castellanos reworks the parameters of the discourse on captivity and expands the expectations of Iberian readers, especially those who were all too familiar with the genre and the phenomenon of Barbary captivity but did not yet possess sound and widespread knowledge about the New World. Indeed, when we examine the fissures where Castellanos alters the existing mold of captivity stories, we can find a less intransigent discourse about Amerindians than the one postulated overtly through cultural oppositions. To be sure, Juan de Salas's tale is carefully constructed not only on the premise that the exploration and conquest of the New World constituted a continuation of the war against the infidels in North Africa but also upon the assumption that Barbary captivity and captivity at the hands of Carib Indians were somewhat commensurate experiences. For this analogy to work the profits awarded to Barbary captors from selling or ransoming Iberian Christians would have to be equivalent to the rewards gained by Caribs from consuming human flesh. In other words, in Salas's story cannibalism replaces the expectation for financial gain that motivated Barbary captors to turn Iberian Christians into valuable commodities.[17] The tension between the rewards that resulted from an economy of ransom on one side of the Atlantic and the practice of cannibalism on the other informs the description of the peculiar exchange that occurs when Juan de Salas is abducted and his captors inform him that their motivation is not what he (and perhaps even some readers) might have expected. In the following stanza, the Caribs' choice to take Salas as their prisoner would confirm that they are not savages but rather savvy connoisseurs of the multiple services that captives could provide on the far edge of the Atlantic world, other than as a source of flesh to be consumed or merchandise to be sold or ransomed:

> *Visto tan grande número de gente,*
> *y cierto su morir si se defienden,*
> *hablóles Juan de Salas blandamente*
> *en lengua guayquerí que bien entienden:*
> *respóndenle también incontinente*
> *diciendo que comerlos no pretenden,*
> *sino que se les dé por cautivo,*
> *si quiere de esta guerra salir vivo.*[18]

> Seeing such a large number of people,
> and their death certain if they resisted,
> Juan de Salas spoke to them with courtesy
> in the Guayquerí language that they understand well:
> they answered him without delay
> saying that their intent was not to eat them
> but for him to surrender as a their captive
> if he wanted to escape this war alive.

The instrumental approach to captives and captivity that informs this stanza and the contributions that explorers and soldiers such as Juan de Salas have provided to empire building are some of the main points Castellanos wants to get across to Iberian readers in this section of his writings. In particular, Salas's command of an aboriginal language immediately casts him as someone who can mediate the alterity of the New World for Iberians readers. But since Juan de Salas did not provide a personal account of his experience, nor is the tale narrated by Salas in the first person, the captives' worth as intermediary as well as his firsthand knowledge of the New World are then transferred throughout the narrative to Castellanos as a writer, the person who assumes the role and assigns himself the authority of speaking on behalf of the captive.

Several other writers before and after Castellanos appropriated a similar generic structure and seized the platform that captivity tales offer to explore the intricacies of cultural contact and exchange, reflect on the lasting scars of intense trauma, or explore the inadequacies of language to express it. Miguel de Cervantes, arguably the most famous Spanish captive of them all, was the first Iberian author to dramatize the experience of captivity on the theatrical stage, and throughout his career he returned often to the topic of captivity to create texts that even today continue to inspire readers to reflect on boundaries of human freedom or on the effects that prolonged and close contact with foreign societies can have on a person's sense of religious, cultural, and national identity.[19] When compared with Cervantes's brilliant reformulations of the discourse of captivity, the brief tale about Juan de Salas can appear formulaic and even lacking in psychological depth, but on Castellanos's behalf one can argue that Salas's story is not a meditation on the experience of captivity per se but above all an illustration of certain premises that justify the exploration and conquest of the New World from the perspective of the conquistadors. It is for this reason that the narrator can skip altogether the details of the specific tribulations that accompanied Salas's imprisonment (there is actually no mention of beatings, torture, hunger, or insults) and focus instead in turning the stages of Salas's captivity into an allegory for the conquest of the New World to be understood as a redeeming act to save the natives. Nonetheless, Juan de Salas's story encapsulates eloquently some of the cultural transformations experienced by explorers and colonists during Europe's expansion simply by reiterating that the protagonist's home is to be found in the same place where he has been made captive, the New World. Such a concept is somewhat foreign to Cervantes's captives, who typically depart from and return to Spain. In the case of the hilarious story of the two counterfeit captives from *The Trials of Persiles and Sigismunda*,[20] the two captives turn out to be students from the University of Salamanca who have never had the chance to leave Spain in the first place. In summary, it is in the gesture of situating the departure and return of the Spanish (American) captive in the unstable and contested geography of the New World as early as 1550 where this tale destabilizes the function that heroic poetry and the discourse of captivity were serving within the larger Iberian discourse of empire and exploration, hence predating and prefiguring the depth and complexity of the discourse of captivity in the hands of writers like Miguel de Cervantes.

THE CAPTIVE CONQUISTADOR AS A CHRISTLIKE SAVIOR

Jorge Cañizares-Esguerra places Castellanos's *Elegías* under the category of "satanic epics," a term he uses to refer to epic poems written in Spanish, Portuguese, Italian, and English during the sixteenth and seventeenth centuries, and whose plots revolve around the portrayal of Christian heroes fighting satanic enemies.[21] Cañizares-Esguerra contends that Castellanos's heroic poems are "organized around the premise that the 'discovery' and settlement of America pitted the forces of evil against the conquistador Christian he-roes."[22] To support this interpretation, he provides a typological and allegori-cal interpretation of the frontispiece of the first volume of the *Elegías* and eloquently argues that the image "makes explicit the Biblical inspiration for the holy violence unleashed by the Spaniards on the natives [of the New World]," and "colonization becomes a fulfillment of Biblical, apocalyptic prophesies, [and] an act of liberation and wrathful divine punishment."[23] According to Cañizares-Esguerra, the frontispiece exalts the navigational prowess of Hapsburg Spain and its definitive triumph over Satan (as the dragon Leviathan), who "had prevented Europeans from crossing the Atlan-tic and had kept America's native people tyrannized and the resources and marvels of the New World hidden."[24]

In light of the analysis of the *Discurso del capitán Francisco Draque* offered in the previous two chapters, it's clear that later on in his career Castellanos adopted a less triumphalist view of Spain's navigational prowess and a more critical view of Hapsburg monarchs than the one advertised in the frontispiece of the first volume of his writings. But there is no doubt that the biblical and providential elements of the view of colonization that Cañizares-Esguerra finds in his typological and allegorical interpretation of the image inform the bulk of the *Elegías*. The tale of Juan de Salas in particular is written with a Christian readership in mind, and it is steeped with biblical references and symbolism, chiefly notions of death, resurrection, and salva-tion. The protagonist of this tale is first and foremost a steadfast Christian and an instrument of God in a fight against evil. The notion that the explora-tion and conquest of the New World confronted the forces of good against evil is first alluded to in the words used by Amerindians to characterize their assault as part of a much larger confrontation: "sino que se les de por cautivo / si quiere desta guerra salir vivo"[25] (but for him to surrender as a their captive / if he wanted to escape this war alive). Similarly, the sense that this is an ongoing struggle is reiterated a few stanzas later when the narrator describes the intensity of the mother's supplications to God through the Virgin Mary as an actual battle: "fue tal el gran hervor de esta batalla / que tuvo Dios por bien el consolarla"[26] (the intensity of this battle was such, / that God eventually consoled her). On several occasions, Castellanos refers to Salas's faith, and it is after all through God's direct intervention that Castellanos attributes the exceptionally benevolent conduct of the Caribs toward their captive, particularly in their decision to spare him from being killed and eaten. Moreover, it is from God that Salas receives the understand-ing and clarity of mind ("buen entendimiento" and "lumbre") to win the Caribs over:

> *y ansi fue que después del vencimiento*
> *en esta miserable servidumbre,*
> *le hicieron un blando tratamiento,*

Figure 5.1. Frontispiece from Juan de Castellanos's *Primera parte de las elegías de varones ilustres de Indias* (Madrid, 1589). *Source:* Image courtesy of the Biblioteca Nacional de España.

fuera de lo que tienen por costumbre;
valiose de su buen entendimiento
y Dios fue servido darle lumbre
para saber ganar las voluntades
a gentes llenas de cien mil maldades. [27]

And so it was that after the defeat
in this miserable servitude
they treated him more kindly,
quite different to their usual habit;
he made use of his good understanding
and God gave him light
to know how to win over the will
of people full of a hundred thousand evils.

Evidence that Castellanos wanted readers to see Salas's misfortunes as an allegory for a redemptive view of colonization can also be found in the fact that the protagonist himself is likened to Christ. Salas's Christlike features emerge for the first time in the scene describing his mother's reaction to the news of his captivity and her requests for assistance from the Virgin Mary. By describing her son's captivity as a type of death ("sin vida tú, yo della mal pagada" [you, lifeless, and I've been badly rewarded by life]) and establishing an analogy between her son and Christ when addressing the Virgin ("dadme mi hijo ya, señora mía, / y por seguras prendas ese vuestro" [Give me my son now, my lady, / and as a gift I shall receive yours too]),[28] Salas's mother sets the stage for the three years that Salas spends in captivity to be viewed as a sort of reenactment of the three days that Christ spent in the tomb.[29] However, it is especially through Salas's role in the liberation of Amerindian captives that he reaches his full stature as a redeemer. Here we may recall that Salas shares his captivity with a group of Amerindian captives (presumably Taino), and that while planning his own escape he voluntarily assumes a leadership position by warning the other captives of their imminent death and inciting them to follow him to safety: "No tenéis hora segura / y todos moriréis despedazados / huyámonos a tierras de cristianos / que buen tiempo tenemos en las manos"[30] (You encounter perils all the time / and will all die dismembered / let's escape to Christian lands / now that we have good weather in our hands). Juan de Salas would then go on to jeopardize his escape and to risk his own life in order to bring the Amerindian captives into safety. Salas's concern for the well-being of the other captives tinges his entire experience with a providential aura and offsets other sections of the tale that could suggest he had acculturated into Carib society or that his conduct was motivated solely by self-interest, pragmatism, or necessity.

Through the successful liberation of a group of Amerindian captives, the narrative about Juan de Salas rationalizes the conquest as an act of kindness and generosity toward Amerindians; and the protagonist's misfortunes, as part of God's providential plan to save them. Salas's proposition, "huyámonos a tierras de cristianos / que buen tiempo tenemos en las manos"[31] (let's escape to Christian lands / now that we have good weather in our hands), speaks of establishing a trust and an alliance between two groups that would otherwise have remained alien to each other. As such, Salas's words convey an itinerary for voluntary intercultural contact that goes in the reverse direction of the forced captivity of the protagonist who came to live among the Caribs against his will. In other words, Salas's proposition carries with it an agenda for the insertion of some indigenous tribes into Colonial Spanish American society, and it presents that experience as one of relenting their cultural values and practices so that they would come willingly to join Colonial Spanish American society, or "tierras de cristianos," as Castellanos calls it. In sum, to the question of why should Amerindians trust Juan de Salas (or any other Spanish explorer for that matter), this captivity tale proposes that from the perspective of Amerindian societies victimized by the Caribs, becoming a Christian was a far better option than slavery or death at the hands of cannibalistic tribes who were under the control of the devil.

Since at the beginning of Juan de Salas's story Castellanos indicated that he had met the protagonist while they were both on the island of Cubagua, the irony of Salas's proposition lays in the fact that from around 1510 until its destruction by an earthquake in 1541, Cubagua, or the *isla de las perlas* (island of pearls) as it was then known, was the site of massive indigenous captivity and enslavement.[32] The reason is that a considerable supply of expendable captives was needed to extract from the ocean bed the highly prized pearls sought after in Europe. This irony is compounded further if we interpret Castellanos's recollection of facing danger while in the company of Juan de Salas as acknowledgment that the two of them had participated in the type of slave raids that supplied the forced labor of Amerindian captives to the exploitative and unsustainable economy of the Caribbean: "Y en medio de los tiros y las valas / en mocedad fue compañero nuestro / ejercitándonos por tierra y agua / en las crueles de Cubagua" (And in the midst of gunshots and bullets / in younger years he was our companion / and we would endeavor in land and sea / in the cruel ones of Cubagua).[33] On the other hand, since Cubagua was also the base from which Spanish slave raiders would harass Fray Bartolomé de las Casas's utopian colony at Cumaná, the reference to Cubagua could encode an ideological message that marks Las Casas's writings as a privileged subtext for this particular section of the *Elegías*. In fact, Juan de Salas's narrative shares a very similar cartography with the chapter of the *Brevísima relación de la destrucción de las Indias* dedicated to the coast of Venezuela ("De la costa de las perlas y de Paria y la isla de Trinidad").[34] But instead of rejecting the practice of enslaving Amerindians or condemning the methods used by Spanish colonists as barbaric, Salas's tale completely elides Spanish enslavement and captivity of indigenous people in the Caribbean and conveys the message that the larger enterprise of conquest, colonization, and evangelization of the New World was a mission for resourceful, self-reliant, and determined Christian warriors and not for idealistic peacemakers.

CAPTIVITY NARRATIVES AND THE AUTHORITY OF THE EYEWITNESS ACCOUNT

As noted earlier, Castellanos interpolated the tale of Juan de Salas's captivity in the 1550s in the middle of a poem dealing with events that had taken place almost sixty years earlier. Far from being unwarranted, this digression fits in well as a preamble to the story of the fate of Diego de Arana and the colonists at Fuerte de Navidad inasmuch as it allows Castellanos to start to clear the reputation of the first explorers and conquistadors by suggesting that the customs of the tribe that abducted Juan de Salas were similar to those of the tribe that killed Diego de Arana and his men (see chapter 2). The narrator sets the tale of captivity to function in this way by explaining in its introduction that Salas's captivity took place in the same geographic area where events related to the early phase of the "discovery" had unfolded ("y de las dichas [Caribbean] islas no me salgo"[35]), thus urging readers to see Juan de Salas's experience as a mirror image of the experience faced by Diego de Arana. Yet, since the historical and testimonial aspects of the narration are anchored in Castellanos's assertion to have known personally the protagonist and to have participated with him in some sort of military campaigns, readers are also urged to see the narrator as a double of both of these two explorers and conquistadors as well.

Critics have read these type of statements as a confirmation of the factual origin of Castellanos's writing, when in reality they are part of an all-encompassing rhetorical strategy to ground his poems in a new kind of knowledge, a knowledge that was challenging the authority of classical sources and professional historians and that came from firsthand experience and prolonged residency in the New World. Given that Castellanos is making controversial claims about the nature of the inhabitants of the New World and presenting the early phase of exploration and conquest from quite a different angle than the one offered by well-known contemporary critics such as Fray Bartolomé de las Casas, the need for boosting the empirical authority of his writing must have presented itself as a requirement. As noted earlier, Castellanos also lacked the type of proximity to the Spanish court that allowed writers such as Alonso de Ercilla to authorize his epic poems by invoking the authority of the monarch (see introduction and chapter 1). From these perspectives, the genre of captivity tales fits like a glove, because, by stating that he knew personally and had shared vital experiences with the protagonist, Castellanos comes as close as he can to actually anchoring his claims on supposedly firsthand empirical knowledge retrieved by an eyewitness. Therefore, the narration of a tale of captivity early on in the *Elegías* is essential for Castellanos in order to construct his own identity as a seasoned veteran of the conquest and to boost his authority to narrate vis-à-vis the epistemological changes derived from Europe's encounter with the New World, particularly the "increasing valorization of the eye-witness testimony."[36] In this sense, there is nothing ancillary concerning this digression, and its narration instead is central to Castellanos's literary self-authorization and self-fashioning.

This having been said, the actual historical evidence that supports many of the statements made by Castellanos about his first three decades in the New World is at best precarious and, in many cases, nonexistent. The portion of Castellanos's life about which we can speak with some certainty is the period from his ordination to the priesthood in Cartagena in 1554 until his death in Tunja in 1607, for which there are sources external to his own poems. In fact, the most logical conclusion one could reach after examining the testimonies of witnesses included in the dossier that was sent to Spain to request Castellanos's appointment as beneficiary of the cathedral in Tunja is that either he had no military experience whatsoever or any involvement in the campaigns of exploration and conquest was too insignificant to mention. Several of the witnesses attest to Castellanos's piety, to his background as a *cristiano viejo* (old Christian), and to his merits as priest, preacher, and citizen of the New Kingdom of Granada, but none of them recalls any specific service provided to the Spanish Crown other than working as vicar at the Nuestra Señora de los Remedios parish in the town of Río de la Hacha prior to being assigned to the cathedral in Tunja. This image of Castellanos essentially as a member of the clergy is confirmed by the portrait that appears on the page adjacent to the opening of the first poem of the *Elegías*. It is not clear whether this is in fact a portrait from life of Castellanos, but the Latin phrase around it dates the image (1588) and names the individual in it as Juan de Castellanos. The subject in the portrait appears half-body in front of a blank background and is depicted as a member of the regular clergy, with a breviary in his hands and wearing the typical attire of a priest. This interpretation is confirmed by the second half of the Latin phrase that states Castellanos had received a religious benefice at the city of Tunja in the New Kingdom of Granada. Nothing from this composition conveys that Castellanos had been a soldier or that he had been a participant in the campaigns of exploration of the New World.

Although circumstantial, this evidence speaks volumes, especially when we take into account the frequency with which individuals who had actually been involved in the campaigns of exploration brought up that pretext when requesting some type of compensation from the Spanish Crown, or the obstinacy with which throughout his poems Castellanos would argue that partici-

Figure 5.2. Photograph of the first page of Juan de Castellanos's *Elegías de varones ilustres de Indias* (1589). *Source:* Image courtesy of the Biblioteca Nacional de España.

pating in the campaigns of exploration and conquest had entitled the conquistadors to social and economic prerogatives. Incidentally, as late as the first decade of the seventeenth century, three out of the four priests who applied for the post of beneficiary of the cathedral in Tunja after Castellanos died mention their connection to that type of service in their applications.[37] Francisco Vivas, for example, points out that "es hijo de uno de los primeros descubridores y conquistadores de aquella tierra"[38] (he is the son of one of the first discoverers and conquerors of that land); Alonso Gutierrez Escovar, on the other hand, mentions that he risked his life many times while preaching the gospel:

> *Celebraba misa armado y en las entradas y correduras iba entre los soldados animándolos y por su persona prendió un cacique que inquietaba la tierra con que se apaciguó y al presente se halla con el presidente Don Juan de Borja en la jornada contra los indios rebeldes que le llevó por administrador del hospital del ejército y capellán del por su mucha experiencia.[39]*

> He would celebrate mass armed. During campaigns and incursions into enemy territory, he would be amongst the soldiers reassuring them, and he captured an Indian chieftain who was spreading unrest throughout the land, and later the land became peaceful. At the moment he is with President Don Juan de Borja participating in the campaign against rebel natives, and the president assigned him as manager of the army's hospital and chaplain because of his broad experience.

In summary, the strategic insertion of autobiographical references; the notion that the narrator was an eyewitness to many of the events he narrates; and the presumption that Castellanos knew personally many of the individuals that he writes about and received from them the accounts he is transcribing are some of the most important narrative strategies Castellanos exploits throughout the *Elegías*, often taking them to a level of complexity not easily found in his contemporaries or predecessors. Most critics have assumed that Castellanos's first experience in the New World was actually somewhat similar to what he attributes to his friend Juan de Salas. If that were the case, with the brief and schematic tale of captivity of a friend, Castellanos has been able to provide one of the most impressive *Relación de méritos y servicios* (Relation of merits and services) any explorer or writer at the time could aspire to.

CAPTIVITY AND MOTHERHOOD: THE DEPICTION OF SPANISH AMERICAN COLONIES AS A WOMAN IN DISTRESS

Like other captivity and shipwreck tales coming out of the Spanish American colonies, Juan de Salas's is the story of a male captive, and the only two female figures in this narrative are the protagonist's mother and the Virgin

Mary. Since there is no indication that during his captivity Salas established any type of relationship with an indigenous female captor, this story precludes the possibility of seeing Salas's captivity as a model for cultural syncretism or its depiction of the early encounter between Spaniards and Amerindians as a foundational myth of *mestizaje* along the line of the manner in which the story of Gonzalo Guerrero's immersion to Maya society in Yucatán has been constructed.[40]

As a co-protagonist, Salas's mother is mentioned at the key stages of the narrative: first, in the moment when she receives the news of her son abduction; then, when the narrator describes her kneeling in front of an altar at a church and transcribes at length her distressed pleads to God and the Virgin Mary; and finally, at the conclusion of the story in a scene of reencounter and (mis)recognition when the mother faints upon the unexpected return of her son. Given the intensity of her suffering and her unwavering commitment to her son's liberation, it is not difficult to imagine the mother's ordeal as a form of imprisonment and to cast her in the role of a metaphorical captive. To be sure, the mother's role as a figurative captive allows us to grasp more clearly the fact that captivity in the sixteenth century was an unstable signifier that could have simultaneously positive and negative connotations. Captivity could bring to mind the detrimental effects of losing one's freedom to religious or military adversaries but could also have positive connotations when used as a metaphor for love in Petrarchist/Garcilacist language and symbolism, not to mention the use of references to captivity to express the depth of a person's faith.[41] As we saw earlier, Castellanos does not hesitate to use the notion of captivity (as imprisonment) in a favorable sense when he rejects the favor of Calliope and Clio and requests the protection of the Virgin Mary: "Pues como vos [Virgin Mary] seáis presidio mío / No quiero más Calíope ni Clío."[42] Likewise, Salas's mother seems very much at home exploring the multiple nuances of the meaning of captivity (but especially as consumption) when she refers to her own womb ("mis entrañas") as the original place that held her son "captive" (in the sense of nurturing him) in contrast to the guts and other inner body parts of the cannibals that threaten to consume him: "!Hijo! que te trajeron mis entrañas, / y ahora las de bestias tan crueles!"[43] (Son! product of my womb, / and now of the entrails of those of cruel beasts!). The connection Castellanos establishes between the mother's womb and the practice of cannibalism among Caribs merits attention inasmuch as it would appear to confirm Las Casas's writing as a privileged subtext. Las Casas had used the same term and the love of a parent for his child as examples to illustrate the level of hospitality of the inhabitants of the Caribbean Islands offered to Spanish explorers:

Los indios recibiéronlos como si fueran sus entrañas y sus hijos , sirviéndoles
señores y súbditos con grandisima afección y alegría, trayéndoles cada día de
comer tanto que les sobraba para que comieran otros tantos. [44]

The natives welcomed them as if they were their marrow parts and their
children, nobles, and commoners serving them with great affection and joy,
bringing them each day so much food that there would be leftovers to feed
many more.

As the main overarching maternal figure in the story, Salas's mother
symbolizes the protagonist's connection to Spain as his original motherland.
This allegorical function is underscored by the fact that readers never learn
the mother's name and that the space assigned to her in the story is inside a
church, which is the only specific location (other than the Caribbean archipelago) that is demarcated and described in the story. The mother's presence
at the church and the favorable response from the Virgin Mary and God
symbolize the successful transplantation of Christianity to the New World.
Such understanding of the New World as a place made sacred by the presence of Christianity is in alignment with the message conveyed in the frontispiece of the first volume of Castellanos's writing as well as with the metaphor Castellanos uses at the beginning of his *Discurso del capitán Francisco*
Draque to refer to the New World under the threat of English piracy: "En
éste nuestro recental aprisco"[45] (in this our new sacred sheepfold; see chapter
3). When all is accounted for, Salas's literal return to his mother and his
figurative return to her womb confirms unequivocally the fact that his identity as a Christian, as a Catholic, and as a (heterosexual male) Spaniard has
not been threatened or destabilized during his three years of captivity.

It would be fair to say that Castellanos is compelled to emphasize Salas's
return to his mother as representative of an unblemished Spanish identity not
only because losing one's faith and/or identity was a concrete risk for captives but also because, in order to increase Salas's worth as a captive, at one
point in the story Castellanos appears to be suggesting that Juan de Salas had
in fact adopted the cultural norms of his captors. The issue of the cultural and
social identity of the captive is brought to the fore in the following stanza,
which offers some of the most puzzling information to determine exactly
what transpired during Salas's three years of captivity:

> *Cuando guerra con indios se movía*
> *daba su parecer en el viaje,*
> *arco, macana, flecha se ponía,*
> *sus meneos, posturas y su traje;*
> *sucedióles bien lo que decía,*
> *en señalar lugar, tiempo, paraje,*
> *y ansí no rehuyó mozo ni viejo*
> *de tomar en la guerra su consejo.* [46]

> When war against the Indians started
> he used to express his views about the journey,
> arc, club, arrow he would wear,
> their jolts, postures and outfits;
> whatever he had said happened,
> pointing out setting, place and time,
> so neither youth nor old escaped
> from taking his advise on war.

In these lines, the narrator enhances Salas's worth as a captive by attributing to him an exceptional ability to cope with the circumstances. Salas is depicted not only as a prisoner turned military advisor for the Caribs but also as someone who has detailed knowledge of the region and has become skilled in the use of indigenous weapons ("arco, macana, flecha"). Unlike Diogo Álvares, the hero of the eighteenth-century Brazilian epic poem *Caramuru: Poema épico do descobrimento da Bahia* (1781),[47] Salas is able to survive and even distinguish himself while being a captive not because he carries a firearm or relies on gunpowder but because he has mastered the more rudimentary style of warfare of the Caribs. While in the story of the two fake captives in the *Trials of Persiles and Sigismunda*, Cervantes would turn the genre of captivity upside down by suggesting that captivity could be performed, in this stanza Castellanos is enhancing the value of the captive in a transatlantic context by suggesting that Salas's worth is increased further by his ability to perform being an Amerindian. Yet, if we take dress (or the lack thereof) as a signifier of acculturation, the question of whether Salas has actually crossed over is briefly left open when the narrator states that the captives' manner of walking, his demeanor, and his attire are the same as those of the Caribs: "Se ponía sus meneos, posturas y su traje"[48] (he would put on their demeanor, posture, and attire). In regard to the issue of identity, the key term from this line is the verb *ponerse* (to put on), which would indicate that when Salas dressed (or perhaps undressed?) as an Indian he is only pretending to be one. However, Salas's thorough knowledge and appropriation of the customs of his captors would beg the question of whether an individual who speaks, walks, acts, dresses, and goes to war like a Carib could actually be performing being a Spaniard upon his return to *tierras de cristianos*. It is then to avoid this type of slippage, and particularly any suspicion of apostasy, that the mother has to literally come to rescue her son and to assure readers not only that her son is alive but also that at all times he remained a Spaniard, inasmuch as being a Spaniard is not something extrinsic or visible through clothing but is more an inner and intrinsic attribute that derives from being a Christian. In this regard, it is telling that when Salas is abducted, the mother is the one responsible for identifying Salas as a Christian who uses all his strength and cunning ("fueza y mañas") to fight against the infidels, thus allowing Iberian readers to recognize the person who has been taken as a captive among Carib Indians as one of them: "¡Hijo! mío! ¿Qué nuevas tan extrañas! / De las que tú, mi bien, enviar sueles? / ¡Hijo! ¿Do están las fuerzas y las mañas / que tenías con estos infieles?"[49] (My son! What odd news, my dear, / unlike the ones you typically send me? / Son! Where are the strength and cunning / you had against these infidels?). Notice that the traits used by the mother to identify her son are essentially the same Cervantes will ironize in the *Trials of Persiles and Sigismunda* when the counterfeit captives identify themselves as individuals who plan to join the Spanish Royal Army in order to "break, smash, maim, and kill [all the] enemies of the holy Catholic faith [they] might run into."[50] Equally important is the fact that any threat of apostasy (in this case equivalent to emasculation) possibly derived from prolonged residency in the New World or immersion into an Amerindian tribe, as implied in the mother's initial interrogation of her son's virility ("¿Do están las fuerzas y las mañas / que tenías con estos infieles?"), is resolved with Salas's successful return to his community of origin and to his mother.

Nonetheless, in the tale of Juan de Salas's captivity, the mother also stands for Spanish America, both as an emerging new identity and as a contested territory in reality and in paper. In this respect, the important thing to notice is that the mother is a resident of the island of Margarita and that neither she nor her son anticipates ever returning to Spain. Quite the contrary, what is made evident from her supplication to the Virgin is that her locus of enunciation (and that of the entire poem) is the New World, the place where she lives and expects to die. Notice that when Castellanos inserts the plea of the distraught mother, he reminds readers on two separate occasions of the very favorable and compassionate reception her requests had among the Spanish American residents who witness her tears and her suffering:

> *No hay duro corazón que no se mueva*
> *oyendo los clamores que está dando:*
> *tales y tantas lástimas decía,*
> *que el pecho más cruel enternecía.*
>
> *¡Hijo mío! ¿Qué nuevas tan extrañas*
> *de las que tú, mi bien, enviar sueles?*
> *¡Hijo! ¿Do están las fuerzas y las mañas*
> *que tenías con estos infieles?*
> *¡Hijo! que te trajeron mis entrañas,*
> *y agora las de bestias tan crueles!*
> *¡Hijo! ¿Quién te llevó? ¿Cómo me dejas?*
> *¿Dó estás? ¿Cómo no oyes estas quejas?*
>
> *Perdíte yo, dejásteme perdida,*

sin vida tú, yo della mal pagada.
¡Oh madre para tanto mal nacida!
¡Oh hijo de la madre desdichada!
Pues que sin ver la tuya ve su vida
con tanta desventura rematada,
eclipse padeció mi llena luna,
menguada por mal orden de fortuna.

La cual no se compone ni concierta
según pide razón que se concierte,
antes a sinrazones abrió puerta
cuando su variedad echó la suerte;
dilatando los días a la muerta,
y al merecedor dellos dando muerte
para que en la morada deste suelo
eterno llanto sea mi consuelo.

sus venerables canas van sin toca
ante la imagen del Juez eterno,
a dolorosas lágrimas provoca
a cuantos viven en aquel gobierno;
y ansi los golpes de su blanda boca
el duro corazón tornaban tierno,
y en tres años continuos de demora
el templo visitaba cada hora.

Allí hablaba con la Virgen pía,
cuyos brazos tenían su maestro;
las palabras formales que decía
aquí se ponen sin color siniestro:
"Dadme mi hijo ya, señora mía,
y por seguras prendas ese vuestro."
Fue tal el gran hervor desta batalla,
que tuvo Dios por bien en consolarla. [51]

There is no harsh heart that remains unmoved
listening to her cries:
such and so many sorrows she expressed
that the cruelest chest softened.

My son! What odd news, my dear,
unlike the ones you typically send me?
Son! Where are the strength and cunning
you had against these infidels?
Son! Product of my entrails,
and now of those of cruel beasts!
Son! Who took you? How can you leave me?
Where are you? Can't you hear these complaints?

I lost you, and now I'm lost,
you, lifeless, and I've been badly rewarded by life.
Oh, mother born for so much sorrow!
Oh, son of a wretched mother!
who without seeing your life, she sees hers
with so much misfortune finished off,
my full moon has suffered an eclipse,
waned by an evil set of fortune.

Fortune is not repaired nor does it improve,
as reason would require it to improve,
instead it opened the door to injustices
when the dice rolled this uncertainty;
delaying the days of the deceased,
and killing he who deserved them
so that in this ground's abode
eternal cry be my comfort.

And with her venerable grey hair uncovered
she would go in front of the image of the eternal Judge
triggering painful tears
to all those who reside in that location;
and so the blows of her gentle mouth
softened the harshest heart,
and in three full years of delay
she visited the temple every hour.

There she talked to the pious Virgin,
whose arms had her own Lord;
the formal prayer she spoke
is here set without bias:
"Give me my son now, my lady,
and as a gift I shall receive yours too."
The intensity of this battle was such,
that God eventually consoled her.

Castellanos wrote "Elegía II" and the tale of Juan de Salas at a time when the indigenous population of the Caribbean basin posed no significant military threat as it had already been drastically decimated through disease, captivity, excessive labor, and genocide. By 1570, Spaniards had been able to gain the upper hand in securing military control of the Caribbean archipelago and were well on their way in the process of colonizing the mainland. For this reason, it seems logical to assume that the urgency conveyed through the mother's tears as well as her distress must be directed toward something other than the Caribs as an actual military threat. Incidentally, the second half of the sixteenth century was a period when several calls for reform came out in the open, including those by individuals such as Fray Bartolomé de las Casas and Alvar Núñez Cabeza de Vaca, who had used narratives that relied heavily on the symbolism and language of captivity and shipwreck to propose more benign and peaceful methods of colonization.[52] In my view, the introduction of the mother's suffering within a tale and a series of poems that validates military conquest reveals that conquistadors turned encomenderos, and the writers at their service, found creative ways to convey the recognition and autonomy they sought in relation to Spain while at the same time seeking a favorable disposition toward their claims and even pleading for more support and protection. The roles assigned to Juan de Salas and his mother oscillate between assertion and submission by suggesting that the New World was a territory that had been conquered from the devil by heroic and Christlike conquistadors but that was now in jeopardy and in need of more protection. In her role as representative of Spanish America, the lengthy supplication of the distraught mother is pivotal to awaken a compassionate response from Iberians readers, similar to the one the narrator attributes to God, to the Virgin Mary, and to all Spanish American colonists who witness her suffering.

CONCLUSION

Throughout the entire narrative there is a clear sense that Juan de Salas has provided a service and that he is reliable enough to provide even more important contributions to God and to the Spanish monarchy. In terms of material rewards, Salas returns from his captivity empty handed, but there is no doubt that he is more valuable because of the experience of dwelling among natives for a prolonged amount of time. In terms of spiritual gains, on the other hand, Salas is able to achieve the liberation of numerous Amerindian captives and prevent their souls from eternal damnation. If, as suggested earlier, the captivity tale is read as a *Relación de méritos y servicios* (Relation of merits and services), Salas's experience and credentials are impeccable. The tale attests that he was an exceptional soldier, sailor, and leader who not only spoke an indigenous language but also demonstrated loyalty to God, the Spanish Crown, his mother, and his community. Moreover, Salas emerges as a generous, resourceful, determined individual, who only appeals to violence in self-defense or in the most extreme conditions. In fact, his true worth is found after he has surrendered his weapons. This virtuous, heroic, and noble image of conquistadors is quite different from the violent and greedy tyrants that populate the pages written by Fray Bartolomé de las Casas. Furthermore, there is also the sense that tryouts and failures are very much a stage toward success, as made evident in the stanza that recounts how Salas was finally able to escape by finding tools and weapons (and clothes!) scattered on the beach from a previous shipwreck:

> *Había por la isla derramadas,*
> *parece ser de naos allí perdidas,*
> *número de machetes y de espadas,*
> *barriles, lienzos, ropas ya podridas,*
> *y otras algunas armas enastadas,*
> *que perdieron sus dueños con las vidas:*
> *desto tomaron lo que les convino,*
> *el y aquel español que con él vino.* [53]

> Scattered around the island,
> seemingly from vessels lost therein,
> there were a number of machetes and swords,
> barrels, canvasses, already rotten clothes,
> and other shafted weapons,
> that lost their masters with their lives:
> from this they took whatever they wanted,
> him [Salas] and that Spaniard that came with him.

In sum, what this tale of captivity tells us is that like his most immediate predecessor and rival, Alonso de Ercilla, Castellanos also faced the daunting challenge of offering one of the earliest poetic representations of the inhabitants of the New World when he set out to write his heroic poems. And like Ercilla, Castellanos appealed to preexisting discourses to help Iberian readers grasp the alterity of the New World. However, instead of employing such discourses in a manner that could serve to idealize indigenous cultures or present indigenous resistance as heroic, Castellanos tailored the discourse of captivity in a way that allowed him to cast the inhabitants of the New World in the role previously occupied by the longtime enemies of Spain and Christendom: the Muslims and the devil, hence dislodging and reshifting the setting where the war against the infidels was taking place, from the shores of the Mediterranean and North Africa to the islands in the Caribbean basin. Yet, if some aspects of Juan de Salas's captivity reveal how his *Elegías* is conditioned by Castellanos's religious and cultural prejudices, as well as his bias toward explorers and conquistadors, his construction of the protagonist as an alter ego confirms to what extend he strove to infuse his *Elegías* with a new type of authority that valued eyewitness accounts and firsthand experience. Similarly, in Castellanos's poems, prolonged residency in the New World does not lead to moral degeneration as some Iberian authors were beginning to argue but served instead as an asset to legitimate knowledge about lands, cultures, and people that until recently had remained unknown to Europeans. Although in hindsight it is possible to find gaps and contradictions in this strategy, his poems and his use of the discourse of captivity, in particular, remain just as eloquent in conveying the portrait of an individual who settled in the Spanish colonies in the New World for good, a possibility that escaped court-bound writers such as the author of the *Araucana*. Moreover, the intriguing nexus between author, narrator, and protagonist and the notion that the written text could offer a mirror image of the self will be issues that will continue to captivate many subsequent modern readers and writers.

NOTES

1. *Elegías*, 1:127.
2. Meo Zilio, *Estudio sobre Juan de Castellanos*, 141.
3. There is a clear affinity in the manner in which Castellanos narrates Juan de Salas's misfortunes and his version of the wreck of Christopher Columbus's largest vessel, the Santa María, as well as his account of the disastrous fate of the first colony at Fuerte de Navidad (which he will narrate in canto 2 of the same poem). In these three separate but related episodes, Castellanos mines the motif of adversity as a metaphor for a Christian triumph and interprets the calamities of an individual or a group as a sign of a Spanish imperial victory.
4. Voigt, *Writing Captivity*, 1–2.
5. In his will Castellanos writes, "Item mando para redención de cautivos que están en tierras de moros doce pesos de oros de veinte quilates" (I provide twelve pesos in gold of twenty carats to be used towards the liberation of (Christian) captives in North Africa). See Rojas, *El beneficiado*, 301.
6. The story of Juan de Salas was included in the first volume of the *Elegías*, which was published in Madrid in 1589.
7. Meo Zilio, *Estudio sobre Juan de Castellanos*, 146.
8. *Elegías*, 1:61.
9. Father Alberto Pedrero writes, "Tal es nuestro poeta Castellanos, / Pues va cantando hechos excelentes / Trabajos increibles y sucesos, / Que sobrepujan cuanto pinta Homero, / Y exceden a los naufragios del troyano" (*Elegías*, 1:54; Such is our poet Castellanos, / who sings of outstanding and incredible deeds / and events that surpass anything depicted by Homer, / and outshine the shipwrecks of the son of Troy).
10. *Elegías*, 1:127.
11. Ibid., 1:126–27.
12. Ibid., 1:128–35.
13. Ibid., 1:129–35.
14. Ibid., 1:126–31.
15. Ibid., 1:127. On the topic of friendship in Renaissance literature, see Daniel T. Lochman, Maritere López, and Lorna Hutson, *Discourses and Representations of Friendship in Early Modern Europe, 1500–1700* (Burlington, VT: Ashgate, 2011).
16. Homer, *The Iliad*, trans. Richmond Lattimore (Chicago: University of Chicago Press, 1951), bk. 1.
17. On the topic of cannibalism in Colonial Spanish America, see Carlos A. Jáuregui's *Canibalia: Canibalismo, calibanismo, antropofagia cultural y consumo en América Latina* (Madrid: Iberoamericana, 2008).
18. *Elegías*, 1:129.
19. The Barbary captivity was staged by Cervantes in several plays, including *El Trato de Argel* and *Los baños de Argel*, and different approaches to the theme of captivity also appear in the novelas *El amante liberal*, *Los baños de Argel*, and *La gran sultana*. On the topic of captivity in Cervantes, see María Antonia Garcés, *Cervantes in Algiers: A Captive's Tale* (Nashville: Vanderbilt University Press, 2002); Cory Reed, "Harems and Eunuchs: Ottoman-Islamic Motifs of Captivity in *El celoso extemeño*," *Bulletin of the Hispanic Studies* 76, no. 2 (April 1999): 199–214; and Ellen M. Anderson, "Playing at Moslem and Christian: The Con-

struction of Gender and the Representation of Faith in Cervantes' Captivity Plays," *Cervantes: Bulletin of the Cervantes Society of America* 13, no. 2 (1993): 37–59.

20. Miguel de Cervantes Saavedra, *The Trials of Persiles and Sigismunda: A Northern Story*, trans. Cecilia Richmond Weller and Clark A. Colahan (Berkeley: University of California Press, 1989), bk. 3, chap. 10.

21. In relation to Iberian satanic epics, Jorge Cañizares-Esguerra traces the use of the discourse of demonology not only in canonical works such as Luis Vaz de Camões's *Os Lusíadas* (1572) and Alonso de Ercilla's *La Araucana* (1569, 1578, and 1589) but also in lesser known poems such as Jose de Anchieta's *De Gestis Meude de Saa* (1563), Gabriel Lobo Lasso de la Vega's *Mexicana* (1594), and Lope de Vega's *La dragontea* (1598), among others. It is clear that the author's goal is not to historicize each source but to highlight the overarching motifs that are present in the normative Spanish poems and later resurface in British texts such as Edmund Spenser's *Faerie Queen* (1590), John Milton's *Paradise Lost* (1667), or William Shakespeare's *Tempest* (1623).

22. Cañizares-Esguerra, *Puritan Conquistadors*, 40.

23. Ibid., 35.

24. Ibid., 39. For further analysis of the frontispiece to the first volume of the *Elegías*, see Jason McCloskey, "Spain Succored by Religion: Titian and Lope de Vega's *La Dragontea*," in *Signs of Power in Habsburg Spain and the New World*, ed. Jason McCloskey and Ignacio Lopez Alemany, 199–221 (Lewisburg, PA: Bucknell University Press, 2013).

25. *Elegías*, 1:129.

26. Ibid., 1:130.

27. Ibid.

28. Ibid., 1:129–30.

29. Anderson reminds us that in the "theology and literature of the time," a Christian held captive by Muslims was often referred to as a "dead man, a thing without a soul" ("Playing at Moslem and Christian," 41). On this topic, see also George Camamis, *Estudios sobre el cautiverio en el Siglo de Oro* (Madrid: Editorial Gredos, 1977), 102.

30. *Elegías*, 1:131.

31. Ibid.

32. The rise and fall of Cubagua are the topic of "Elegía XIII," entitled "Elogio de la isla de Cubagua, donde se trata la gran riqueza que allí hubo y su perdición y asolamiento."

33. *Elegías*, 1:127.

34. Bartolomé de las Casas, "De la costa de las perlas y de Paria y la isla de Trinidad," in *Brevísima relación de la destruccion de las Indias*, ed. Jean-Paul Duviols, 145–54 (Buenos Aires: Stockcero, 2006).

35. *Elegías*, 1:127.

36. Voigt, *Writing Captivity*, 34.

37. The testimonies of the witnesses were found by Ulises Rojas at the Archivo General de Indias in Seville. See "Documentos" in Rojas's *El beneficiado*.

38. Quoted in Rojas, *El beneficiado*, 317.

39. Quoted in ibid., 316.

40. For the evolution of Gonzalo Guerrero's story in Early Colonial Latin American texts, see Adorno, *Polemics of Possession*, 246–78.

41. In the poem entitled "Vivo sin vivir en mí" (I live without living in me), Saint Terese of Ávila writes, "Esta divina prisión, / del amor en que yo vivo, / ha hecho a Dios mi cautivo, / y libre mi corazón; / y causa en mi tal pasión / ver a Dios mi prisionero, / que muero porque no muero" (this divine prison / of love in which I dwell, / has turned God into my captive, / and free my heart; / and prompts such passion in me / to see God as my prisoner / I die because I'm not dying). See Teresa de Ávila, *Obras completas de Santa Teresa*, ed. Tomás Alvarez, 17th ed. (Burgos, Spain: Editorial Monte Carmelo, 2014), 1482. In "O llama de amor viva" (O flame of living love), Saint John of the Cross, on the other hand, writes, "!Oh cautiverio suave! / ! Oh regalada llaga!" (O gentle captivity / O dear and generous wound). See San Juan de la Cruz, *Poesía*, ed. Domingo Ynduráin, 10th ed. (Madrid: Cátedra, 1997), 263. Finally, in poems such as "Ode ad florem Gnidi" the use of word "cautivo" to refer to the distraught lover has rich

sexual connotations. See *Garcilaso de la Vega y sus comentaristas*, ed. Antonio Gallego Morell. (Madrid: Editorial Gredos, 1972) 138.

42. *Elegías*, 1:61.
43. Ibid., 130.
44. Casas, *Brevísima relación*, 56.
45. *Discurso*, 1–2.
46. *Elegías*, 1:131.
47. José de Santa Rita Durão, *Caramuru: Poema épico do descubrimiento da Bahia* (São Paulo, Brazil: Edições Cultura, 1945).
48. *Elegías*, 1:131.
49. Ibid., 129.
50. Cervantes, *Trials of Persiles and Sigismunda*, 249.
51. *Elegías*, 1:129–30. In a recent study about Silvestre de Balboa's seventeenth-century heroic poem *Espejo de paciencia*, Raúl Marrero-Fente establishes an intertextual relation between Castellanos's and Balboa's poems paying special attention to the prayer by Salas's mother to the Virgin Mary and the prayer by Bishop Cabezas Altamirano in front of the altar after regaining his freedom. See Raúl Marrero-Fente, *Epic, Empire, and Community in the Atlantic World: Silvestre de Balboa's Espejo de Paciencia* (Lewisburg, PA: Bucknell University Press, 2008), 60.
52. On the so-called peaceful conquest, see José Rabasa, *Writing Violence on the Northern Frontier: The Historiography of Sixteenth-Century New Mexico and Florida and the Legacy of the Conquest* (Durham, NC: Duke University Press, 2000).
53. *Elegías*, 1:132.

Coda

As mentioned earlier in this book, at the end of chapter 6 of the first part of Miguel de Cervantes's *Don Quixote*, the parish priest saves a copy of Alonso de Ercilla's *Araucana* from being thrown into a fire by exclaiming that Ercilla's poem, together with Juan Rufo's and Cristóbal Virués's poems, were some of the finest jewels Spain had produced in heroic poetry. As with many other sections of Cervantes's novel, the words uttered by the priest are open to interpretation, not the least because they appear in a chapter with clear undertones regarding the censorship and public burning of books practiced by the Spanish Inquisition, and in which Cervantes includes ironic remarks and self-deprecating humor about the task of literary criticism and his own achievements as a novelist. In addition, some readers could find in the priest's words evidence of Cervantes's first attempt to explore issues regarding literary genres, a topic that will come into the forefront later in chapter 47.[1] On a more immediate level, one could argue that the words of the priest simply convey a favorable opinion of the *Araucana* shared by many contemporary Spanish readers. The editorial success of the *Araucana* could be offered in support of this interpretation, as several editions of Ercilla's poem appeared in the sixteenth and seventeenth centuries, and the enthusiastic reception of the love affair between Lautaro and Tegualda alone inspired six romances by different authors.[2] If that is the case, the analysis presented in this study shows that not all contemporaries of Cervantes shared the views expressed by the priest and that the act of reading and interpreting the *Araucana* could change significantly depending on whether a reader's livelihood, social standing, and sense of identity hinged on a different depiction of the campaigns of conquest. To put it succinctly, like the priest in Cervantes's *Don Quixote*, the conquistadors turned encomenderos and the writers at their service read the *Araucana* as a poem that narrated the deeds

of Spaniards engaged in building an empire through war. However, the encomenderos did not share the celebratory enthusiasm of the priest, as what they
found in the pages of Ercilla's poem was not necessarily the type of war they
had been willing to fight, nor the empire they had envisioned.

The advantages of approaching Juan de Castellanos's writings from complementary perspectives are manifold. To begin with, since Castellanos could
be considered a quintessential example of a colonial Spanish American *letra-
do*, this book shows how the link between writing and power was more fluid,
and the ideological field more fragmented, than what was articulated by
Angel Rama when he first coined that term.[3] Second, while some critics have
pointed out the abundant factual inaccuracies in Castellanos's poems and
others have rushed to discard the *Elegías* as nothing more than a rhymed
chronicle devoid of any poetic merits, the unveiling of the inventive methods
employed by Castellanos to recalibrate the poetic language of Francesco
Petrarca and Garcilaso de la Vega and to increase the authority of his writings begins the process of explaining why ensuing historians were drawn to
the pages of the *Elegías* when writing their own versions of the exploration
and conquest of the New World, including Fray Pedro Simón (1574–1628),
Antonio de Herrera y Tordesillas (1549–1626), Lucas Fernández de Piedra-
hita (1624–1688), Juan Bautista Muñoz (1745–1799), and Joaquín Acosta
(1800–1852), among others.[4] In addition, some of the findings of this book
are also useful to recognize how the interplay of historical facts and poetic
license continues to inform Latin American literature today. For example,
long after the institution of the *encomienda* has been abolished, and at a time
when eyewitness testimonies have been largely discredited and we have the
theoretical tools to decipher the political and literary ambition hidden behind
gestures of servility, novelists such as William Ospina have opted to return to
the pages of Juan de Castellanos's *Elegías* in an attempt to boost the verisimilitude of their own historical fictions.[5] Ospina's interest in the *Elegías*
confirms that some versions of the past continue to have more weight than
others and illustrates the enduring allure and the persuasive force of the
discourse of sincerity and friendship to produce partisan narratives about the
colonial past. The relationship between the *Elegías*, Ospina's novels, and
new models of domination in contemporary Colombia falls beyond the scope
of this book and will be the topic of a new study.

The long narrative poems about the conquest of the New World have
become a focus of increasing attention over the past three decades, but there
is a lot of work that remains to be done to fully understand the connection
between this form of writing and colonial institutions and social practices, as
well as to more subtle but equally pervasive manifestations of violence. Such
findings, in turn, would allow us to assign due prominence to heroic and epic
poetry within a more inclusive and less hierarchical canon of Spanish Golden
Age and Early Colonial Spanish American literatures. With this in mind, in

these closing remarks I offer two possible avenues of inquiry to further explore the significance of Juan de Castellanos's poems.

Interpreting, reassessing, and resignifying the not-so-distant past played a major role in establishing the colonial regime in Spanish America in the sixteenth century, particularly as those individuals who participated in the exploration and conquest sought creative ways to ensure a privileged social and economic position in the adverse environment created by the promulgation of the New Laws, the decimation of the indigenous population, and the increasing pressure to compete against representatives of the Spanish Crown. Juan de Castellanos's seemingly endless poetic toils constitute a focal stage in the process of securing domination through writing, as his *Elegías* construct a complex poetic discourse that denies (their own) history to Amerindians and reinforces an asymmetrical scheme of ethnic, religious, and gender differences. After the Wars of Independence from Spain in the nineteenth century, it was not merely the initial phase of the conquest but also the entire colonial experience that needed to be reinterpreted, reassessed, and resignified, this time as part of nation-building projects that included a renewed "will to civilization" that in the case of Colombia was inherently violent.[6] Not surprisingly, Colombian creole literati involved in the construction of a (Hispanic) national identity focused on the life and works of Juan de Castellanos as a vehicle and a sounding board to construct a favorable vision of the colonial past and of the role of Spain and the Catholic Church in the New World. A pivotal moment in the development of this tradition came with the publication of Castellanos's writings as part of the *Biblioteca de autores españoles* (Madrid, 1847), which not only made available parts of the *Elegías* that had remained unpublished but also elevated Castellanos's literary status by placing him in the company of esteemed Spanish authors such as Miguel de Cervantes Saavedra and Leandro Fernández de Moratín. The tradition I am alluding to developed subsequently in the writings of José María Vergara y Vergara (1831–1871) and Miguel Antonio Caro (1845–1909), who were some of the first literary critics to cast Castellanos as a national writer.[7] Vergara y Vergara was a historian, a diplomat, a journalist, a writer, and the author of the first literary history of Nueva Granada, *Historia de la literatura en Nueva Granada* (1867). Caro was a Latinist, a philologist, the president of Colombia, and the author of a biographical sketch of Juan de Castellanos, which was published in 1879 in the *Repertorio Colombiano* and reprinted in the 1955 edition of the *Elegías*. Vergara y Vergara's and Caro's evaluation of Castellanos's work offers fertile ground to understand the contributions of a patriotic literary historiography to fraught nation-building efforts in the nineteenth century. More pertinently, the examination of Caro's and Vergara y Vergara's acceptance of the categories constructed by Castellanos, their endorsement of the ethnographic validity and historiographic accuracy of the *Elegías*, and their timely formulation of Castellanos as an embodiment of the best attributes of an immutable Spanish chivalric spirit (the adjectives Caro uses to describe Castellanos include generous, magnanimous, pious, humble, etc.) can throw light onto the role of literary criticism in the complex nexus between the "will to civilization," violence, and representation, particularly as the task of defining civilization lays at the core of Caro's and Vergara y Vergara's work as writers and historians, as had been the case with Juan de Castellanos three centuries earlier.[8]

Finally, in this study I addressed several misconceptions about Juan de Castellanos's writings, including the stark differences between Castellanos's heroic poems and Alonso de Ercilla's *Araucana*. The impetus for my approach sprang from the recognition that epic and heroic poetry played a key role in what Rolena Adorno has termed the "polemics of possession," and the conviction that the explicit and implicit dialogue Castellanos establishes with the work of Ercilla had been vastly misunderstood by critics. To address this case of critical myopia I illuminated the larger transatlantic scope of Castellanos's poems as well as the transformation of epic and Petrarchist/Garcilacist tropes after Europe's encounter with America. Nevertheless, Castellanos's *Elegías* also engages head on with a more immediate and local discursive tradition, which includes the writings of *mestizo* indigenous chieftain Diego de Torres, whose work has only until recently started to receive critical attention.[9] Diego de Torres spent his formative years in the cities of Santafé de Bogotá and Tunja and, like Castellanos's, his writings offer an assessment of the institution of the *encomienda* and of the shortcomings of the colonial regime in the New Kingdom of Granada. Torres traveled to Spain on two occasions to present Philip II a *relación* that dramatizes the plight of the native population at the hands of encomenderos. If the relationship between Castellanos's and Ercilla's poems allows us to recognize the ideological fractures among the individuals who carried out the conquest and the divergent literary project advanced on behalf of the encomenderos, the relationship between Castellanos's and Diego de Torres's work can show us how Early Colonial Spanish American texts produced within the "polemics of possession" were shaped by an effort to respond or silence *mestizo* writings.

NOTES

1. I'm indebted to Ellen Anderson for sharing her interpretation and bibliographic suggestions regarding chapters 6 and 47 of *Don Quixote*.

2. Nicolopulos, "Reading and Responding," 227.

3. In his introduction to the English translation of Angel Rama's *La ciudad letrada* John Charles Chasteen describes *letrados* as members of a "lettered elite closely associated with the institutions of state and invariably urban in orientation" (Rama, *The Lettered City*, ed. and trans. John Charles Chasteen [Durham, NC: Duke University Press, 1996], vii).

4. In regard to the historical inaccuracies present in the *Elegías* and the difficulty of relying on these poems to reconstruct the trajectory of Castellanos's life, see Marcos Jimenez de la Espada's *Juan de Castellanos y su historia del Nuevo Reino de Granada* (Madrid: Tipografía de la Manuel Ginés Hernández, 1889). Historians Fray Pedro Simón and Antonio de Herrera y Tordesillas borrowed heavily from the *Elegías* to write sections of *Noticias historiales de las conquistas de Tierra Firme en las Indias Occidentales* (Bogotá, Colombia: Biblioteca de Autores Colombianos, 1953), and *Historia general de los hechos de los castellanos en las Islas y Tierra Firme del mar Océano que llaman Indias Occidentales* (Madrid: Imprenta Real, 1601–1615), respectively.

5. William Ospina is a Colombian poet, award-winning novelist, and the author of three historical novels that narrate the expedition of Pedro de Ursúa in search of El Dorado and the land of cinnamon: *Ursúa* (Bogotá, Colombia: Alfaguara, 2005); *El país de la canela* (Bogotá, Colombia: Editorial Norma, 2008); and *La serpiente sin ojos* (Bogotá, Colombia: Mondadori, 2012). Ospina's novels are largely based on the account of Ursúa's expedition offered by Castellanos in "Elegía XIV." Ospina is also the author of a study entitled *Las auroras de sangre: Juan de Castellanos y el descubrimiento poético de América* (Bogotá, Colombia: Grupo Editorial Norma, 1999), which offers an alternative assessment of Castellanos's work.

6. Cristina Rojas, *Civilization and Violence: Regimes of Representation in Nineteenth-Century Colombia* (Minneapolis: University of Minnesota Press, 2002).

7. José María Vergara y Vergara refers to Castellanos as "primogénito de nuestra literatura" (firstborn of our literature; *Historia de la literatura*, 30); and Miguel Antonio Caro considers Castellanos "un escritor en cierto modo nacional" (a national writer to some degree; Caro quoted in "Prologue," in *Elegías*, 1:10).

8. See Iván Vicente Padilla Chasing, *El debate de la hispanidad en Colombia en el siglo XIX: Lectura de la Historia de la literatura en Nueva Granada de José María Vergara y Vergara* (Bogotá, Colombia: Universidad Nacional de Colombia, 2008); and Rojas, *Civilization and Violence*.

9. See Joanne Rappaport, *The Disappearing Mestizo: Configuring Difference in the Colonial New Kingdom of Granada* (Durham, NC: Duke University Press, 2014); and the works of Luis Fernando Restrepo, "El cacique de Turmequé o los agravios de la memoria," *Cuadernos de literatura* 14, no. 28 (July–December 2010): 14–33; "Narrating Colonial Interventions: Don Diego de Torres, *Cacique* of Turmequé in the New Kingdom of Granada," in *Colonialism Past and Present: Reading and Writing About Colonial Latin America Today*, ed. Alvaro Félix Bolaños and Gustavo Verdesio, 97–117 (Albany: State University of New York Press, 2002); and *El estado impostor: Apropiaciones literarias y culturales de la memoria de los muiscas y la América indígena*. Medellín, Colombia: Editorial Univesidad de Antioquia, 2013.

Appendix

Exordium to Juan de Castellanos's "Elegía I"

A cantos elegiacos levanto
con débiles acentos voz anciana
bien como blanco cisne que con canto
su muerte solemniza ya cercana:
No penen mis amigos con espanto,
por no lo comenzar mas de mañana;
pues suelen diferir buenos intentos
mil varios y diversos corrimientos.

Para dar orden a lo prometido,
orbe de Indias es el que me llama
a sacar del sepulcro del olvido
a quien merece bien eterna fama:
Diré lo que me fuere permitido
por la que descompone nuestra trama,
pues para correr vías tan distantes
había de tomarla mucho antes.

Iré con pasos algo presurosos,
sin orla de poéticos cabellos
que hacen versos dulces, sonorosos
a los ejercitados en leerlos ;
pues como canto casos dolorosos,
cuales los padecieron muchos dellos,
parecióme decir la verdad pura
sin usar de ficción ni compostura.

Por no darse bien las invenciones

de cosas ordenadas por los hados,
ni los dioses de falsas religiones,
por la vía láctea congregados,
en el Olimpo dando sus razones
cada uno por sus apasionados;
ni por mi parte quiero que se lea
la deshonestidad de Citerea.

Ni me parece bien ser importuno
recontando los celos de Vulcano
ni los enojos de la diosa Juno,
opuestos al designio del troyano;
ni palacios acuosos de Neptuno,
ni las demás deidades de Océano,
ni cantaré de Doris y Nereo,
ni las varias figuras de Proteo.

Ni cantaré fingidos beneficios
de Prometeo, hijo de Japeto,
fantaseando vanos edificios
con harta mas estima que el efecto;
como los que con grandes artificios
van supliendo las faltas del sujeto;
porque las grandes cosas que yo digo
su punto y su valor tienen consigo.

Son de tan alta lista las que cuento
como veréis en lo que recopilo,
que sus proezas son el ornamento,
y ellas mismas encumbran el estilo,
sin mas reparos ni encarecimiento
de proceder sin mácula el hilo
de la verdad de cosas por mi vistas
y las que recogí de coronistas.

Porque si los discretos paran mientes,
de suyo son gustosas las verdades
y captan atención en los oyentes
mucho mas que fingidas variedades;
demás de ser negocios indecentes
matizar la verdad con variedades
la cual no da sabor al buen oído
si lleva de mentiras el vestido.

Así que no diré cuentos fingidos,
ni me fatigará pensar ficciones
a vueltas de negocios sucedidos
en índicas provincias y regiones;

y si para mis versos ser pulidos
faltaren las debidas proporciones,
querría yo que semejante falta
supliese la materia, pues es alta.

Mas aunque con palabras apacible,
razones sincerísimas y llanas
aquí se contarán casos terribles,
reencuentros y proezas soberanas:
muertes, riesgos, trabajos invencibles,
mas que pueden llevar fuerzas humanas,
rabiosas sed y hambre perusina
más grave, más pesada, más continua.

Veréis romper caminos no sabidos,
montañas bravas y nublosas cumbres.
Veréis pocos y ya casi perdidos
sujetar increíbles muchedumbres
de bárbaros crueles y atrevidos
forzados a tomar nuevas costumbres
do flaqueza temor y desconfianza
afilaban los filos de la lanza.

Veréis ganarse grandes potentados
inexpugnables peñas, altos riscos,
no con cañones gruesos reforzados
ni balas de fumosos basiliscos;
mas de solos escudos ayudados
y puntas de acerados obeliscos
siendo solo los brazos instrumentos
para tan admirables vencimientos

Veréis muchos varones ir en una
prosperidad que no temió caída
y en estos esta misma ser ninguna
de su primero ser desvanecida,
usando de sus mañas la fortuna
en los inciertos cambios desta vida
otros venir a tanta desventura
que el suelo les negaba sepultura.

Ya pues que cosas de Indias celebramos,
para no proceder sin fundamento ,
parece cosa justa que digamos
algo de su primer descubrimiento:
porque de la raíz saquemos ramos
que hagan al lector estar atento;
pues edificio de cimiento falto

mal se puede subir a lo muy alto. (*Elegías*, 1:61)

* * *

To mournful verses I raise
with weakened stress my aging voice
just like the white swan
that solemnizes its approaching death with song
do not be overpowered with fear my friends
for not having begun [this task] earlier;
for fair attempts tend to be postponed

By a thousand diverse obligations.
So as to fulfill what has been promised
the world of the Indies beckons me
to release from the tomb of oblivion
those that truly merit eternal fame.
I shall speak of what I have been permitted
by the one who wrecks our plot,
for in order to traverse such distant paths
one ought to start from as far back as possible.

I shall proceed with fairly hasty steps
without the embellishment of poetic adornments
that make sweet and harmonious verses
for those who are competent to read them;
and since I sing of sad and mournful events
such as many of them were suffered
it seemed fitting to speak the sole truth
without the use of neither fiction nor style.

Since it is not fitting
to speak of things decreed by fate
nor by the gods of false religions,
gathered around the Milky Way,
each one proclaiming their wisdom
to their followers on Mount Olympus;
nor do I want to confront readers
with the dishonest acts by Cythera.

Nor do I find it proper
to recount the jealousies of Vulcan
nor the fury of the goddess Juno,
bent against the design of the son of Troy;
nor of the aqueous palaces of Neptune,
or the rest of deities in the Ocean,
nor will I sing of Doris and Nereus,
or of the various forms of Proteus.

Nor will I sing feigned praises
of Prometheus, son of Iapetus,
formulating empty works
that have less effect than their [actual] worth;
such as those that with great artifice
compensate for the limitations of their subject;
because the great deeds that I speak of
carry in themselves an intrinsic worth and significance.

Those acts of which I speak carry such merit
as you shall witness in what I have compiled
that their own heroic feats are their adornment
and they themselves increase style
without any further objections or praise
by proceeding without tainting the thread
of the truthful things I have witnessed
and what I gathered from chroniclers.

For upon reflection the prudent person will see
that truths in themselves are pleasurable
and capture the listeners' attention
much more effectively than artifice
apart from being offensive and improper
to tinge the truth with false digressions
for truth is no longer pleasant to the ear
if it is covered in deception.

And so I shall not speak of false tales
nor will I endeavor to devise fabrications
surrounding the affairs that have taken place
in the provinces and regions of the [West] Indies;
and if my verses are lacking the required qualities
to be considered fine poetry
I would hope that such fault
be remedied by the content that is of the highest order.

Yet though with gentle words
with most sincere and unadorned reasoning
terrible events shall be narrated here
as well as magnificent accounts and heroic deeds
deaths, bravery, insurmountable toil
more than human fortitude can withstand
wrathful thirst and Peruvian hunger
heavier, more burdensome, more persistent.

You shall witness the treading for unknown paths
perilous mountains and hazy summits

you shall witness the few and almost defeated
subdue incredible hordes
of cruel and fearless barbarians
forced to adopt new customs
where weakness, fear, and mistrust
would sharpen the blades of the spears.

You shall witness the conquering of great potentates
impregnable rocks, tall cliffs
not with thick cannons
nor bullets from fiery basilisks; yet aided only by shields
and the spikes of iron obelisks
with their arms as the sole instruments
for such admirable victories.

You shall witness many men
achieve such prosperity that feared no loss
and among them the inexistence of it
vanished from the start
using the trickery of fortune
in life's uncertain changes
others fall to such misfortune
that even the earth refused their burial.

And since we celebrate the affairs of the [West] Indies
so as not to proceed without a foundation
it seems just to state
something about its first discovery
so that from the root we may obtain branches
that will make the reader attentive;
for a structure without a base
cannot be raised to great heights.

Bibliography

Adorno, Rolena. "Literary Production and Suppression: Reading and Writing About Amerindians in Colonial Spanish America." *Dispositio* 11, nos. 28–29 (1986): 1–25.

———. *The Polemics of Possession in Spanish American Narrative*. New Haven, CT: Yale University Press, 2007.

———. "The Warrior and the War Community: Constructions of the Civil Order in Mexican Conquest History." *Dispositio* 14, nos. 36–38 (1989): 225–46.

Alvar, Manuel. *Juan de Castellanos: Tradición española y realidad americana*. Bogotá, Colombia: Instituto Caro y Cuervo, 1972.

Anderson, Ellen M. "Playing at Moslem and Christian: The Construction of Gender and the Representation of Faith in Cervantes' Captivity Plays." *Cervantes: Bulletin of the Cervantes Society of America* 13, no. 2 (1993): 37–59.

Bhabha, Homi. "Of Mimicry and Man: The Ambivalence of Colonial Discourse." In *Tensions of Empire: Colonial Cultures in a Bourgeois World*, edited by Frederick Cooper and Ann Laura Stoler, 152–60. Berkeley: University of California Press, 1997.

Bolaños, Alvaro Félix. *Barbarie y canibalismo en la retórica colonial: Los indios Pijaos de Fray Pedro Simón*. Bogotá, Colombia: Centro de Estudios de la Realidad Colombiana, 1994.

Brading, D. A. *The First America: The Spanish Monarchy, Creole Patriots, and the Liberal State, 1492–1867*. New York: Cambridge University Press, 1991.

Camacho Guizado, Eduardo. *La elegía funeral en la poesía española*. Madrid: Editorial Gredos, 1969.

Camamis, George. *Estudios sobre el cautiverio en el Siglo de Oro*. Madrid: Editorial Gredos, 1977.

Cañeque, Alejandro. "The Emotions of Power: Love, Anger, and Fear or How to Rule the Spanish Empire." In *Emotions and Daily Life in Colonial Mexico*, edited by Javier Villa-Flores and Sonya Lipsett-Rivera, 89–121. Albuquerque: University of New Mexico Press, 2014.

———. "Imaging the Spanish Empire: The Visual Construction of Imperial Authority in Habsburg New Spain." *Colonial Latin America Review* 19, no. 1 (April 2010): 29–68.

———. *The King's Living Image: The Culture and Politics of Viceregal Power in Colonial Mexico*. New York: Routledge, 2004.

Cañizares-Esguerra, Jorge. *Puritan Conquistadors: Iberianizing the Atlantic, 1550–1700*. Stanford, CA: Stanford University Press, 2006.

Casas, Bartolomé de las. *Brevísima relación de la destrucción de las Indias*. Edited by Jean-Paul Duviols. Buenos Aires: Stockcero, 2006.

Castellanos, Juan de. *Discurso del capitán Francisco Draque*. Edited by Angel González Palencia. Madrid: Instituto de Valencia de Don Juan, 1921.

———. *Elegías de varones ilustres de Indias*. 4 vols. Bogotá, Colombia: Editorial ABC, 1955.

———. *The Narrative of the Expedition of Sir Francis Drake to the Indies and the Taking of Carthagena*. Translated by Walter Owen. Buenos Aires: Walter Owen Institute, 1991.

———. *Primera parte de las elegías de varones ilustres de Indias*. Madrid: Casa de la viuda de Alonso Gómez, 1589.

Castiglione, Baldassarre. *El Cortesano*. Edited by Mario Pozzi. Translated by Juan Boscán. Madrid: Cátedra, 2003.

Castillo de Bobadilla, Jerónimo. *Política para corregidores y señores de vasallos, en tiempo de paz y de Guerra*. Madrid: Luis Sanchez, 1597. Reprint, Madrid: Imprenta Real de la Gazeta, 1775.

Cervantes Saavedra, Miguel de. "El celoso extremeño." In *The Complete Exemplary Novels*, edited by Barry Ife and Jonathan Thacker, 337–89. Oxford, UK: Oxbow Books, 2013.

———. *El ingenioso hidalgo Don Quijote de la Mancha*. Edited by John Jay Allen. Vol. 1. 10th ed. Madrid: Cátedra, 2000.

———. *La Galatea*. Madrid: Espasa-Calpe, 1961.

———. *The Trials of Persiles and Sigismunda: A Northern Story*. Translated by Cecilia Richmond Weller and Clark A. Colahan. Berkeley: University of California Press, 1989.

Cevallos, Francisco Javier. "Don Alonso de Ercilla and the American Indian: History and Myth." *Revista de Estudios Hispánicos* 23, no. 3 (October 1989): 1–20.

Colombí-Monguió, Alicia de. *Petrarquismo peruano: Diego Dávalos y Figueroa y la poesía de la miscelánea austral*. London: Tamesis, 1985.

Concha, Jaime. "El Otro Nuevo Mundo." In *Homenaje a Ercilla*, edited by Luis Muñoz G. et al., 31–82. Concepción, Chile: Universidad de Concepción, 1969.

Covarrubias Horozco, Sebastián de. *Tesoro de la lengua castellana o española*. Madrid: Iberoamericana, 2006.

Cruz, Anne J., ed. *Material and Symbolic Circulation between Spain and England, 1554–1604*. Aldershot, UK: Ashgate, 2008.

Curtius, Ernst Robert. *European Literature and the Latin Middle Ages*. New York: Pantheon, 1952.

Davis, Elizabeth B. *Myth and Identity in the Epic of Imperial Spain*. Colombia: University of Missouri Press, 2000.

Díaz Rengifo, Juan. *Arte Poética Española*. Salamanca, Spain: Casa de Miguel Serrano de Vargas, 1592.

Diccionario de Autoridades. 3 vols. Madrid: Editorial Gredos, 1969.

Diego Dávalos y Figueroa, *Primera parte de la miscelanea austral*. Lima, Peru: Antonio Ricardo, 1602.

Domínguez Camargo, Hernando. *Obras*. Caracas, Venezuela: Biblioteca Ayacucho, 1986.

Drake, Francis. *Sir Francis Drake's West Indian Voyage*. Edited by Mary Frear Keeler. London: Hakluyt Society, 1981.

Durand, José. "El chapetón Ercilla y la honra araucana." *Filología* 10 (1964): 113–34.

Durão, José de Santa Rita. *Caramuru: Poema épico do descubrimiento da Bahia*. São Paulo, Brazil: Edições Cultura, 1945.

Ercilla, Alonso de. *La Araucana*. Edited by Isaías Lerner. 3rd ed. Madrid: Cátedra, 2002.

Florit, Eugenio. "Los momentos líricos de *La Araucana*." *Revista Iberoamericana* 33, no. 63 (January–June 1967): 45–54.

Galperin, Karina. "The Dido Episode in Ercilla's *La Araucana* and the Critique of Empire." *Hispanic Review* 77, no. 1 (Winter 2009): 31–67, 69–70.

Garcés, María Antonia. *Cervantes in Algiers: A Captive's Tale*. Nashville: Vanderbilt University Press, 2002.

Gerassi-Navarro, Nina. *Pirate Novels: Fictions of Nation Building in Spanish America*. Durham, NC: Duke University Press, 1999.

Greene, Roland. *Unrequited Conquests: Love and Empire in the Colonial Americas*. Chicago: University of Chicago Press, 1999.

Guzmán, Rodolfo M. "City, Writing, and Identity: Emergence and Consolidation of the Creole in Santafe de Bogotá (1586–1808)." PhD diss., John Hopkins University, 2002.

Herrera y Tordesillas, Antonio de. *Historia general de los hechos de los castellanos en las Islas y Tierra Firme del mar Océano que llaman Indias Occidentales.* Madrid: Imprenta Real, 1601–1615.

Homer. *The Iliad.* Translated by Richmond Lattimore. Chicago: University of Chicago Press, 1951.

Jáuregui, Carlos A. *Canibalia: Canibalismo, calibanismo, antropofagia cultural y consumo en América Latina.* Madrid: Iberoamericana, 2008.

Jiménez de la Espada, Marcos. *Juan de Castellanos y su historia del Nuevo Reino de Granada.* Madrid: Tipografía de Manuel Ginés Hernández, 1889.

Kelsey, Harry. *Sir Francis Drake: The Queen's Pirate.* New Haven, CT: Yale University Press, 1998.

Lerner, Isaías, ed. "Introducción." In *La Araucana,* by Alonso de Ercilla, 9–51. Madrid: Cátedra, 2002.

Lochman, Daniel T., Maritere López, and Lorna Hutson. *Discourses and Representations of Friendship in Early Modern Europe, 1500–1700.* Burlington, VT: Ashgate, 2011.

Manrique, Jorge. *Coplas a la muerte de su padre.* Madrid, 1799.

———. *Poesía.* Edited by María Morrás. Madrid: Editorial Castalia, 2003.

Marrero-Fente, Raúl. "Épica, Fantasma y Lamento: La retórica del duelo en *La Araucana.*" *Revista Iberoamericana* 73, no. 218 (January–March 2007): 211–26.

———. *Epic, Empire, and Community in the Atlantic World: Silvestre de Balboa's Espejo de Paciencia.* Lewisburg, PA: Bucknell University Press, 2008.

Martí, José. "Nuestra América." In *Obras completas,* 6:15–23. Havana: Editorial Nacional de Cuba, 1963.

———. *Obras completas.* 28 vols. Havana: Editorial Nacional de Cuba, 1963–1975.

Martínez, Miguel. "Género, imprenta y espacio social: Una 'poética de la pólvora' para la épica quinientista." *Hispanic Review* 79, no. 2 (Spring 2011): 163–87.

Martínez-Osorio, Emiro F. "En éste nuestro recental aprisco: Piracy, Epic and Identity in cantos I–II of *Discurso del capitán Francisco Draque* by Juan de Castellanos." *Calíope: Journal of the Society for Renaissance and Baroque Hispanic Poetry* 17, no. 2 (2011): 5–34.

———. "¿Imitación o subversión? La representación de heroínas indígenas en las *Elegías de varones ilustres de las Indias.*" *Cuadernos de Literatura* 14, no. 28 (December 2010): 34–52.

Mayers, Kathryn. *Visions of Empire in Colonial Spanish American Ekphrastic Writing.* Lewisburg, PA: Bucknell University Press, 2012.

McCloskey, Jason. "Spain Succored by Religion: Titian and Lope de Vega's *La Dragontea.*" In *Signs of Power in Habsburg Spain and the New World,* edited by Jason McCloskey and Ignacio López Alemany, 199–221. Lewisburg, PA: Bucknell University Press, 2013.

Medina, José Toribio. *Vida de Ercilla.* Mexico City: Fondo de Cultura Económica, 1948.

Mena, Juan de. *Obra completa.* Edited by Angel Gómez Moreno and Teresa Jiménez Caliente. Madrid: Turner, 1994.

Menéndez y Pelayo, Marcelino. *Historia de la poesía Hispano-Americana.* In *Obras completas.* Edited by Enrique Sánchez Reyes. Vol. 27. Santander, Spain: Consejo Superior de Investigaciones Científicas, 1948.

Meo Zilio, Giovanni. *Estudio sobre Juan de Castellanos.* Florence, Italy: Valmartina, 1972.

Middlebrook, Leah. *Imperial Lyric: New Poetry and New Subjects in Early Modern Spain.* University Park: Pennsylvania State University Press, 2009.

Miramontes Zuázola, Juan de. *Armas antárticas.* Edited by Paul Philipp Firbas. Lima, Peru: Pontificia Universidad Católica del Perú, 2006.

Montemayor, Jorge de. *La Diana.* Edited by Juan Montero. Barcelona: Crítica, 1996.

Murrin, Michael. *History and Warfare in Renaissance Epic.* Chicago: University of Chicago Press, 1994.

Navarrete, Ignacio. *Orphans of Petrarch: Poetry and Theory in the Spanish Renaissance.* Berkeley: University of California Press, 1994.

Nicolopulos, James. "Pedro de Oña and Bernardo de Balbuena Read Ercilla's Fitón." *Latin American Literary Review* 26, no. 52 (July–December 1998): 100–119.

———. *The Poetics of Empire in the Indies: Prophecy and Imitation in La Araucana and Os Lusíadas*. University Park: Pennsylvania State University Press, 2000.

———. "Reading and Responding to the Amorous Episodes of *La Araucana* in Colonial Perú." *Calíope* 4, nos. 1–2 (1998): 227–47.

Olivares, Julián. "Soy un fue, y un será, y un es cansado: Text and Context." *Hispanic Review* 63, no. 3 (Summer 1995): 387–410.

Oña, Pedro de. *Primera parte de Arauco Domado*. Lima, Peru: Impresso en la Ciudad delos Reyes, 1596.

Osorio de Negret, Betty. "Juan de Castellanos: De la retórica a la historia." *Texto y Contexto* 17 (1991): 36–49.

Ospina, William. *El país de la canela*. Bogotá, Colombia: Editorial Norma, 2008.

———. *Las auroras de sangre: Juan de Castellanos y el descubrimiento poético de América*. Bogotá, Colombia: Grupo Editorial Norma, 1999.

———. *La serpiente sin ojos*. Bogotá, Colombia: Mondadori, 2012.

———. *Ursúa*. Bogotá, Colombia: Alfaguara, 2005.

Ovid. *Metamorphoses*`. Translated by Charles Martin. New York: Norton, 2004.

Padilla Chasing, Iván Vicente. *El debate de la hispanidad en Colombia en el siglo XIX: Lectura de la Historia de la literatura en Nueva Granada de José María Vergara y Vergara*. Bogotá, Colombia: Universidad Nacional de Colombia, 2008.

Padrón, Ricardo. "Between Scylla and Charybdis." In *The Spacious Word: Cartography, Literature, and Empire in Early Modern Spain*, 185–230. Chicago: University of Chicago Press, 2004.

Pardo, Isaac J. *Juan de Castellanos: Estudio de las Elegías de varones ilustres de Indias*. Caracas, Venezuela: Biblioteca de la Academia Nacional de Historia, 1991.

Parker, Geoffrey. "David or Goliath? Philip II and His World in the 1580s." In *Spain, Europe and the Atlantic World: Essays in Honour of John H. Elliott*, edited by Richard L. Kagan and Geoffrey Parker, 245–66. Cambridge: Cambridge University Press, 2002.

Pastor Bodmer, Beatriz. *Discursos narrativos de la conquista*. Hanover, NH: Ediciones del Norte, 1988.

Pierce, Frank. *Alonso de Ercilla y Zúñiga*. Amsterdam: Rodopi, 1984.

———. *La poesía épica del Siglo de Oro*. 2nd ed. Madrid: Editorial Gredos, 1968.

Pittarello, Elide. "Arauco Domado de Pedro de Oña o la vía erótica de la conquista." *Dispositio* 14, nos. 36–38 (1989): 247–70.

Porqueras Mayo, Alberto. *El Prólogo como género literario: Su estudio en el Siglo de Oro español*. Madrid: Consejo Superior de Investigaciones Científicas, 1957.

Quevedo Alvarado, María Piedad. *Un cuerpo para el espíritu: Mística en la Nueva Granada, el cuerpo, el gusto y el asco, 1680–1750*. Bogotá, Colombia: Instituto Colombiano de Antropología e Historia, 2007.

Quint, David. *Epic and Empire: Politics and Generic Form from Virgil to Milton*. Princeton, NJ: Princeton University Press, 1993.

Rabasa, José. *Writing Violence on the Northern Frontier: The Historiography of Sixteenth-Century New Mexico and Florida and the Legacy of the Conquest*. Durham, NC: Duke University Press, 2000.

Rama, Angel. *The Lettered City*. Edited and translated by John Charles Chasteen. Durham, NC: Duke University Press, 1996.

Rappaport, Joanne. *The Disappearing Mestizo: Configuring Difference in the Colonial New Kingdom of Granada*. Durham, NC: Duke University Press, 2014.

Reed, Cory. "Harems and Eunuchs: Ottoman-Islamic Motifs of Captivity in *El celoso extemeño*." *Bulletin of the Hispanic Studies* 76, no. 2 (April 1999): 199–214.

Restrepo, Luis Fernando. "El cacique de Turmequé o los agravios de la memoria." *Cuadernos de literatura* 14, no. 28 (July–December 2010): 14–33.

———. *El estado impostor: Apropiaciones literarias y culturales de la memoria de los muiscas y la América indígena*. Medellín, Colombia: Editorial Univesidad de Antioquia, 2013.

———. "Entre el recuerdo y el imposible olvido: La épica y el trauma de la conquista." In *Epica y Colonia: Ensayos sobre el género épico en Iberoamérica (siglos XVI y XVII)*, edited by Paul Philipp Firbas, 41–59. Lima, Peru: Fondo Editorial Universidad Nacional Mayor de San Marcos, 2008.

———. "Narrating Colonial Interventions: Don Diego de Torres, *Cacique* of Turmequé in the New Kingdom of Granada." In *Colonialism Past and Present: Reading and Writing About Colonial Latin America Today*, edited by Alvaro Félix Bolaños and Gustavo Verdesio, 97–117. Albany: State University of New York Press, 2002.

———. "Sacred and Imperial Topographies in Juan de Castellanos' *Elegías de varones ilustres de Indias*." In *Mapping Colonial Spanish America: Places and Commonplaces of Identity, Culture, and Experience*, edited by Santa Arias and Mariselle Meléndez, 84–101. Lewisburg, PA: Bucknell University Press, 2002.

———. "Somatografía Épica Colonial: Las *Elegías de varones ilustres de Indias* de Juan de Castellanos." Hispanic issue. *Modern Language Notes* 115, no. 2 (March 2000): 248–67.

———. *Un nuevo reino imaginado: Las Elegías de varones ilustres de Indias de Juan de Castellanos*. Bogotá, Colombia: Instituto Colombiano de Cultura Hispánica, 1999.

Retratos de los Españoles Ilustres con un epítome de sus vidas. Madrid: Imprenta Real, 1791.

Rivers, Elías L. *Boscán y Garcilaso: Su amistad y el Renacimiento en España*. Seville, Spain: Sibila, 2010.

Rodríguez Freyle, Juan. *El carnero*. Caracas, Venezuela: Biblioteca Ayucacho, 1979.

Rojas, Cristina. *Civilization and Violence: Regimes of Representation in Nineteenth-Century Colombia*. Minneapolis: University of Minnesota Press, 2002.

Rojas, Ulises. *El beneficiado Don Juan de Castellanos, cronista de Colombia y Venezuela*. Tunja, Colombia: Biblioteca de Autores Boyacenses, 1958.

———. *El Cacique de Turmequé y su época*. Tunja, Colombia: Imprenta Departamental, 1965.

Romero, Mario Germán. *Aspectos literarios de la obra de Don Juan de Castellanos*. Bogotá, Colombia: Editorial Kelly, 1978.

———. *Joan de Castellanos: Un examen de su vida y de su obra*. Bogotá, Colombia: Banco de la República, 1964.

Sabat de Rivers, Georgina. "*La Araucana* bajo el lente actual: El noble bárbaro humillado." In *La cultura literaria en la América virreinal: Concurrencias y diferencias*, edited by José Pascual Buxo, 107–23. Mexico City: Universidad Nacional Autonoma de México, 1996.

———. "Introducción, Esta, de nuestra América pupila: Estudios de poesía colonial." *Calíope: Journal of the Society for Renaissance and Baroque Hispanic Poetry* 4, nos. 1–2 (1998): 7–17.

Sánchez de las Brozas, Francisco. *Obras del excelente Poeta Garci Lasso de la Vega: Con anotaciones y enmiendas*. Salamanca, Spain: Pedro Lasso, 1574.

San Juan de la Cruz. *Poesía*. Edited by Domingo Ynduráin. 10th ed. Madrid: Cátedra, 1997.

Schwartz de Lerner, Lía. "Tradición literaria y heroínas indias en la *Araucana*." *Revista Iberoamericana* 38, no. 81 (October–December 1972): 615–25.

Sigüenza y Góngora, Carlos. *Infortunios que Alonso Ramírez, natural de la ciudad de San Juan de Puerto Rico padeció*. Edited by J. S. Cummins and Alan Soons. London: Tamesis, 1984.

Simón, Pedro. *Noticias historiales de las conquistas de Tierra Firme en las Indias Occidentales*. 7 vols. Bogotá, Colombia: Biblioteca de Autores Colombianos, 1953.

Teresa de Ávila. *Obras completas de Santa Teresa*. Edited by Tomás Alvares. 17th ed. Burgos, Spain: Editorial Monte Carmelo, 2014.

Valencia, Felipe. "Las 'muchas (aunque bárbaras)' voces líricas de *La Araucana* y la índole poética de una 'historia verdadera.'" *Revista Estudios Hispánicos* 49, no. 1 (March 2015): 147–71.

Vega, Garcilaso de la. *Garcilaso de la Vega y sus comentaristas*. Edited by Antonio Gallego Morell. Madrid: Editorial Gredos, 1972.

———. *Obras completas con comentario*. Edited by Elías L. Rivers. Madrid: Editorial Castalia, 1981.

Vega, Lope de. *La dragontea*. Valencia, Spain: Pedro Patricio Mey, 1598.

———. *La dragontea*. Edited by Antonio Sánchez Jiménez. Madrid: Cátedra, 2007.

———. *Laurel de Apolo con otras rimas*. Madrid: Juan González, 1630.

Vergara y Vergara, José María. *Historia de la literatura en Nueva Granada*. Bogotá, Colombia: Editorial ABC, 1867.

Vilches, Elvira. "Coins, Value, and Trust: The Problematics of *Vellón* in Seventeenth-Century Spanish Culture." In *Signs of Power in Habsburg Spain and the New World*, edited by Jason McCloskey and Ignacio Lopez Alemany, 95–112. Lewisburg, PA: Bucknell University Press, 2013.

———. *New World Gold: Cultural Anxiety and Monetary Disorder in Early Modern Spain*. Chicago: University of Chicago Press, 2010.

Vitulli, Juan. "Blanco pequeño de ambos mundos: Una lectura del 'Agasajo' de Hernando Domínguez Camargo." *Caliope: Journal of the Society for Renaissance and Baroque Hispanic Poetry* 18, no. 2 (2013): 139–60.

Voigt, Lisa. *Writing Captivity in the Early Modern Atlantic: Circulations of Knowledge and Authority in the Iberian and English Imperial Worlds*. Chapel Hill: University of North Carolina Press, 2009.

Wagschal, Steven. *The Literature of Jealousy in the Age of Cervantes*. Colombia: University of Missouri Press, 2006.

Wright, Elizabeth. "El enemigo en un espejo de príncipes: Lope de Vega y la creación del Francis Drake español." *Cuadernos de Historia Moderna* 26 (2001): 115–30.

———. "From Drake to Draque: A Spanish Hero with an English Accent." In *Material and Symbolic Circulation between Spain and England, 1554–1604*, edited by Anne J. Cruz, 29–38. Aldershot, UK: Ashgate, 2008.

———. *Pilgrimage to Patronage: Lope de Vega and the Court of Phillip III, 1598–1621*. Lewisburg, PA: Bucknell University Press, 2001.

Wright, Irene A., ed. and trans. *Further English Voyages to Spanish America, 1583–1594*. London: Hakluyt Society, 1951.

Zárate, Agustín de. *Historia del descubrimiento y conquista del Perú*. Antwerp, Belgium: Martin Nucio, 1555.

Index

Adorno, Rolena. *See* polemics of possession
Aeneid (Virgil), xxxvin3, 11, 20, 63
Alvar, Manuel, 19
Alvares, Diogo, 121
aprisco, 45, 46, 48; *recental aprisco*, 45, 46–47, 50, 64, 65, 80, 120
Arana, Diego de, 22, 38n13, 115
La Araucana, xi; analysis/critic of, xxxiii, xxxvin3, xxxvin20, 1, 2, 5, 9–10, 15n55, 18, 19–20, 37, 131; apostrophe, use of, xxiv; Battle of Andalicán, 90; Battle of Lepanto, xxxvin3; Battle of Penco, 36; canto 21, 36, 72–73, 83, 84, 87, 94; and Castellanos' writing, xii, xiv, xv–xvi, xxviii–xxxi, 4, 8, 10, 13, 17, 18–19, 21, 28, 31, 74, 88, 92, 134; characters, xxiii, xxv, 2, 13, 17, 25, 38n20, 74; clothing in, 92; dedication to Philip II, xxxi; and Ercilla's portrait, xxx, xxxviin30; geography of, 13; and heroes, xxxii, xxxiv, 10, 23, 84, 94, 132; and history, xxviii, 22, 131; political and literary context, xxxi, xxxii, 9; practice of *imitatio*, xviiin9; and protagonism, 2, 37, 127; public reception, xxvi–xxvii; rhetoric of mourning, 10; sensuality and, 26; time span, xiii; *See also dulce*; Ercilla, Alonso; Lerner, Isaías
Argus Panopte, 53, 67n34

authority (-ies, -ative) : baton of, 82–84, 86, 96n4, 97n31; and Castellanos, xiv–xv, xxxiv, 64, 72, 101–127; and captives, 109; and empirical evidence, xxxii; and *encomendero*, 82–84, 86; of eyewitness, xxxii, xxxiv, 71–72, 115–118, 126; and firsthand experience, 103; and friendship, 107; from colonial periphery, xiv, xxxiv; of Judge Francisco Guillén Chaparro, 73, 77–78, 80, 83, 89; literary, xii, xxviii, 5–6, 12; local, 41, 46, 50, 57, 60, 107; of monarchs/royalty, xxvii, xxxi, xxxii, xxxiii–xxxiv, 5–7, 72, 76, 95, 96n2, 97n31, 99n55; and motherhood, 118–125; poetic discourse/voice, xvii, 71, 132; political, xvii, 72–73, 94, 95; sources of, 115; textual, 73, 80, 84, 94–95

barbarism (-iarns, -ic), xvii, 1–2, 7, 8, 29, 33, 35, 105, 115. *See also* captivity; Barbary
Bautista Muñoz, Juan, xviin1, 132
baquiano, 50, 76, 77–78
Bellona, xxxi, xxxiii

Cabeza de Vaca, Alvar Nuñez, 103–104, 125
Calliope, 104, 119

About the Author

Emiro Martínez-Osorio holds a doctoral degree in Hispanic literature from the University of Texas at Austin. An associate professor of Colonial Latin American Literature at York University (Canada), he has published articles in *Calíope: Journal of the Society for Renaissance and Baroque Hispanic Poetry*, *Revista Canadiense de Estudios Hispánicos*, and *Cuadernos de Literatura*. Along with epic poetry, he works on Caribbean literature, historical novels, and contemporary visual art from Colombia. He is currently working on a bilingual (English/Spanish) critical edition of the *relación* presented by mestizo chieftain don Diego de Torres to King Philip II of Spain in 1586.